How to Watch Soccer

PENGUIN BOOKS

HOW TO WATCH SOCCER

Ruud Gullit was born in Amsterdam in 1962. He was the captain of the Netherlands team that won the 1988 European Football Championship and played in the 1990 World Cup. He was named "European Footballer of the Year" in 1987 and "World Soccer Player of the Year" in 1987 and 1989. After he retired from the field, he managed the LA Galaxy and several other teams around the world. He currently works as a broadcaster regularly covering soccer matches on television in the United States, the United Kingdom, Germany, France, the Netherlands, and across the Middle East.

How to Watch Soccer

RUUD GULLIT

Translated from the Dutch by
Sam Herman

PENGUIN BOOKS

PENGUIN BOOKS

An imprint of Penguin Random House LLC
375 Hudson Street
New York, New York 10014
penguin.com

First published in Great Britain under the title *How to Watch Football*
by Viking (UK), a division of Penguin Random House UK, 2016
Published in Penguin Books 2017

ISBN 9780143130741 (paperback)
ISBN 9781524704575 (e-book)

Printed in the United States of America
1 3 5 7 9 10 8 6 4 2

Set in Dante MT Std

Contents

Foreword

All soccer players have their own style. That goes for soccer analysts too. Some analysts are provocative, some analysts are loud, and some analysts try to stay friends with everyone. When covering soccer, broadcasters like to present a mix of all these styles of commentary to give viewers a complete picture.

When I appear as an analyst, I watch the game as a *manager* rather than as a player. By contrast, many fans tend to watch as spectators. It's natural, but it's the difference between watching a game and watching the ball.

The first thing I look at is how the manager has lined up each team. That tells you immediately what his intentions are and how he plans to hurt the other side. Then as the match starts you watch whether each team manages to execute its game plan, and how the other side has anticipated this plan. From the pattern of play you can see which team is dominating and is able to take an advantage on the basis of its formation and tactics. Now you're already a few minutes into the game and you've hardly even looked at the ball.

As the game continues, I watch for details and look for reasons why things go wrong. Everyone can see the mistake; the point is, why did it happen? Where and why do teams slip up? Often the fault is not with the person who made the error, such as the last defender or the goalkeeper; it starts way before. Not everyone watching the screen can see that. And that's where the analyst comes in: to show things which may not be obvious but that have a crucial impact on the course of the game. I also try to explain how a mistake should have been avoided. I do this without looking for scapegoats. I'm critical, I base my comments on what I see, and stay respectful. There's no need to score points in the media with your remarks.

My approach to soccer is positive. After all, I owe soccer a lot. The sport has given me everything. I've no desire to air dirty laundry in public; I try to analyze as objectively as possible. I must admit that it's hard to talk about some former teammates such as Frank Rijkaard, Carlo Ancelotti and Marco van Basten objectively. I'm always positive about these guys—I give them the benefit of the doubt, maybe even support them.

I prefer technical, well-planned, attacking soccer, yet the objective must always be to win. It's great to see teams throwing everything into the attack. But it doesn't always pay off, so last season it was not the favorites, FC Barcelona and Borussia Dortmund, who won the Champions League and Europa League. Both teams lacked the shrewdness of the bread-and-butter player whose overriding objective is to win. Even if that means going against the grain and taking on a different identity should the situation demand it.

I enjoy watching Barcelona, but at the same time I hate it when other sides lie down and submit to the supremacy of Messi & Co. You have to do everything that's necessary to win, within the rules, even against Barça.

That's why I loved watching Atlético Madrid in the quarterfinals of the 2015/16 Champions League. What possible reason could Atlético have had to play Barcelona's game and offer themselves up to the slaughter? Because that's what neutral spectators wanted? If there's no way to win by playing soccer, other weapons besides sheer talent have to make up the difference: such as tactics, and mental and physical strength. It's all about winning.

Diego Simeone's team adapted on various levels to make sure it got through to the semifinals of the Champions League; eventually Atlético managed to outmaneuver the supposedly indestructible Barcelona with tough, macho soccer.

At the same time I also enjoyed watching Manchester City in those quarterfinals. Unlike Atlético, Manuel Pellegrini's side didn't look to defend, but went on the attack to eliminate Laurent Blanc's stronger Paris Saint-Germain.

Circumstances forced Jürgen Klopp's Liverpool to choose another approach to beat a superior Borussia Dortmund side in the Europa League quarterfinals. Twice Liverpool found themselves lagging behind by an almost hopeless margin (2–0 and 3–1) at Anfield only to pull out all the stops in an all-or-nothing offensive. Under constant attack by a Liverpool team fired by boundless energy and a never-say-die mind-set, the Germans found themselves 4–3 down deep into injury time.

Without denying Liverpool's obvious achievement, it was no less Borussia Dortmund's fault for allowing the English side to wreak unbridled havoc. By failing to finish them off by scoring more goals or by slowing down the pace to frustrate the other side, they allowed themselves to be drawn into an open game and simply forgot to close it down. There were no minor infringements by the German side: no time-wasting or silly tricks at the corner flag, no one rolling about theatrically on the ground. Those kinds of tactics may not be fun to watch, but after all there's a Europa League semifinal at stake, and that's as good an excuse as any. To allow yourself to be drawn into an English game against an English side is asking for trouble, and in this case the result was defeat and elimination.

I find it fascinating to watch teams stretch themselves to their maximum potential. Atlético Madrid are a great example. They may not be the best players individually, but they manage to go deeper than other teams and to play with more discipline than the other side on the day.

When they play a weaker team that then in turn adapt to their game, it's Atlético that find it difficult to dominate. It is always easier to respond to the other side's game. In the round of sixteen of the Champions League, Atlético were on the point of collapse. PSV almost had the Madrilenians on the floor, only to be defeated in the penalty shootout. While PSV adapted, Atlético had to take the initiative and that's what the team found problematic.

As an analyst watching Atlético Madrid–Barcelona, I was looking to see if Barça had a response to Atlético's driven soccer. Clearly not, since they never really got going and never showed the same level of commitment as their opponents. Barcelona's forwards kept dribbling the ball; that's exactly what you *shouldn't* do in a confined space. The result is that you lose the ball. Instead you should be trying to keep possession as long as possible, with one or two touches, keeping up the pace. Waiting to create a space and to exploit it. That's how to avoid tackles and fouls. I was disappointed to see a great team like Barcelona with all those world-class stars unable to use common sense as the game developed. Plan A had been perfected, but it wasn't working, and there was no plan B. Well, in fact sending their tall center back Gerard Piqué to use his height up front turned out to be plan B. It was a desperate measure that they obviously hadn't practiced, since Piqué's teammates barely fed him any long, high balls from the touchline or the back. For me, this exposed Barcelona's true weakness.

Tactics is about responding to the specific qualities of those who determine play, whether in your own team or in the opposing side. Paris Saint-Germain thought they could camouflage the absence of various midfield players by fielding a 3-5-2 formation against Manchester City while still providing support for Zlatan Ibrahimović. Laurent Blanc's tactical adjustment caused chaos in the squad. I suspect that no one at PSG had ever played in that formation. Each player's position and task are different. As a result, their automatic reactions were all wrong. By piling pressure on the three defenders, Manchester City were able to gain the advantage.

Feeling lost in their 3-5-2 formation, PSG were unable to achieve any depth in their game. Manchester City played their familiar 4-2-3-1 formation and waited patiently for their chance. Paris Saint-Germain hardly got started. The solution should have been to move one of the three defenders forward to provide more structure. They could afford to do that, since City were playing with a single striker, Sergio Agüero, which meant that two French defenders would have been sufficient.

But they didn't do that, with the result that Zlatan, their best player, remained marooned in the French half. He threatened on only two occasions—two set pieces—and PSG were unable to stop Manchester City eliminating them from the competition.

As you can see with Atlético, Man City and Liverpool, there's more than one way to skin a cat. Sometimes the solution is not technique, or tactics, or strategy, but simply giving it everything you've got. Soccer purists don't like to hear that, but if you're not the better side in absolute terms then it may be the only way to win that crucial game.

How to Watch Soccer

Getting to the top

In the end, soccer is all about winning. That's how you play, how you train, how you coach, how you watch. But that's not how it begins. It begins with the ball.

The ball is sacred when you're a youngster. It's totally different from the way you experience the game later, as a professional soccer player, manager/coach or analyst. Supporters and fans view soccer like I did as a kid. They watch the ball. That's the essential beauty of the game. It's why I loved going to the playground when I was growing up in Amsterdam. I'd spend the whole day there, from early morning until late evening, until the light faded and my mother came and dragged me home. That's how I got into soccer as a young lad. The ball was my obsession.

Junior at Meerboys, DWS and Young Orange

When I was eight, I used to mess about with the ball in the local playground with little sense of what was happening around me. I developed skills with the ball, moves, tricks, trying to outsmart the others. In those tiny playgrounds in Amsterdam I wasn't the star. On a real pitch I found playing much easier: I was big for my age and there was plenty of space to sprint past everyone with my long legs. That was at Meerboys, a stone's throw from the Ajax stadium. Three years later I moved from Amsterdam's Jordaan to West Amsterdam and joined DWS, well-known in those days as a small professional club, though now amateur.

The manager put me in defense. I got the ball from the keeper, started to run, and kept going until I saw the other goal up ahead. My legs at full stretch. That was my tactic, although I didn't know it was a tactic. A tactic with an expiry date, however. Because when you're playing at the highest professional level, you can't get away with that kind of unorthodox style. In fact it isn't really soccer. Still, the scouts noticed those huge sprints. And so I ran my way into all kinds of teams, from Amsterdam's juniors to the Dutch youth team, and I just kept on running past everyone. All the way from the back. With no idea about positions on the field, or coordination with other players; I didn't even see the other side: I ran past them all.

It was in Amsterdam's youth team that I first encountered players from Ajax, while I was a youngster from small, modest DWS. Those Ajax players had an air of superiority. And they could play well, but they were a bit too self-assured, a little arrogant even. Being big and able to run fast, I held my own quite easily. It was when I tried to get involved in the quick, technical combinations of the Ajax players that they had me at a disadvantage, but they had no answer to my physical approach and my speed. I had little trouble making my presence felt among kids who had far more talent with the ball than I had. It was all going so smoothly that by the time I was twelve I was thinking: hey, maybe I'm a soccer player. It had never occurred to me before, but finding a way to respond to this new style of playing had enabled my own qualities to surface.

A natural progression in 1978 was to the Dutch youth team, but I had to work hard to fit in at that level. This time more was expected of me than physical strength and pace. Once again I discovered that I had to become a better soccer player, technically and in close combinations.

I was surprised when the Dutch managers didn't automatically put me in defense. They saw me more as a midfielder and a forward. Yet how could I release my energy in these positions? From central defender at DWS to midfielder for the Dutch youth team was quite a change. Out in midfield, I was in unfamiliar territory. I didn't really understand the positions and I hardly knew what to do. But I was big and strong, so I thought: if I just start running and keep on running, it'll drive the other side crazy. The tactic worked and I held my own on the pitch. I could easily keep going the whole game, I was so big and strong compared to others of the same age.

The Netherlands were known in those days for technically refined combination soccer. I was different. So it was hardly surprising that I spent much of my first year with the Dutch youth team—for players aged twelve to fourteen—on the bench. They always sent me on later in the game, though. Another player in that team was Erwin Koeman, older brother of Ronald Koeman and later his brother's assistant at Southampton and Everton. Erwin was a technically skilled midfielder with an excellent left foot. In 1988, we won the European Championship together.

In the Dutch youth sides they moved me all around the pitch. I played in many different positions, mostly as a sub. The way you play depends when you're sent on, and whether the team is behind or ahead. I had to be able to adapt to the situation, and I also had to play in different positions on the field. When I was young that could be frustrating, but as a professional it became my real strength.

Having carved out a place in the Dutch youth squad, I was shifted to a higher age group. I was only fourteen and suddenly I was playing in a team with sixteen-, seventeen- and eighteen-year-olds. Once again I had to adapt. I was a kid, but I didn't let anyone intimidate me. Not physically, and not mentally either. At that age I had to prove myself on the pitch and to find a place in the team hierarchy. I was always ready with a quick reply. Growing up in Amsterdam—a big city where you had to act tough on the streets—that came easy.

First professional club: Haarlem

In 1979, Dutch first-division club Haarlem snapped me up from DWS and I got my first professional contract. As the last outfield defender:

center back. For the first time I came face-to-face with people who played for a living. A whole other world than the one I was used to, messing about with kids of the same age. This was far more intense. The manager, Barry Hughes, a Welshman who had played for West Bromwich Albion, had found out that Ajax were considering signing me. So he waited outside our door all night to get me to sign for him.

Hughes took me under his wing. I was seventeen years old, and he put me in the heart of Haarlem's defense; I was their John Terry. On the pitch I did whatever came naturally. It was pure intuition. Hughes loved it whenever I went on one of my runs. He was old-school English style: more motivation than tactics. Hughes got us all worked up and made sure the whole team was ready to devour the other side. Now whenever we get together he tells fantastic stories about the old days. "A long ball came in from the other side, Ruud chested it down in his own penalty area. He controlled the ball, a capital crime so close to your own goal of course, but Ruud could get away with it. And then he started to run and run and run until he reached the goal at the other end and smashed the ball into the top corner." Hughes tells it as if I knew exactly what I was doing. That's not how it felt though. Often I just did stuff and because it worked I kept doing it over and over. For the other players, it was fine as long as we kept winning: that meant a bigger bonus and bread on the table.

In my second season at Haarlem, Hans van Doorneveld joined as manager. He moved me up front. Precisely the position I had never played before. With my pace and strength I soon made the center-forward role my own. I scored a lot of goals. I had no trouble adapting to new situations. I still can't explain why.

In those days I was often surrounded by older players on the pitch. Some were twice my age. They liked having a kid on their side, a cheeky youngster who wasn't afraid to answer back. The older guys always helped me.

The orange shirt and Feyenoord

At the age of eighteen, two years a professional, I was selected for the Dutch national side. A huge step at a totally new level. Those players were older, more experienced, they knew more about life, they appeared for major clubs that regularly played in Europe. And there was I, the new kid from Haarlem, a tiny outfit by comparison.

Ruud Krol, already a record-breaking international, and his Ajax teammate Tscheu La Ling formed the backbone of the national side and ran the show. Ling tested me out straight away, the way older players do in teams. Being from Amsterdam, I wasn't going to let him get the better of me and I gave as good as I got. They were supposed to supply me with a suit for my first international. Me and Frank Rijkaard were together and I came into the dressing room wearing my trainers. There were no shoes to go with the suit, so I kept my trainers on. Krol and Ling both tried baiting me, but I danced out of the room, way ahead of my time.

So I passed their test. Ling and Krol were smart; they realized I had quality and thought: we won't get the better of him—nothing gets past him. Gradually I was learning how things worked at the top in the soccer world. I began to get it.

I was a forward in the Dutch team, like I was at Haarlem. I was doing pretty well, although without being a real team player. So it was a logical move when I transferred from Haarlem to Feyenoord, my first real top club.

At Rotterdam, my free-and-easy days came to an end. Here it was all about performance. Now I was no longer a talented newcomer; I was a fixed asset. Even so, my first season at Feyenoord in 1982, aged twenty, was more of a warm-up. I mainly played on the far right, sometimes as a midfielder and sometimes as an outside right in a 4-3-3 formation.

Cruijff

The following season, the legendary Johan Cruijff moved from his beloved Ajax in Amsterdam to archrivals Feyenoord in Rotterdam. It was not the manager (Thijs Libregts) but Cruijff the player who dictated tactics and positions. My place in his ideal Feyenoord lineup was as a pure outside right. The winger's job was to keep the game wide, to create chances and supply passes. To get some chalk on your boots, as they say. Once again a whole new situation to adapt to, because I had been used to a lot more space as a striker, but Cruijff's will was law.

We had a good option on the left: Pierre Vermeulen. He could beat defenders, pass the ball and score regularly: a superb player on the ball, but the demands were too much for him and he was dropped from the squad (later he appeared for Paris Saint-Germain). Cruijff replaced him with the defender Stanley Brard. As a left back, Brard's job was to keep things organized whenever we lost possession. When we had the ball, he hardly needed to do anything; but when we lost it, it was Brard who had to clean up for Cruijff. That gave Johan a moment to rest, until we regained possession.

Johan Cruijff knew where to place players and was always talking, on and off the pitch. Johan was full of ideas, about my position as an outside right and how to combine with right midfielder André Hoekstra. Hoekstra had amazing stamina: he kept on running, constantly turning up in front of goal to meet passes. He scored plenty of goals, yet some said he wasn't good enough for the top. However, with the tactics that Cruijff developed, Hoekstra came into his own. Cruijff gave me a new insight into tactics through his coaching and his way of talking about soccer. He showed there was more to it than knowing your own position on the pitch.

With Cruijff as player, the 1983/84 season finished with Feyenoord winning the Dutch championship and the cup. After the season ended, Cruijff opened my eyes to my own personal role in soccer, in the clubs and squads I would come to play in. It was on a trip with the squad. We happened to get into the elevator together and started talking. We carried on for hours in our hotel room and that prepared me for the rest of my career.

"Ruud, if you get a transfer to another club now, they'll expect far more from you. You'll be arriving as someone special, the great footballer with a huge personality. Take a striker like Ruud Geels—a goal machine at Feyenoord, Ajax, PSV, Anderlecht, Club Brugge—no one bats an eyelid when he transfers, as long as he scores goals. But you, you're going to get a pile of shit dumped on you if you change clubs now. Like the shit I got when I left Ajax for FC Barcelona in 1973. They'll accuse you of all kinds of things—filling your pockets, betrayal—and they'll call you all sorts of names. Just because you have more qualities than the average player."

According to Cruijff, there was only one way to tackle that problem: by putting other players where they would perform better. As an inexperienced 22-year-old, I had trouble understanding what Cruijff was telling me. I still had no real idea how things worked. The wisdom of his words became apparent the following season. When I transferred from Feyenoord to PSV, it caused a furor, as did the move from PSV to AC Milan. Many resented those transfers and the epithet money-grubber was perhaps one of the more flattering.

Cruijff's words set me thinking and for a long time I tried to understand what they really meant: he had shown me a completely different approach to the game. Since each manager I'd played under had played me in a different position and had forced me to adapt my game, I had been able to focus only on myself.

From Feyenoord to PSV

When I got to PSV, I instantly understood the importance of what Cruijff had said. It wasn't that PSV wanted to become champions; no, it was imperative that they won the championship. There was no other option. And the responsibility for that mission lay with me. They made that publicly clear at the start. How I handled the pressure was up to me.

Happily, PSV is a quiet, friendly club, and so I had little difficulty making my presence felt; in fact I may have been a little overzealous at times. I piled all the pressure on my shoulders and took on the weight of responsibility of winning the league. I wanted to win so much, to be champion, to fulfil the expectations, that I involved myself in every minute detail.

I even got them to change the kit. PSV used to play in red shirt, black shorts and red socks. To me it looked ugly: so depressing, so dark, it radiated none of the strength and freshness I wanted. So we switched to a new kit: red shirt, white shorts and white socks. It sent a powerful signal to ourselves and the opposing side. We felt bigger and stronger.

I also got involved with the players and persuaded them that they needed to improve their team performance: that we had to work on this together. For example the right back, Erik Gerets, had no love for the outside right, René van der Gijp. Van der Gijp was always larking about, a fun guy and a good player, though you had to keep him under control. Gerets was really serious, always put soccer first and had no time for Van der Gijp's practical jokes. Gerets depended on his work ethic—he never gave up—while René would sometimes lean on his talent.

René was always causing controversy, while Gerets was the captain of Belgium's national team. I needed them both if PSV were going to win the championship, so I started working with the two players away from the manager, to get the most I could out of them. Even though their personalities were completely different their soccer qualities were an excellent match, because Gerets could close the defensive gap that Van der Gijp left open, while René would create space whenever Erik ran up along the touchline and would pass perfectly timed balls that Erik would cross beautifully.

It was against Cruijff's Ajax that the pieces of the puzzle came together. Cruijff had just been appointed manager, and Ajax had made a dream start to the season with a string of victories. The sky was the limit. Ajax were on a roll, winning competitions, everything. PSV arrived in Amsterdam like lambs to the slaughter. We were lagging behind in the league and bookmakers were doing well with 4–0 and 5–0 scorelines. Moreover, Ajax had always been the favorites, while PSV were still looked on as multinational Philips's glorified factory club. It was a real motivation for me that everyone had already written us off before we even arrived at Amsterdam's Olympic Stadium.

In the end, we turned out to have progressed a lot further, and we were much more mature as a team even that early in the season. We won 4–2. I scored twice. A wonderful game, which I played with great clarity, consciously keeping an eye on the team. It confirmed for me that I was on the right path in my development as a player. The lessons I had learned at Feyenoord under Johan Cruijff were beginning to bear fruit.

It was not just my proactive approach that made a difference, it was also the space the manager, Hans Kraay Senior, gave me to influence the players. I used that space because I had begun to realize my responsibility. They looked to me. I would get the blame if it all went wrong for PSV and if we failed to win the championship. Fine, but at least it would be my way. Having a tight grip on the team's tactics felt good.

Every corner of the pitch

I started that season at the back and scored fifteen goals. In the last ten matches I moved up front and in the final five games I scored ten goals. I never stayed in my comfort zone, even though that would have been safer. I put my own interests after those of the team. Adaptation is a theme that runs through my career. In the Netherlands, later in Italy and England, and in the Dutch national side too.

If you're able to adapt to different positions and systems at the highest level then you can develop quickly as a player. I was used to playing 4-3-3 at Haarlem and Feyenoord—Cruijff stuck to that formation rigidly—then at PSV I switched to 4-4-2. As a central defender I could move into midfield and would often dash from there into an attacking position. Willy van de Kerkhof, a Dutch international and part of the country's first team at the 1978 World Cup in Argentina, immediately filled the gap. So the balance in midfield was preserved, as too in the team as a whole.

In the Dutch national side I switched back to 4-3-3. These tactical changes made me a more mature player as I learned what was going on in my opponent's head. As a defender you can read the striker's thoughts, and as a striker you understand how a defender thinks.

To Italy

When PSV met AC Milan in the Gamper Trophy in Barcelona, I was playing in defense. I must have made quite an impression because, after the game, the Italian technical manager, Ariedo Braida, looked me up in the dressing room. "Next season. You, play Milan? You play Milan?" Naturally I felt flattered. "Si, si," I answered and in the months that followed we spoke regularly, until Braida and the club's president, Silvio Berlusconi, submitted an official request to PSV. Hans Kraay Senior, the manager, didn't want to let me go, but PSV's board settled on a transfer sum of 16.5 million guilders (7.5 million euros), a record at the time. At Milan they asked me what I thought of Marco van Basten, with whom I'd played in the Dutch squad. A few weeks later, the club snatched up Marco from Ajax.

At AC Milan—just as Cruijff had predicted, the entire Netherlands had turned against me—the manager, Arrigo Sacchi, put me on the right wing in a 4-3-3 formation. Pietro-Paolo Virdis was the center forward and Marco van Basten was on the left. Our success with Milan came when we moved to a 4-4-2 formation, but that came about quite by accident, as it often does in great teams.

The Milan puzzle

Marco van Basten, one of our best players, injured his ankle in a game against Fiorentina. The next week we met Milan's archrivals, Verona, without Marco. With Virdis and me up front together, we demolished Verona. So Sacchi switched permanently to a 4-4-2 formation, with

Virdis and me in the attack. In the end Van Basten's ankle injury forced him to remain on the sidelines for most of the season.

From outside right in a 4-3-3 lineup to striker in a 4-4-2 formation requires a switch in thinking and playing, both for the team and for individual players. We picked it up in no time at AC Milan. The new system fit like a tailor-made Italian suit. As a player I had little trouble with the physical demands of the new system, although it meant more confrontation: confrontation with the other side's central defense.

Towards the end of the season, Marco returned to the side for the game against Napoli, then Italy's champions with two stellar players, Diego Maradona and Gianfranco Zola. Van Basten took Virdis's place up front and scored as well. Two Dutchmen in the attack. On the pitch I had a natural rapport with the striker Van Basten, right back Mauro Tassotti and midfielder Rijkaard. The three of them were always close by and we would pass in triangles. We tuned it so finely that we were almost impossible to defend against, however well the other side prepared.

Later, I moved to the right of midfield at AC Milan. Once again I had to adapt. The advantage for me as a runner was that there was plenty of space to do my thing along the touchline. I still found it difficult to exploit my skills when I was boxed in. With all that space on the right I knew what to do. Although every team invariably played defensively against AC Milan, we still created space by tempting the other side out. Once we had the ball, we surged forward quickly and deep down the touchline, from where I would cross to the advancing Van Basten or Virdis.

Training for crosses

My cross was a trained cross. It hadn't come naturally. At Feyenoord I had practiced crossing continually, because it's a key weapon in the 4-3-3 arsenal. Feyenoord aimed to play in the other side's half, where space was limited, so you often had to cross without having gone past your opponent.

Germans call that kind of curve ball in front of the defender's stretching leg a *Bananenflanke*. HSV's Manfred Kaltz was known as a specialist. Peter Houtman—a superb striker and a great header of the ball—and I would spend hours practicing crosses and finishing. Houtman practiced scoring, me the cross: always at full speed, the full 100 percent, while most players normally train at about 60 percent.

My physical build posed a problem. I run with long strides. That meant it was essential to judge my pace exactly. There was no room for a bit of dribbling in between. Where space was limited, my physique created another problem. I couldn't correct my stride by taking a quick extra step, like shorter players can. So timing was everything.

If there's no one to take account of, then it's fine. But there's usually someone trying to stop you. And what about the striker, who's expecting a cross? What's he doing? Where has he moved to? Which post is he going to choose? That's why I always practiced with Houtman, our regular center forward, to develop an automatic connection.

When we trained I tried to find the best way to kick the ball, which part of the foot to use, to be able to pass the ball so that it didn't arrive too close to the goal, and not too high either. I found that striking the ball halfway up the inside of my foot was the most effective, and actually lifted the ball. Moreover, I had to learn to give the ball the perfect weight. If I kicked it too hard, the ball would sail over everyone and everything. If I didn't give it enough power, then I wouldn't be able to control where the cross went. It's a fine line, but with enough practice you soon start to improve.

After a while, I was able to place crosses for Houtman with my eyes shut—I could time them and plant them perfectly, and at full speed. I didn't even have to look up for him or any of the players. I put my vision into a sort of widescreen mode: I could see the different-colored socks of the players in the penalty box out of the corner of my eye, and knew exactly who to aim for. When you're crossing you have to take account of the other player's forward motion. So you have to make sure that the ball arrives just ahead of the striker, so that he meets the ball at precisely the right time for a header.

Forward runs

When you cross, you have to anticipate how your teammates are going to run in. You have to go over these runs in detail with the striker. They have to be automatic. So if the striker makes a dummy run to the near post, you send your cross to the far post, and vice versa. You each need to know what the other is doing, because a cross to the near post requires a different touch to a cross to the far one. The first should be tighter and lower, while the second should have more power and slightly more height. Often there'll be two tall central defenders in the way so the ball has to arrive over their heads.

Strikers use dummy runs to shake off their markers. If you stand still or you run to the front post without dummying, then you make it really easy for the defenders. All they need to do to block the striker is to keep up or run at the player. In that case, if the cross doesn't reach the striker, then it's always the striker's fault, not the player crossing. It's up to the striker to keep the defender guessing, to wrong-foot the opponent, but without surprising your teammates. Eventually, you no longer need to discuss these things: they work automatically.

Lionel Messi and Cristiano Ronaldo both score often, and almost always after a run. When their side has possession they are constantly moving around to keep their opponents wondering what they're going to do. Before they get into a scoring position, they've already shaken off their markers with any number of dummies and fake runs. These top players have to evade not one, but sometimes two or three defenders whose job is to mark them, before they find a free position in the box. Once you realize that, you know the answer to the constant complaint of television commentators: "How on earth could they have given Messi (or Ronaldo) so much space?" Then you know: that's what makes them so special.

It's fantastic to watch Messi and Ronaldo dummying and faking even as they run with the ball, dribbling at full speed toward a defender. With subtle movements of the body they leave their opponent barely standing, while they continue running, completely balanced. That's how top players create time and space for themselves to be able to give the ball that decisive touch past the defender, to shoot directly at goal.

Defenders know the ploy is coming, and they still sprint off in the wrong direction. The explanation is simple: when you're running backward you have far less control over your body and you quickly lose balance with the slightest twist or turn. When you're running forward you have far more control, and when you have the ball, you're the one who sets the pace.

In the AC Milan front line, Marco van Basten was a past master when it came to dummying and faking. As a teammate, you have to be able to anticipate that. On the right at Milan, I knew exactly where the attack was heading when Paolo Maldini was defending at the back on the left. Instead of to Van Basten as striker, the pass would come to me, or vice versa. I preferred Marco to be on the receiving end because then I knew the ball would go in.

Of course we weren't supposed to go straight to where the ball was going to arrive; we had to find our way there bit by bit. Paolo Maldini or midfielder Carlo Ancelotti would play to Van Basten up front and he would pass back to midfielder Demetrio Albertini. I'd run in with a defender hanging on to my coattails and feint toward Albertini, before sprinting away, deep. All Albertini needed to do was feed the ball into space and I was off.

Switching roles after losing possession

Attacking in the way I've described here is like playing without an opposing team. It's a theoretical attack, an ideal situation that you try to re-create in practice. In reality you have to be continually aware that you may lose the ball at any stage of the attack.

As a player you had to know exactly what to do, what your task was, if Ancelotti, Van Basten or Albertini lost the ball while moving forward. At AC Milan we constantly practiced how to switch roles as soon as we lost possession in the middle of a coordinated attack. It is basically about organizing the team to prevent a goal being scored. (When regaining possession, it's less about organization and there's more space for intuitive play.)

Rule 1: Never lose possession in the center when building an attack

You see it so often, even at the highest level: triangle passes between two central defenders and the keeper. Irresponsible if your aim is to win matches, because it is far too risky. Yet it seems practically endemic in the Netherlands. In other countries, teams in that kind of situation simply kick the ball as far as they can upfield.

Even FC Barcelona regularly commit the cardinal sin of building up through the center. It caused a major problem last season against Celta de Vigo. Gerard Piqué was taking far too long, lost the ball, and Celta scored: 1–0. If Barcelona can't do it, then lesser teams shouldn't even try. So what should you do if everyone is tightly marked? Pass back to the keeper, who'll send the ball into the other half for the strikers to battle for possession. After all, it's not always possible to build up from the back.

Rule 2: Never let the other side attack through the center

This starts with the forwards. They have to force the other side to attack along the wing, because there you have more chance of closing down a player and regaining possession by using the touchline like an extra defender. In the center, in midfield, you're more vulnerable and it's easy to find yourself outflanked; after all, the other side can move either left or right or simply go forward. This is where the manager plays a key role. Whatever the team's system, it's the manager's job to find a solution to this problem.

These two defensive rules were our basic creed at AC Milan. It was drilled into me and fine-tuned during my first season (1987/88); in my second season we won the European Cup and played brilliantly. No opposing side could find an answer. By next season, every team we played had analyzed our game and adapted its strategy. That made it much harder and forced us to develop as a team.

Changing the selection is the usual way to achieve this: some players disappear and others with specific skill-sets are brought in to maintain the element of surprise. It's an extremely difficult process. Managers and coaches are loath to break up a winning team. As a result, even top clubs like Bayern Munich and Barcelona find it almost impossible to win the Champions League twice in a row.

The only way to succeed two seasons in succession is by a thorough analysis and adjustment of the team and by ensuring that players maintain their concentration, hunger and passion. A key aspect is to have players with exceptional individual qualities in the attacking lineup.

European Champions 1988

Before we qualified for the 1988 European Championship in what was then still West Germany, the Dutch national side had experienced some major disappointments. In 1983, we had failed to qualify for the 1984 Championship in France on goal difference when Spain beat Malta 12–1, and two years later we missed our chance to compete in the World Cup in Mexico after Georges Grün scored just before full time in the play-off against Belgium.

So we arrived as untried newcomers that year in West Germany, although the squad was packed with experience. Ajax had just won the European Cup Winners Cup; shortly before the European Championship, PSV had won the European Cup and in Italy Marco van Basten and I had won the league championship with AC Milan.

Bizarrely, we lost our first game, against Russia (the Soviet Union as it was), 1–0. Despite the initial setback, we had a stroke of luck in our last group game against Ireland, which we won with a goal scored by Wim Kieft—who was offside—with a quite unorthodox header.

For the Netherlands, the semifinal against Germany was the real final. Fourteen years before, the whole country had sat weeping in front of the television as they watched the Dutch suffer the ignominy of defeat to Germany in the World Cup final of 1974. We had come to put that right.

The game had taken a strange course, with a penalty awarded quite correctly to Germany, while our penalty was a gift from the Romanian referee, Ioan Igna. In Germany against the Germans, with a gift like that in a European Championship semifinal: strange things are bound to happen. Ronald Koeman made sure of the penalty and that gave the team such a boost that Van Basten soon guided the winning goal home.

With that the championship had been won as far as we were concerned, our revenge was complete and I organized a huge party in Hamburg. We were on top of the world. The next day we left for the final in Munich and the whole squad went to watch a Whitney Houston concert. Inconceivable today. It was not until the coach, Rinus Michels, came to review tactics that we started focusing on the actual final, when we would again face the USSR: "You have achieved something fantastic, but now that we've come to Munich, we might as well win the final. Then we'll really have done something."

That was the gist of it, as if it was taken for granted that we would win even though the Russians were the stronger team. I don't really have a plausible explanation; it just felt that way. Our keeper, Hans van Breukelen, even stopped a penalty. A sweet symmetry: in the opening game we were stronger but Russia won; in the final, Russia were stronger and we won. The scoreline was 2–0, with goals from Van Basten and myself.

My own role in the European Championship was modest, despite being the captain. I played either as second striker or on the left or right in a 4-4-2 formation, depending on where we could hurt the other side more. I was exhausted, broken after that intense first season at AC Milan. Mentally and physically I was totally worn out after the relief of winning the Italian title.

When I arrived for the tournament I was too tired to play with the energy I had shown at AC Milan, however badly I wanted to. Michels even stopped me taking free kicks. But happily Van Basten recovered his form for the tournament following months of injury and after waiting on the bench during the opening game against Russia. Marco was fresh so I was constantly passing to him.

I put my ego on hold and knuckled down for the team and for the result. My form returned in the final, and as a reward Michels let me take the free kicks. That led indirectly to the opening goal. My free kick was followed by a corner from which I scored with a header: 1–0. Later, Van Basten volleyed in a world-class shot that epitomized the championship. In the French media, *L'Équipe* would later call my first goal "the forgotten goal."

At last, in 1988, a Dutch national side had won a major trophy after the lost World Cup finals of 1974 and 1978. Later, in 2010, we reached the final of the World Cup in South Africa. I'm extremely proud of our achievements in the soccer world. The Netherlands may be a small country, but in 1974 we transformed the game with our total soccer concept. We were pioneers, and although we didn't qualify for the European Championship in France in 2016, we are still considered one of the giants of international soccer.

The peak

It was at AC Milan that I developed into a mature player. To a large extent that was down to my new surroundings. Italy was attracting top players in the late 1980s and early '90s. Clubs were allowed to have up to three foreign players under contract and money was no object— Italy then was like England today. Italian clubs bought up the world's best: guys like Maradona, Rijkaard, Van Basten, Zico, Falcão, Daniel Passarella, Lothar Matthäus, Zbigniew Boniek, Michel Platini, Jürgen Klinsmann, Preben Elkjær Larsen, Andy Brehme, Michael Laudrup and many others. And Italy itself also had world-class players such as Franco Baresi, Carlo Ancelotti, Roberto Baggio, Paolo Maldini, Giuseppe Bergomi, Pietro Vierchowod and Roberto Mancini.

The level of soccer played in Italy's Serie A was far superior to that of any other European league. It was similar to the difference between Spain's Primera División and Europe's other leagues today. Good players improve each other and raise the competition to a higher level.

For strikers, Serie A could be grueling; every Italian knew how to defend, whether playing for Juventus or for Cremonese, Lecce, Ascoli or Cesena. You had to be fast to even create the possibility of a chance.

At Fiorentina, they had Daniel Passarella, captain of the Argentinian side that had won the World Cup in 1978. There's a photo in which he elbows me straight in the face. I had just headed a ball onto the bar and one on target, so he took over from Giuseppe Bergomi or Riccardo Ferri as my marker. "Welcome to Serie A," he barked. Passarella was so intensely vicious, a real Argentinian killer. "You were a big fellow, so I had to do something about it," he confessed when we ran into each other recently. We laughed about it.

Vierchowod, at Sampdoria, was one of the best defenders I ever came across. Ask Van Basten what he thinks of Vierchowod. Marco managed to get past him only once when we played against the star defender. A lucky goal after the ball had bounced back off the bar. Marco just nodded it in.

Switching roles

Dutch clubs don't focus on training players in how to switch roles after losing possession. Strikers can find that difficult because their focus is on the ball. During my first year at AC Milan as a striker, whenever I missed a chance I would stay where I was, absorbing the disappointment or just taking a moment to rest. To correct this I had to tell myself: Ruud, first get back into position, then you can reflect or rest. At Milan, players like Sacchi, Ancelotti and Baresi would soon bring you back down to reality if you were lost in thought and forgot your place in the organized team.

Standing still after an attack is deadly for a team. Some players look down at the ground in shame after missing a shot and walk back. Instead, you should really look up and run straight back to your position, otherwise the keeper will throw the ball over your head to the right or left back and they'll have all the time they need to start a counterattack. At AC Milan every player switched roles automatically whenever we lost possession. If you didn't work like that, you simply didn't get selected. By playing with discipline we nullified every surprise that the other team had prepared for us. At AC Milan there was no way we could be surprised, because we were so well organized. It took truly great players like Maradona, Zola, Careca, Zico or Klinsmann to be able to give us a run for our money with their incredible individual skills.

Pressure

Being so tightly organized we first had to give the other side space to play forward. By forcing players to the side, we made them build up from their right or left back. Then when they passed the ball into midfield, all ten of us were ready to pounce on it, to regain possession.

In a sense we paved the way for Barcelona. They do exactly what we did. In fact they penetrate even faster and deeper to build pressure in the other half. A key reason for giving the other side space was that if we attacked too soon the ball would go straight back to the keeper. So there was no point putting the other side under pressure too early. In those days keepers could still pick up a ball from a back pass. The rule wasn't changed until 1992.

The new rule makes it easier for a team to put the other side under pressure. You can go twenty or thirty meters closer to the opposing goal: which leaves the other side far less space to build. And the faster you regain possession, the nearer you are to goal and the less distance you need to make up.

How to beat the wall

At that time, there was no team outside Italy that knew how to deal with the way we pressed. Even good players make mistakes under pressure. At training sessions we practiced pressing and sticking close together, keeping within five meters of each other, perfecting our tactics.

We would practice playing for offside, with eleven men against seven defenders. The seven were the keeper, Sebastiano Rossi; the four defenders, Franco Baresi, Filippo Galli (later Alessandro Costacurta), Paolo Maldini and Mauro Tassotti; and two midfielders, Carlo Ancelotti and Frank Rijkaard. I was out on the right opposite Maldini. We fought hard, but we never got through, not even with long-distance shots.

Later we played eleven against five defenders, including the keeper, and even then it was impossible to get through the defense, not even with a through ball.

When we were at the height of our game, we trained eleven against eleven on a half-size pitch no wider than the sixteen-meter area. You have to be able to combine, because it's impossible to dribble. It was not always fun but it forced you to make quick decisions. It was vital to practice like this because other teams were digging themselves in further and further when they played AC Milan, leaving ridiculously little space. You had to be able to make a decision in an instant if you wanted to get through the defense. It was not the most picturesque way to play, but it was necessary.

Creativity in attack

In addition to an organized defense you need a plan of attack. This has to include plenty of space for players to use their intuition, particularly the strikers. You can't rely on prepared moves. Everyone knows them. Kids get them spoon-fed from childhood at their local club. The right winger moves to the center, meets an opponent, knocks back to the right midfielder, and the right back moves over as third. Intuitive players are able to break through these standard patterns with unexpected, creative moves.

Best of all is when you have two players of that quality in your team. As long as they can work together, that is, because, in the end, you have to have an instinctive, infallible understanding. They say that good soccer players can always play well together, but sometimes the combination simply doesn't work and different qualities of various players don't match. At FC Barcelona they have at least three amazing players: Messi, Luis Suárez and Neymar. The way they work together is exceptional.

Rituals

The whole process leading up to the match itself—the bus ride, arriving at the stadium, dressing-room problems, the warming up and the national anthems or the Champions League hymn—forms a kind of ritual for the players. Everyone experiences it in their own way, but it's a ritual nonetheless.

Whether you sit with your headphones on listening to music, or you read a book, go to the toilet three times or make sure you're last on the pitch, everyone is in their own cocoon. I don't try and figure out whether a player is going to play well or not. The way they behave in the tunnel says nothing about how they'll play. You often hear players, managers and analysts come up with all kinds of explanations for the result based on what they could see before the game started. I don't believe in those crystal ball theories. It's a retrospective romanticized view that often bears no relation to what really happens before the match. Many people, especially those who aren't directly involved, think they see more going on than meets the eye, but it's usually not that complicated.

It's nothing more and nothing less than a ritual that you have to go through in order to get to what really matters: the game.

To England

In 1995, I moved from Italy (after AC Milan, and Sampdoria in Genoa) to England and began playing in London for Chelsea. Once again I had to adapt. This wasn't about the English 4-4-2 game, or even the 5-3-2 that we sometimes played; it was more that most others at the club didn't play at the same level I had experienced in Italy. They were good players, but at a different level. I went from European top to English average. But I quickly adjusted my expectations to accept the new situation instead of allowing it to become frustrating.

Some of the Chelsea players were less quick with the ball and they were not always moving, unlike my former teammates in Italy, which is what made them average. For developing players, English soccer is a tough place: it's difficult to learn to play faster and to always be moving, while staying out of trouble and avoiding the kicking and shoving of the other side. I still had the speed in my mind and my legs. That was fortunate, because I was everyone's favorite target, especially Vinnie Jones, who got me in his sights more than once.

Teammate Mark Hughes and I—he had played at Manchester United and Barcelona—took the squad under our wing. Experienced players see everything a lot quicker, you can tell what's going on and what's about to happen so you have more time to talk, to tell players what to do and to coach. Eventually other players start to get it and to play the way you want.

English soccer

The manager, Glenn Hoddle, put me in central defense, as I had suggested when we discussed my move from Sampdoria to Chelsea. Great idea, said Glenn. Until I chested down the first couple of deep balls, let the ball fall to my feet and passed to the nearest teammate. The fans loved it. "Whoah," came the response from the stands. But Hoddle was aghast. No one in the Chelsea side had ever played like that. Someone like Michael Duberry, a killer at the back, was expecting me to kick the ball straight back upfield, and suddenly there it was at his feet: "What the f*** are you doing?" he shouted as he skied the ball blindly into the stands.

It's true I thought we could set up an attack by building from the back. But at halftime Glenn said: "Ruud, I know what you were trying to do and it's great, but not here and not now. Would you please move up into midfield?" Clearly, the tactics you choose have to match the individual qualities of the other players.

In England, the midfield area is where players fight for the ball. With my insight I managed to avoid those duels. After one game Gavin Peacock, a midfielder who had joined from Newcastle United, asked: "Ruud, how come you're always in free space?" I couldn't explain it, but with ten, fifteen years' experience at the top you know where to go and where not to go.

For me, the Premier League was the ideal place to be at that time. Everyone was saying that the pace was so fast and every game was a battle, but I felt like I had more than enough time and space to develop as a player. And a bit of confrontation was no problem. Until someone floored me with a really brutal tackle and I broke my ankle. I carried on playing for a bit, but that didn't go well of course, so I was off the pitch for a couple of months.

I loved England. Naturally I had to speak English, so we could communicate with each other effectively. At AC Milan no one spoke

English, so I had to get by with a minimal amount of Italian. Even the manager, Arrigo Sacchi, could hardly make himself understood in English. When he came to me to suggest some tactical change he'd tell me in English with his heavy Italian accent: "I am Gullit, I come and I go in zone dangerous." For emphasis, he described it with his hands and promptly pulled a muscle in his neck; it was hilarious. Sacchi would always want to hold discussions in his office. I preferred talking on the pitch, when the moment was still fresh in the memory and everyone could picture the situation you were talking about.

While there was a huge gap between English and Italian soccer at that time, as a player I really enjoyed playing in England. English club soccer was at a low ebb, but better days lay ahead. Premier League clubs had begun raising their income in the mid-nineties with lucrative television contracts, enabling them to buy up expensive players from abroad: Eric Cantona, Jürgen Klinsmann, Dennis Bergkamp, David Ginola and Faustino Asprilla all went for English pounds sterling.

Managers also found themselves in an international market: English managers increasingly made way for foreigners, the supreme example being Arsène Wenger. In 1996, I also joined the managers' guild as player-manager at Chelsea.

English grass

In England, clubs in the lower divisions often employed a tactic that involved letting the grass in the corners of the pitch grow a little longer. During the 1998/99 season, when I was coaching Newcastle United and we played Tranmere Rovers at Prenton Park, the corner flags were almost overgrown. Their manager was John Aldridge, the famous former Liverpool striker, and his central defenders had orders to kick every ball into the long grass in our corners. Since the ball rolled to a halt there, it hardly ever went over the line. From there they would cross the ball toward our goal. It was a difficult tactic to defend against. And if our defenders kicked the ball over the touchline then one of their players would throw it in all the way to the goalmouth.

Talking about throw-ins: they had a clever ploy at Tranmere. There was a door in the advertising hoardings there and the ball boys had towels at the ready. I couldn't believe my eyes. As I watched, a Tranmere player disappeared from view, drying the ball. I stepped out of the dugout to see where he had gone and there he was, standing among the spectators. With that door open he had an extra couple of meters' run-up and he threw the ball right up to the penalty spot. Like a free kick! I asked the ref if that wasn't against the rules, but he allowed it.

Later, when we had a throw-in near there, the door remained resolutely shut of course, and there were no towels to be found either.

Rocket man

Later on in my playing career at Sampdoria and Chelsea I felt as if I had been released from my chains, I played free and easy. I could see everything three times as fast and flew like a rocket. I had the most fun as a player at Genoa. All my experience came into its own. I wanted a completely free role up front, and that is precisely what the Sampdoria manager, Sven-Göran Eriksson, gave me. At Chelsea, it was exactly the same under Glenn Hoddle, although Glenn kept me out of the defensive lineup because I took too many risks.

The package I brought with me from AC Milan was perfect for Sampdoria and Chelsea. In Genoa I was a striker alongside Mancini and I scored sixteen goals in thirty-one league games in the 1993/94 season. At AC Milan I had never got more than nine in the net.

Yet nothing compares to the feeling of winning and the professionalism they evinced at AC Milan. It was hard work, but that club is the best thing that ever happened to me. However, it was at PSV and

Sampdoria that I enjoyed playing the most. At Eindhoven I was the star practically every week, whatever position I was playing in. Of course, I tended to dominate the team, the whole club actually, yet I had a lot of fun too, with everything I did.

Feyenoord, at the start of my career, was where I learned most, especially under Johan Cruijff. I realized that it was the team that mattered. An obvious example is my place in the Dutch team at the 1988 European Championship in West Germany. In the group stage against England I was on the left wing and in the final against the Russians I was up front. It could be frustrating sometimes, but you have to sacrifice your own interests for the team, even when you disagree with your coach's tactical vision. Especially if you're captaining the national side.

Although, of course, I understood that the team was the priority, I never played to my true ability in an orange shirt.

At the 1992 European Championship I was on the right wing in the group stage against Germany and I faced Michael Frontzeck as my direct opponent. He was constantly going forward, and with me chasing after him. At halftime I asked our coach, Rinus Michels, whether someone else could take over for me. All he said was: "You keep dogging that Frontzeck." "That" Frontzeck was as pleased as Punch and more than glad of my company. His job was to make sure I came nowhere near the German penalty area. Frontzeck had the easiest task possible; and we had made sure ourselves that I wasn't part of the attack thanks to the defensive provider Michels had given me. The Netherlands won 3–1 and the whole country was in ecstasy, but for me the game was totally unsatisfying.

When it comes to positions and tactics, I always had a kind of love–hate relationship with the Dutch squad. The tactics that the various national coaches chose were not always what suited me, even though players are selected for the squad for their specific qualities. My problem was that I could play in several positions and my basic level was so high I could be used for all kinds of tactics, so that I often had to put my own ambitions second in the service of the team. I often played as a pure right winger for the Netherlands, even though I didn't have the specific qualities for that role in a 4-3-3 formation.

Looking back, it all came easy to me. Cruijff made me conscious of my responsibility as a team player and persuaded me that I could develop into someone who could lead a side, both on and off the pitch.

Manager

After my first year at Chelsea, in 1996 the chairman, Ken Bates, asked me if I wanted to be a manager, to succeed Glenn Hoddle. Hoddle had been appointed to coach the England side and the fans were calling for me to be the new guy. I hesitated at first, because it signaled the end of my playing career. Being a manager-coach and a player at the same time is almost impossible. You have to divide your attention, so you do both half well. It's an illusion to imagine that you can manage a major club and also play in every game. At the top, you have to do either one or the other. At some point, Gullit the player would have to make way for Gullit the manager.

Although I was just a beginner as a manager, Bates gave me all the space I wanted. I hadn't even taken a course in youth coaching when I took the helm at Chelsea. It was only after Chelsea that I took a Professional Football Coach's course in the Netherlands. At first I had to rely on my experience as a player and the lessons I had learned from managers such as Arrigo Sacchi, Fabio Capello, Rinus Michels and Sven-Göran Eriksson.

It was all in my head; nothing on paper. Since I was working with top players I didn't need to bother with practice exercises and plans. The main thing was to create a connection between the players and help them complement each other's qualities. It's about searching for the ideal combination of players until you have a squad that gels together as a team.

I organized various combinations to play each other for prizes, to foster automatic responses between players, which increases the pace and keeps everyone on the pitch sharp. For a prize of ten pounds the sparks flew. From experience I knew that players loved this kind of thing and they really enjoyed themselves.

At a preseason competition, we once played against Ajax. The fantastic Ajax side that Louis van Gaal had built, which had won the Champions League. I knew Ajax's 4-3-3 system like the back of my hand. My immediate concern was what to do to make a difference. "Play the ball to Hughes and keep the midfielders moving forward."

Not a particularly revolutionary, intelligent idea, but I knew that the Ajax midfielders hated having to run after their opponents. They weren't used to such distances, since Ajax always try to play deep in the opponents' half. Their game is all about possession. They're always thinking ahead and whatever happens at the back, that'll take care of itself.

A serious miscalculation. Sure, Ajax had their chances, but we won the game. Patrick Kluivert, the Ajax forward who later played for AC Milan and FC Barcelona, found me and congratulated me on the result, and especially on our tactics. "You got it right, Ruudje."

Naturally, after all my years in Dutch soccer, I knew how to play Ajax to win. More to the point is whether you have the players to do the job. It wouldn't have worked without Hughes.

Hughes's specific qualities made all the difference because Ajax didn't know how to deal with him. In fact Van Gaal soon started making substitutions and explained afterward that he was still working on building his team . . . well, I didn't buy it, of course.

You should always deploy players on the basis of their qualities, and I tried to do that as much as possible. When we did technical exercises at training sessions guys like Zola, Roberto Di Matteo and Franck Leboeuf would join in. They could do anything with the ball. On the pitch they took the other players under their wing. As a manager you can direct, but it's up to the players to work together. I just showed the way to go. I must have done something right because we won the FA Cup that season.

Image

Both as player and manager I dealt with tensions differently. I looked for the positive and added a sense of fun. Not everyone appreciated that approach though, inside or outside the club. Many in the soccer world have a hard time accepting people with a sense of humor. They seem to think: he can't be serious about his work, which I always found hard to understand. As if walking around with a frown and making a fuss about everything makes you serious. As a manager I had to find a golden mean. Not easy, because you soon lose touch with the real you. And when you lose touch with yourself, you don't perform well. Examples of managers who put on a façade and then failed to live up to expectations are legion.

When my friend Robby Di Matteo was head coach at Schalke 04, he was at the club from seven in the morning to eight at night. Whenever anyone asked if he wanted to go out to eat, Robby would say: "No, people would think I'm not serious." It didn't help much. Within a year the directors fired him.

In fact the opposite is true: if you give the directors, the players and your staff the impression that you're always involved with the club, and you lose a few times, you'll be out on your ear just as quick.

Building a team

In retrospect, in my first year at Chelsea I was still learning. I got a look in the kitchen to check which ingredients Chelsea needed to rapidly become a significant force in the Premier League.

To build a team you have to start by creating an axis: from goalkeeper to striker. I brought in Franck Leboeuf, Roberto Di Matteo, Gianfranco Zola and Gianluca Vialli, and a year later keeper Ed de Goey from Feyenoord. Good English players augmented the side, players who knew the ropes. Steve Clarke (Clarky) was an intelligent, skillful defender, and to put a dent in the tough English strikers I had Michael Duberry. Later, we acquired Celestine Babayaro, Tore André Flo, Gustavo Poyet and English international Graeme Le Saux.

The foreign players had to get used to the English, and vice versa; and we also adopted a more European style of playing. For some in the squad it meant a huge change of culture, and for the fans too. In the end, we won them all over and people appreciated the new tailored attacking soccer we played at Stamford Bridge.

Le Saux was a left back who loved to send long passes to the left winger or to the striker. But I wanted Chelsea to play soccer that built up from the back. Poyet, a Uruguayan and a sprinter with two tanks of oxygen on his back, came to me and said: "Rudi, tell this man to play the ball to my feet," because players like Poyet and Dennis Wise are possession players, but they need to have the ball . . . My focus was always on transforming the team. We played hundreds of practice matches, always with something at stake and with a tactical purpose. I had to keep it competitive too, otherwise the transition would have seemed optional and it would never have succeeded.

Le Saux was an excellent player who adapted fast and easily. He had all the qualities necessary for the style of play I had in mind. Our right back was Dan Petrescu. He could run and covered the whole right flank. Up in front was Zola, a Premier League sensation. Impossible to take the ball away from, turning left and right, a superb shot, an easy goal scorer and a wonderfully stylish player. He had learned a lot at Napoli from his teacher, Diego Maradona.

Finding a successor

Italian international Roberto Di Matteo, later my friend, played at Lazio as a defensive midfielder. At Chelsea I asked him to take on a more attacking role. He developed rapidly, and within no time

Robby was regularly scoring goals. He didn't know what had come over him, but I'd already spotted his potential in Italy.

When I found Robby I realized I had the perfect player to take over my role in the team. In the end he also took over as manager and he was responsible for coaching Chelsea to the club's greatest success, winning the Champions League in 2012.

Robby is cosmopolitan: born in Switzerland, he moved to Italy. He speaks Italian, German and English. When I called Robby to invite him to come to Chelsea, he was in the Italian national squad's dressing room. "Sorry, Ruud, I can't really speak here. Let's talk German. Then at least no one will understand what I'm talking about." So I launched into my high school German, and suddenly I'm listening to a real German speaking. I thought he was pulling my leg, as if he had passed the phone to an actual German. I knew Robby and he always spoke with a heavy Roman accent. And he turned out to speak German like a native. "Is that you, Robby?" I asked. It was.

He was eager to join the club and had an amazing time as a player at Chelsea. Like Gianfranco Zola—another magnificent midfielder at the club in those days—Robby has continued to make England his home.

Hidden conflicts

In May 2005 I submitted my resignation to the directors at Feyenoord, following a turbulent period under the media lens. That February we had been eliminated from the UEFA Cup by Sporting Lisbon in the third round, but we still had everything to play for: we had the title in our sights, and the KNVB Cup. Then we lost a postponed midweek game against FC Den Bosch and the mood suddenly switched.

Some fans in Rotterdam started to call me "that Amsterdammer": Rotterdam against Amsterdam, 010 against 020. The rivalry went too far then and it still goes too far today. They used to say things

like: "You're a good guy, but what about that Amsterdam accent?"
Whenever I went to Varkenoord in those days—Feyenoord's amateur
complex—I could feel the looks like daggers in my back. It's so shortsighted. And this while all my life I've been a fan of Feyenoord and I
even played for the club.

A while later, we lost the semifinal of the KNVB Cup when goalkeeper Gabor Babos dropped the ball.

The end wasn't long in coming.

But what had actually happened? There was a lot more at stake than
winning or losing one or two games. My assistant, Željko Petrović,
was invited to appear on TV and was publicly humiliated. It suddenly
got deeply personal. To my mind that must have been orchestrated.
People at Feyenoord must have been leaking information to under-
mine my position.

As a manager I never felt that I had a grip on what was happening in
the club. I was never able to put my finger on it.

The manager's influence

As a manager it can be difficult to close yourself off from the outside
world. Everyone wants to influence you, inside and outside the club.
Mostly the discussions are about how to organize the team and the
tactics to employ, although often it will also be about which players
to sign.

At Chelsea I was constantly being offered players. These were only
available through certain middlemen who tried to influence the manager or club to their own ends. Their ends being: to make money.
Unfortunately, these were nearly always players we didn't really need.
They were forever suggesting that Chelsea buy Chris Sutton. "What
do I need him for?" I'd say. Where I was concerned that was usually
enough to close that particular window. But after I was fired, Sutton
was one of the first players the club bought. With all due respect to

Sutton, he was not the player to help Chelsea grow to the level the club aspired to.

When a club begins to acquire players who bring nothing to the squad then it's usually a clear sign: that ship has more than one captain, and they all want a piece of the pie.

It can be hard to keep tabs on these processes as a manager. Especially since you may only be with a club for a short period, and at first the internal and external lines of communication are all but impenetrable. All sorts of things happen, often behind your back. There are powerful forces in and around the club and the team that it may be difficult to influence. You can't say: "I don't accept that." If you did, you'd be out like a shot. A manager is a passer-by. Only when you get a chance to stay for the long term, like Sir Alex Ferguson at Manchester United or Arsène Wenger at Arsenal, is it possible to influence the organization.

Even José Mourinho had trouble stamping his authority on the club, despite that supposedly being one of the Special One's specialities. Everywhere he works, controversy follows, as if it's part of the way he works. Yet in the end it's always Mourinho who wins, at least as long as the club keeps winning, as in his unprecedented run of success at Chelsea in 2004–7.

Mourinho's downfall

When he first arrived, Mourinho was unique: the way he spoke to players, how he trained and how he prepared them mentally. Players always spoke about him in positive terms, even after they had left. (Although there's always a moment when players rebel. Especially those who aren't being selected.)

In 2013, when he began his second stint at Chelsea, Mourinho's arrival was different. He no longer got away with everything; the media and the English soccer audience took a more critical stance,

especially after the episode involving the first-team doctor, Eva Carneiro. Mourinho had gone too far and for the English everything was
suddenly different. Mourinho even began to criticize certain players,
which he usually didn't do. Clearly a break-up was imminent. At
Chelsea, they dropped him like a brick, despite having just won the
championship.

As Chelsea disintegrated, Mourinho had almost no one to fall back
on beside his first eleven. But no one said a word about his departure.
Later, players' stories began to appear in the media. People like Kevin
De Bruyne and John Obi Mikel revealed that Mourinho had never
spoken to them at all: "He only focused on his core players. He didn't
even see the substitutes." Retrospective comments like that are unnecessary in my opinion. They should have said something when he
was with the squad as their manager. (By the way: that is why De
Bruyne left for the Bundesliga club Wolfsburg, after which the Belgian
midfielder/striker made the perfect move by signing for Manchester
City.)

Mourinho made a few extraordinary remarks in the buildup to the
2015/16 season: "I don't need to buy any new players for the coming
season, because I have a team full of champions." That is bound to get
the substitutes thinking: Will I ever get a chance to play, am I even
part of the plan? And at the same time, it's a warning to all the rival
clubs: Oh yes, they'll be thinking, so they reckon they're the best?

Two ways to win

Although I don't know Mourinho personally, I have a sort of love–
hate relationship with him. I admire him for all the trophies he has won,
for his amazing achievements at FC Porto, Chelsea and Internazionale. Yet I get the feeling with each of Mourinho's teams that, given the
individual qualities of the players, he should have been able to achieve
a lot more. Each of his teams has lacked that extra bit of class that

would have made it so much more attractive to watch. The main reason, in my opinion, is that for Mourinho it's all about the result.
Nothing wrong with that of course, because he can justify his choices
with an array of trophies and the compliments of the players he has
worked with over the years.

At the end of his first period at Chelsea, Mourinho was fired because
it was felt, not least by the owner, Roman Abramovich, that the style
of play was not attractive enough. Even so, the Russian invited him
back six years later and the terms they agreed doubtless also covered
the style of play. Indeed, after the summer of 2014, Chelsea played fantastic soccer under his guidance, the kind of soccer I love. Players had
all the space they needed to display their class and everyone enjoyed
watching.

Yet at the start of the second half of the season the change came:
each time the team had gained a 1–0 lead, Mourinho had taken out his
calculator and locked down the midfield with Kurt Zouma as an extra
defender. Was that really necessary to win the Premier League? After
all, the beautiful, attractive style of the first half of the season had put
Chelsea on top, and with a significant lead. Wouldn't it have been
amazing if Mourinho of all people had continued to produce attacking
soccer all the way?

But as he said himself: "Do you want to win or do you want to play
beautifully?" For him, it's either one or the other, there is evidently no
way of combining the two.

I admit, he's a winner and he's one of the best managers in the
world. His methods are successful and his philosophy is 90 percent
my philosophy. On the other hand: I've played with the world's greatest stars in an extraordinarily tough Serie A, where defense was always
paramount. But at AC Milan we turned that around and we got
results by playing attractive soccer. Like Ajax, Bayern Munich, Liverpool and FC Barcelona used to do, and like Bayern and Barcelona do
today.

Do his victories belong in that same category? Will he be

remembered, with all his trophies, as an innovator? Not in my book, because I only saw that last crucial 10 percent in the first half of his last season at Chelsea. The result was that he left Chelsea a second time due to poor results exacerbated by internal problems.

Charisma and pure luck

A manager needs to exude charisma. Zinedine Zidane may not be much of a talker, but his charisma is obvious. And yet even Zidane, with his Real Madrid background and all his trophies, remains a passer-by. After all, the club's money is on the pitch, and directors will always look to the players in the end. If he wants to stay on as manager in the Spanish capital, he has to succeed.

And even success is no guarantee. Carlo Ancelotti was successful at Chelsea and was given the boot, just like Roberto Di Matteo, who won the Champions League against Bayern Munich. At the same time, there are numerous examples of managers who won nothing and yet remained, like Claudio Ranieri, who brought no trophies to Stamford Bridge and still served out four years.

Luck is a crucial ingredient for any manager to succeed at a club. Often, even the greatest managers can't be particular, because you don't always have a choice. You never know what you're going to find at a club. How will the board respond if the team's performance declines? What is the atmosphere like between the players? And between players and staff, and with the directors, and what is the real financial picture at the club?

You can learn a lot in preliminary discussions, but you get a feel for the actual situation inside the club only once you start work. So luck is an essential factor: have you arrived at just the right moment? Are you the perfect fit for that organization at this point?

At one time, if you were the manager at Manchester United you would have won the Premier League at some point or other, but now the English competition seems to have been blown wide open: there is so much cash being pumped into clubs like Manchester City, Chelsea, Arsenal and Tottenham Hotspur that United no longer have one or two teams competing against them for the title, but five or six.

It was these changing conditions in the Premier League that David Moyes and then Louis van Gaal faced at Manchester United. That is what made it so difficult for them. But the outside world isn't interested in excuses: the expectations of the fans and the press remain unchanged. So the manager's future at the club is in the hands of the directors and the ultimate question is whether the board has the patience to wait for results. Not where Moyes was concerned, as his quick dismissal proved. Van Gaal continued a bit longer, but his credit didn't last forever either.

The toss

When the referee tosses the coin, if you call it right you get to choose which goal you defend in the first half. Clubs always prefer to play toward their supporters in the second half. Liverpool like to play toward the Kop after halftime, Feyenoord to Vak S and Borussia Dortmund to Die Gelbe Wand. Psychologically, playing toward the fans gives a team an additional incentive to score. You can look into their eyes and feel their desire for a goal.

As a captain I always took that into account. I turned it around at away games. Knowing that the home team would want to play toward its own fans in the second half, I'd make sure they did just the opposite if I won the toss. Then we'd be the team playing toward the home fans after halftime. That was fantastic.

The toss is an opportunity to needle the opposition. It's a tactic like any other. Some captains prefer not to do that, out of respect for the home side. But what's the point? They'd do the same if they were the visiting team. The game starts with the toss.

How to watch soccer

Soccer players have to think two or three steps ahead on the pitch. By contrast, analysts look two or three steps back.

Almost everyone knows something about soccer, a little at least, but no two people have exactly the same perspective. Some base their views on statistics and some follow the ball or the movements of the players, while others watch how the players are organized on the pitch. I mainly look at the details that show why things are going well or badly for a team.

Often, errors are not the fault of the person directly involved; usually the cause lies with something that went wrong earlier in the movement. The last player in line usually ends up in trouble because of something another teammate did at an earlier stage. You have to trace it back.

Cause and effect

For the wider public, cause and effect are not always obvious, so that is what I focus on as an analyst. In fact that's how most players and managers watch a game. Whether it's at home in front of the television, at the stadium, or in the TV or radio studio, what I ask is: "Why did it go wrong?"

A good example is Ross Barkley, who the press and the public talked up as one of England's most talented players. I analyzed an Everton game in which the midfielder was running with the ball far too often and constantly losing possession. The longer you run with the ball, the more likely you are to lose it. It's simple probability. But was it the lad's fault that he kept running? Why didn't other players offer to take the ball? Why weren't they making runs?

Everything Barkley did showed he was trying to live up to expectations. In his desire to prove himself he kept calling for the ball, but often lost it too. I show examples, but I wouldn't lay the blame on a young guy like that. On the contrary. Alongside Barkley there was the experienced Gareth Barry, who could have solved Barkley's problem by telling him: "Don't run, Ross, pass the ball, look for an easy option." That's the kind of coaching young players need, not a roasting for losing the ball. Without support from a player like Barry he'll carry on making the same mistakes time and again.

You have to put the blame where the responsibility lies. First point out what Barkley is doing wrong, then discuss why it happens. In effect you're giving viewers a manual and, if they're smart, Barkley and especially Barry will also benefit. That's how I analyze soccer: identifying cause and effect. The player who loses the ball in a tackle may seem to be the one to blame, but in reality the real error was often not his.

As a manager I tried to make sure the less experienced players were never made scapegoats; I put responsibility on the better players. It was up to them to lead the way. Often I had to use tough language. Later I'd take the player aside and explain. If you're as good as you're supposed to be, and you're so confident and classy, then you should be helping the others and warning them about what's going to happen and the mistakes they're making. You're the one who's responsible and you should feel that responsibility. It's easy to abuse inexperienced players. When experienced players make mistakes then it's only fair they take the blame.

In the studio

At the BBC I follow one or sometimes two games. Often they ask me to comment on Chelsea matches, because I played for Chelsea and I was a manager there. Or if there's a key Dutch player or manager, like

Louis van Gaal when he was running Manchester United, I'll be the first in line to analyze their moves.

I'll often be in the Netherlands, England or Qatar, with different analysts in the studio. For *Match of the Day* on the BBC with Gary Lineker, I select moments in the game to show where things go wrong or right later on. Afterward I go to the editing room to review them and discuss what we'll use in the program. Sometimes I ask for arrows to highlight how the players move.

My favorite combination is two analysts and one presenter, as in *Match of the Day*, SBS6's Champions League broadcasts and the beIN Sports subscription channel. Then you get more time to talk about the game and the key moments, and you're able to delve a little deeper, explain a few things. With three analysts it gets less interesting, and with four you hardly get a chance to speak. Especially at halftime, since the advertisements leave you just a couple of minutes to present your analysis.

I usually jot down a couple of names during the game and when I see the pictures later in the broadcast I remember what I wanted to say and I point out the relevant details. For example, a player who fails to make a run, or a player who lets another get away from him, or who fails to coach a fellow player.

I tell these things in my own way, calm and relaxed, and I definitely don't do it with a frown. There's no reason not to joke and have a laugh. I smile and chat with everyone and I'm comfortable whoever I'm talking to.

The main thing is to analyze as originally as possible, and show viewers key aspects of the game and the effect these episodes had, whether for better or for worse: aspects that I see but that many viewers may have missed.

Decisive moments

When analyzing a game I don't just follow the ball. I look at various aspects of formation and pattern, and try to identify decisive moments: why do things happen the way they do?

Perhaps the most decisive, game-changing moment in recent years was Robin van Persie's goal for the Netherlands at the 2014 World Cup against the world champions, Spain, in the opening encounter. That flying header over Iker Casillas reverberated around the world. It was sensational.

But that was not the most important aspect of the goal for the Dutch team. After having struggled through the first forty-five minutes and narrowly escaped a 2–0 deficit when David Silva was caught offside, suddenly the Dutch equalized and went in at halftime back in contention. While Louis van Gaal's team entered the dressing room on a high, the Spaniards left the pitch under a psychological cloud. A cloud that must have seemed darker and darker as the fifteen minutes in the dressing room ticked by. Had they conceded the goal at any other time, they would have carried on with the game and the equalizer would not have had such an impact. But now the Spanish players were sitting in the dressing room, wondering: "How was that possible?" While the Dutch players were thinking: "We're back in!"

This timing can influence the rest of the game in a dramatic way, and indeed the second half saw the world champions demolished 5–1 by an unfettered Dutch team, with Van Persie and Arjen Robben rampant. Spain were unable to rise above that moment just before halftime: it affected their subsequent games too, and they never progressed past the group stage. Meanwhile the Dutch went on to the semifinals, where they met Argentina, only to be eliminated on penalties.

An unforgettable game from an analyst's point of view was the Premier League encounter between two closely matched sides, Liverpool and Chelsea, on April 27, 2014. At stake was the championship. If

Liverpool could draw the game, they would retain their one-point lead against their nearest rivals, Manchester City, then chasing a second title in three seasons. A simple draw was all that Liverpool needed from their manager, Brendan Rodgers, for a first league championship since 1990.

But what did Liverpool do? They decided that they wanted to *win* that game at Anfield in front of their delirious fans, to show why they were the side that deserved to take the Premier League trophy that season. The lasting memory of their delusion came just before halftime as Steven Gerrard slipped in midfield, lost the ball and Chelsea's striker Demba Ba snatched it and tucked it into the Liverpool goal: 1–0.

At that moment the game turned, but did Gerrard's loss of the ball really cost Liverpool the match? No, there was a different reason: Chelsea had set a trap and Liverpool had walked right into it. Liverpool wanted to wrap up the title at home as quickly as possible and went for it from the moment the whistle blew. Chelsea allowed Liverpool to take the initiative and played the league fixture as if it had been a Champions League encounter. Liverpool thought: we've got the ball, we're the team in charge, we're dominating.

But did the course of play tell the real story? To me, Chelsea looked more dominant than Liverpool, even though the Blues had less of the ball in that first half. Chelsea let Liverpool do what they wanted and refused to panic: come on, attack if you like, our defense can deal with anything you have. That was the attitude Chelsea radiated. Sticking to their defensive formation, Chelsea waited remarkably calmly, their organization airtight, ready to pounce at a moment's notice. And the moment came. The moment Gerrard lost his balance and Demba Ba scored.

Conclusion? Brendan Rodgers had made an enormous error of judgment. He and his team should have treated the Chelsea match like a Champions League fixture. It seemingly never crossed Rodgers's mind that he could or should have played a defensive game. He forgot the crucial bottom line, the minimum he needed from the game: a draw.

If Liverpool had played a compact game and left Chelsea to take the initiative, it would have thrown the Londoners completely. By playing a totally unexpected game—giving the ball away—Rodgers could have confused Chelsea. But he failed to deliver the masterstroke.

Lacking the necessary experience, the unsuspecting Rodgers wandered into Chelsea's wide-open trap. Rodgers must have nightmares whenever he remembers that game. Liverpool threw away their chance of winning the title, at home, in front of their own fans.

If you have to win in a do-or-die, all-or-nothing game then, of course, go for victory. But if all you need is *not to lose*, you should never take the risk of throwing caution to the wind and playing only to win. It's a crucial lesson at the top. Sometimes you have to play a negative game, to be shrewd and smart. Instead Liverpool naively gave away the match and the first chance of regaining the title in twenty-five years. And although their approach had been exceptionally negative, Chelsea went home with three points.

In short: Chelsea had allowed Liverpool to think they were dominating. A fata morgana.

A clear message

The greatest first tackle of a game, *ever*, was by Roy Keane in the World Cup qualifier between Ireland and the Netherlands on September 1, 2001. In the first minute he sent Marc Overmars flying with a merciless tackle into his ankles from the back. Helmut Krug blew his whistle, but the German referee kept his red card in his pocket, and didn't even show a yellow. The tone was set; the first blow struck. The intention was clear; the Irish had declared: you're getting nothing here today!

Referees often overlook infringements in the first minutes of the match since they are afraid of overusing their yellow and red cards.

They have to be careful how they dish out the first slap on the wrist. A nice side effect is that a foul like that often leads to some kind of retaliation. And then all you have to do is roll over in pain and groan a little, and wham! Yellow for the other side.

Influencing the referee is a vital aspect of the game. Refs try to be objective robots, but of course they are only human. Sometimes you see players get away with all sorts of infringements. Xabi Alonso (Liverpool, Real Madrid and Bayern) is the best: he almost always gets away with fouls, and these are often crucial. He goes too far sometimes, but he's annoying and irritating rather than unacceptable or dirty.

In my time at AC Milan it was Franco Baresi who often got away with it. He would stand there looking sheepish. Baresi wasn't nasty, but he could be a hard player sometimes. Especially when we played Internazionale and he faced Jürgen Klinsmann, thundering up to him time and again. Baresi would give the German striker a knock or two, just to be rid of him.

Getting involved

Whether a player is in top form or not isn't something you can judge from his expression or attitude, whether his shoulders are drooping or he's dragging his feet on the pitch. That kind of thing is too general to interpret.

You have to concentrate on aspects relating to soccer, which everyone can see but not everyone pays attention to. Is his first touch good or bad? Is he offering to take the ball? Is he hesitating what to do next? Is he prepared to play the ball forward or is he avoiding taking risks? Does he need to touch the ball a second time to place it where he wants it, or does he receive, play and move on? Players who aren't really involved in the game become increasingly insecure and tend to lose the ball unnecessarily or just avoid contact.

The power of goals

The first goal is not always decisive. It all depends on your reaction. And that response depends on the circumstances and the moment in the game.

As a manager I never let a quick goal (whether for my side or against us) confuse me. If you go a goal down, there's still plenty of opportunity to correct the score; and if you go a goal up, the other side has oceans of time to make up the difference. After an early goal, whether as a manager in the dug-out or as a player on the pitch, I approached the game as if the score were still 0–0, not 1–0 or 0–1. At that point it is still too early to draw conclusions or to make dramatic changes and bring on substitutes. Perhaps a minor adjustment in the formation, but only if the other side is employing different tactics from what you anticipated.

A goal in the closing stages of a game can change everything, even though things may still go either way. If you score near the end and take the lead, then you can expect the other side to collapse, physically and mentally. It's basic psychology: you get a goal and then you think— right, we've got what we wanted.

Actually, the opposite often happens. The other side suddenly gets a shot of adrenaline, a sort of primitive instinct drives them to make up the deficit. On the pitch they pick up the second ball more often, and they play a little faster, tougher and harder than you do. And although you're ahead, suddenly you're the weaker side and if they score an equalizer . . .

Sometimes the game takes a different course: a team falls behind after a late goal and pulls out all the stops to equalize; in the unbridled sprint to draw level, players forget their place in the organization, so that a quick counterattack may result in their conceding yet another goal.

The fact remains that a goal in the last fifteen minutes is often followed by another—an equalizer. As the final whistle approaches, panic sets in. Balls are kicked away blindly, the strikers are no longer accessible or are no longer in position because they're helping to defend, or they're spread out too widely. Often when the ball is kicked upfield it is hard to win back. In the dying minutes, teams, even experienced teams, can find themselves in serious trouble.

To steer a game like that to a satisfactory conclusion you need a couple of smart players in the team. Players who know how to provoke a foul, or commit one, how to dive in the corner, fake an injury, waste time with a corner or a free kick, or pretend that a coin struck them on the head. Italians were past masters: anything to win. The English consider it cheating; others don't.

Managers can do little from the touchline. A traditional last-minute substitution is an option, or minor changes to dot the i's while treating an injury. Yet it's hard to speak to the players at this point, especially in a stadium with 60,000 fans shouting wildly. The manager has to rely on one or two key players to keep things under control and to guide the team through the difficult final minutes. A John Terry for example, or Roy Keane, or Franco Baresi.

Dominating the game

My advantage as an analyst is that I used to play at the highest level and in different positions. Someone who has played as a striker can tell a lot about a team's defense, and can talk about how a forward is performing. I also played in midfield. With my experience I understand what's happening since I can empathize with a particular player's role.

As an analyst I begin by assessing the relative strengths of the two clubs. Then as the game progresses I wonder what a team or a manager actually wants. What is their intention? Their strategy? What is the better side going to do to translate its superior strength into goals? What are the players actually doing on the pitch? Are they going for the jugular? Do they want a quick goal? What are the underdogs doing about it? What is the real difference in strength between the teams?

Dominating the game is the buzz phrase in soccer at the moment. It's a twenty-first-century thing. When I was a player we never used to talk about dominance or dominating a game. I see it as a term that describes a team making its intentions clear to the public. An empty term really, because it says nothing about whether you leave the ground a winner, or a loser even. It doesn't say whether you attacked or defended. It suggests attack, but that's not necessarily the case. Think back to that dramatic game between Liverpool and Chelsea in 2014. Liverpool thought they were dominating, which they seemed to be for a long while, but as soon as the façade cracked they disintegrated.

At Manchester United, Louis van Gaal was often criticized for his emphasis on dominating play. He was constantly claiming that his team had played such a dominant game. He always had a list of percentages at the ready: how much more possession United had enjoyed than the other team. But even 60, 70 percent possession doesn't guarantee that you win the game, as Van Gaal found out in the Premier League. When United played Ronald Koeman's Southampton, they easily had 65 percent possession, yet still lost 1–0. It was painful. Ronald Koeman and Van Gaal are compatriots, but hardly best friends.

In defense of his strategy and choice of players, Van Gaal explained to the assembled press yet again how they had dominated possession. In England they laughed, and quite rightly.

Dominating the game often goes hand-in-hand with the concept of positional play. Another holy grail, certainly in the Netherlands. But, like dominance, positional play is no guarantee that a team will win.

The most important thing is to create opportunities and to score. The best chance of winning is to move forward as fast as possible with players who can weave between the lines—between defense and midfield and between midfield and attack—and make themselves available to take the ball while at the same time someone else moves in deep to open up the defense.

With today's video systems and analytical software it is increasingly difficult for attacking teams to surprise their opponents. Every team's attacking strategies have been studied thoroughly with video analysis. A normal attack pattern—passing to the deepest player, who sends the ball to an approaching player who passes to a third player, who goes in deep—need not present a club at the highest level with any problems.

Anyway, it's easier to defend than to attack, since you are tightly organized and the slightest contact with the ball can disrupt the whole attacking buildup. An organized defense should be refined and perfected to the ultimate degree so that it functions even if the players aren't the best. Only really talented individuals on the attacking side can get through a well-organized defense.

FC Barcelona are by definition dominant, on or off the ball. With players like theirs, opponents are not likely to be tempted to try to dominate a game; Barcelona players have such a surplus of individual talent that they have to dominate play. Teams facing Barcelona have to play poker to win. It rarely works, but the two teams that managed to do this went on to win the Champions League: Internazionale in 2010 and Chelsea in 2012.

When a dominant team is at the top of its game, dispatching a weaker opponent usually presents little problem. The first priority is to ensure that the game isn't left to chance. A dominant team should aim to get a 1–0 or 2–0 lead as soon as possible. Then they can turn down the heat and meanwhile look for a third goal. And then freewheel through the rest of the match.

This was the game plan at AC Milan from the moment we kicked off. For Italians it was a revolutionary concept. At that time, 1–0 was a sacred dogma in Italy. Almost every team, wherever it stood in the league, knew how to defend a minimal lead down to the final whistle. Keeping the back tightly shut had been raised to an art form.

Yet to me, coming from the Netherlands, focusing on defense like that seemed unnecessarily stressful. Each time I felt like we were tempting fate. I didn't like it at all. In those first games at AC Milan I continued looking for goals even after we had our 1–0 advantage. I wanted to make sure of victory with a second or third goal, which drove Arrigo Sacchi crazy: he would run up and down the touchline: go back, lock the game up!

In the end we managed to shake off the Italian orthodoxy at AC Milan. Chasing goals became our new tactic and we started looking for opportunities to increase our lead and to guarantee the points. After that strategy had succeeded a few times, the players began to realize that you didn't need to bolt the door and wait after going ahead 1–0; you could decide matches long before the final whistle. And, either way, it was better for your heart.

At first, Sacchi hesitated; eventually, however, on January 17, 1988, he changed his mind. It was at a home match against Como at the San Siro. Mauro Tassotti got sent off in the nineteenth minute. Unprecedented. It never happened so early in the game in Italy. A huge advantage for Como, everyone thought, especially Como. Eleven against ten, with over an hour to go: those three points were in the bag! Como did the worst thing possible: they came forward.

In the first place, Como were totally unused to attacking, since they were always struggling against attacks themselves. And we were extra sharp because we knew that there were only ten of us to do the job. With fewer players, we found ourselves swimming in the kind of space no team ever had in Serie A. AC Milan's ten ran rings around Como's eleven and after ninety minutes it was 5–0. That was when Sacchi realized that attack is the best defense and that it pays to go forward, even with ten, and especially if you already have the lead. That was how we won the Italian championship in my first season at AC Milan and two years later the European Cup.

Counterattacking

If you have the quality to play dominating soccer, then in my opinion you have to be able to counterattack. Leicester City combined the best of both worlds in the 2015/16 season like no other Premier League club. Their Italian manager, Claudio Ranieri, molded an airtight defense and sent his superfast striker Jamie Vardy to wander the open spaces between the lines of the opposing side, backed by the architect Riyad Mahrez. On paper many of those opponents were better than Leicester City. Far into the season, other clubs continued to rely on their presumed superiority and acted accordingly: arrogant, haughty, self-important. Meanwhile, Leicester City profited. Time and again.

The club, especially the manager and his players, proved that it was possible to come a long way with a solid defensive organization, a little aggression, a couple of superquick forwards and one creative player. Even in the world's greatest competition, as they like to call the Premier League. Every time, the big clubs walked into the same Leicester City trap. The trick was to let the other side think it was dominating the game, and was therefore better.

Having underestimated Leicester, opposing teams came in attacking, testing the team's defense, its weakest link, or so they supposed. It was exactly what Leicester City's defenders wanted. They weren't hanging around their own penalty area without a reason. There they felt nice and safe, with little space behind them to defend. Which gave Vardy, Mahrez, Danny Drinkwater and N'Golo Kanté all the space they needed to play their favorite counter-game, dodging between the opponents' lines. That was how even Manchester City, who played in an extremely dominant style at home, suffered a humiliating 3–1 defeat.

No other Premier League manager got as much out of his players that season as Ranieri. And that is what counts when you're coaching. If you can manage that and still lose then you know you were up against a quality team. And the other thing is, you have to go down fighting to the last.

Often a side will appear to dominate because it seems to have the ball most of the time. Yet appearances can be deceptive: possession isn't the same as winning. Often a team will allow the other side to keep the ball because it's harder for players to create options when they are forced into a confined space and easier for the team without the ball to react when they have all that extra space.

In the old days, Arsenal were above all a good counterattacking team. In their best years, with David Seaman, Tony Adams, Martin Keown, Patrick Vieira, Emmanuel Petit and Thierry Henry forming the axis, they had more quality than Leicester City in 2016. Arsenal could reach the other side of the pitch with three passes. Their system was tailor-made for Henry, whose speed made him the ideal striker to spearhead the attack. Arsenal used to be known as boring, but soon lost that epithet in this period, thanks to the brilliant virtuosity of Bergkamp, the determination of Adams, Keown, Petit and Vieira, and the pace and killer instinct of Henry.

I suspect that after a while Arsène Wenger fell in love with Barcelona's game. Too much in love. I reckon he wanted Arsenal to play in Barça's style and to rise to the same level as the Catalans, what he called the new soccer. Laudable, but risky. It seems to me that Wenger went out and bought players specifically to realize his plan to play in that style.

Yet he forgot one simple rule: Barcelona are Barcelona and Arsenal are Arsenal. It is useless to compare two teams; creating a copy of another team is bound to fail. So Arsenal got stuck halfway and Wenger never managed to duplicate Barcelona's style of soccer. It is naive to imagine that buying the same kind of players allows you to play the same kind of soccer. After all, the difference between the style of play in the Premier League and the Primera División is vast. You can't compare it. English soccer is robust and physical, with lots of movement; in Spain they play technical tiki-taka soccer based on a positional game.

Tiki-taka in Germany

Pep Guardiola himself discovered just how difficult it is to adopt Barcelona's style of play. His vision, developing the ideas expounded by Johan Cruijff, is incorporated into the Barcelona game, and he thought he could add two elements when he moved from Barça to Bayern Munich, namely German mentality and determination.

But it's the players who have to do the work. Guardiola has two fabulous players in Arjen Robben and Franck Ribéry. In the first of his three seasons Guardiola came within a hair's breadth of his previous team's top level; for example, at the away game in the Champions League group stage against Manchester City. But Guardiola and his players were unable to maintain that standard for long. They approached it, but they couldn't equal it because the key players for their system, Robben and Ribéry, missed too many games through injury. Victory in the Champions League was a bridge too far. It's not that easy to replace players of that caliber, even if you're Bayern Munich. Being unable to attract the world's top five players, they acquired Douglas Costa and Kingsley Coman for when their two stars were sidelined.

Move and countermove

The best place to analyze a game is at the stadium. There you can view the whole pitch, including the open spaces. That's harder on television, although it's usually possible to gauge a team's intentions quite quickly.

For example, the buildup from the back by teams like Real Madrid or Bayern Munich. There, defenders such as Real's Marcelo and Bayern's David Alaba are similar: perhaps not the tightest in defense, but in an attack they make all the difference as they surge along the flank from their position at left back. Every team knows that Real and Bayern build up along their right and eventually end up on the left with Marcelo and Alaba, who deliver the cross.

Managers of opposing teams have to find tactical solutions. Leave Marcelo and Alaba to orchestrate the attack from the back. Where the ball is, that is where most players are concentrated. That means they are far away from the opposite goal and it should be easy to create a well-organized defense. So well-organized that when the attack comes their forwards are unable to break through. If the attack builds up on the left then the striker or right winger is almost always the final link in the chain. That offers a way to control the opposing team and to take the sting out of their game.

Mission accomplished, you could say. But it's an illusion to imagine that you can keep this up for ninety minutes. Not only that: leading clubs like Bayern and Real have an array of options at their disposal tailored to the qualities of their available players, although it's obviously frustrating if you block their favorite attacking strategy.

Tactical plans and formations like these are often of crucial importance to less well-equipped teams and provide a lifeline when facing stronger opponents. Either way, you can't say: "As long as we play in our own style the results will come." That's not how it works. You have to adapt, although that is no guarantee either.

How to watch defenders

When watching defenders you have to assess how they respond to their opponents as well as the ball. Poor defenders tend to concentrate on the ball. If a forward gets past a right or left back, the defender's natural reaction is to focus on the player with the ball on the wing, yet the real danger lies elsewhere. The danger is the player running toward goal to score. As a defender your focus should not only be on where the ball is: you should have one eye on the other players coming forward. Today's defenders often fail to do that. It is incredible how many defenders allow forwards to get away from them.

That hardly ever happens to Italian defenders. They always know roughly where the ball is, but for the rest their focus is entirely on their opponents. It is part of their instinct and training. Giorgio Chiellini, left back for Juventus and Italy, is a past master. His only concern is: how do I deal with the threat in front of goal?

Players like Chiellini are continually looking at where the strikers are moving to. There is a huge difference between the runs that players like Messi and Ronaldo make and those of so-called ordinary strikers. Runs by these top players are so explosive, so precise and unpredictable, that you wonder as a defender after they have scored: how on earth did they manage to get so much free space? There were at least two or three defenders there . . .

Easy: the defenders were concentrating on the ball and were too far away from Messi or Ronaldo, instead of breathing down their neck.

The best defenders are in constant contact with their opponent. You can't hold him, because you don't want to give away a penalty. But there is always physical contact so you know where your forward is. While you can never completely eliminate a player's threat, a defender's job is to minimize the danger he poses. A ball-watcher is a striker's golden opportunity.

The art of defending

As Chelsea's manager, Roberto Di Matteo was well aware that his team was ill-equipped to play attacking soccer. Moreover the team was not comfortable with itself. His players lacked the creativity and class to play in the opponents' half and at the back they lacked the pace to use the forty meters between the defenders and the keeper. So, true to his Italian roots, Di Matteo raised defense to an art. In the Premier League, Chelsea drifted; but in the Champions League the club stood its ground, scraping through against Napoli and winning twice against Benfica.

Attack would have been suicide in the semifinal against FC Barcelona, even at Stamford Bridge. So Chelsea dug in around the penalty area. The players pushed themselves to the limit at home, and again at the Nou Camp in Barcelona. Eventually, it got them a result that had people perplexed: how was that possible? Because even Fernando Torres, totally out of form, managed to get on the score sheet. For a coach it was world-class achievement.

Unfortunately, most people—apart from Chelsea fans—fail to recognize the amazing accomplishment of the club and its manager, Di Matteo. More accurately: they don't want to see it. Why? Because it's not a pretty sight for a neutral spectator. And, of course, games at that stage of the Champions League are watched by far more neutrals than partisan supporters.

Yet the one paramount consideration in top sport is to do whatever is necessary to win. Especially if your opponent is stronger. Chelsea could never have won against Barcelona on the basis purely of the team's attacking qualities. With a tailored approach to the game, Chelsea stood a much better chance of winning. Di Matteo had devised the perfect tailored tactics and so he managed to win. No, it may not have been beautiful, but that would have been impossible. Di Matteo deserves full credit for Chelsea's one Champions League trophy. He found Barcelona's Achilles' heel, exposed it, caught the Spaniards off balance and eliminated them. Remarkable.

By the way, Chelsea were obviously a superb team with above-average players, otherwise they could never have defeated Barcelona, whatever their tactics. In the end it's the players who determine whether your ideas are feasible. Di Matteo's genius is that he managed to find a perfect balance between his players' qualities and the team's needs as a whole.

Naive defending

Sometimes I get angry at the naivety of Dutch clubs, nationally and internationally. They insist on finding an elegant solution for every situation, taking unnecessary risks as they build their attack. Keepers passing to defenders while there's a player marking them, for example. In international games, it's simply not done. Why do you think forwards pressure defenders? Because they're dribblers? It makes you wonder: what's going on? What on earth are they doing?

Take a look at a few clips of Manuel Neuer. Or Peter Schmeichel, possibly the most accomplished keeper of the last fifty years. He never passed a ball to a defender if he was marked. Instead he would send the ball flying toward the strikers and add for good measure: make something of it over there.

You often see teams trying to find an elegant solution for every situation, especially against FC Barcelona. No club can deal with Barça using only soccer skills. You have to be combative, create one-on-ones, harass and tackle them, and employ compact tactics. Then at least you have a chance. To rely on pure skill is to concede defeat because if any of your players' individual skills were high enough, they would be playing for Barcelona and not for you.

Atlético Madrid, and in 2015 Celta de Vigo and Espanyol as well, never pass in front of their own goal when they play Barcelona. Their weapons are hard work, confrontation, intimidation and a consistent strategy from the edge of the penalty area.

Celta took a risk and sent their forwards in to pressure Barcelona's defenders. They didn't give them the time to play the ball to the midfielders, they kept the passing lines covered. That suddenly exposed Gerard Piqué's vulnerability, revealing his inability to construct.

You can go into the game with a plan like that, but keeping it up for ninety minutes is another story. You have to get goals. Going behind forces Barcelona to play in a more attacking style, to take risks, allowing more space at the back. If you can achieve that, then even they are beatable.

Celta de Vigo won, Espanyol drew and Atlético Madrid lost at home by a hair's breadth.

I'm talking about teams that aren't as strong as Real Madrid, Juventus, Bayern Munich and Paris Saint-Germain. Chelsea tackled the 2012 Champions League semifinal differently. The English locked the back shut and gambled on getting at least one or two breaks. For the first half of the strategy you need a bit of luck. Well, Chelsea had a huge blue angel sitting on their crossbar. Astonishing. You need assassins to make the difference. Which is exactly how it went down at the Nou Camp, with goals by Ramires and Torres.

Traditionally, Barcelona do not have many players who are physical and like to get involved in one-on-ones. Javier Mascherano is really the only player with those qualities, and before him was Carles Puyol. When they play, their aim is to put their opponent under constant pressure, whether they have possession or not: by creating combinations against the other side when they're in possession in their own half, and by chasing after the other side in their half when they lose the ball.

Neither strategy requires a physical approach. But you need someone in the team who can make a serious dent in the other side. Carles Puyol used to be able to do that. Gerard Piqué is not that type of player. He is a clean defender whose main job is to make up for the lack of height in the Barcelona line-up at set pieces such as corners and free kicks.

Adapting to your opponent

Great teams are able to play in phases, to vary their tactics throughout the game. When Roy Keane captained Sir Alex Ferguson's Manchester United, no other team in the world could surpass them. They would entice their opponents with the idea that perhaps there was a chance here; maybe United aren't that much better after all. That gave teams like Chelsea or Newcastle the confidence to create a little space, and then United would come down like a ton of bricks, wherever and whenever they wanted: not once, but practically at will; usually in a 4-4-2 formation, although sometimes it was 4-3-1-2 or 4-3-3. They could switch tactics to match the way the opposing side were playing, taking advantage of weaknesses and grabbing opportunities wherever they occurred. So devious, and so smart.

PSV employed a similar approach between 2002 and 2006. Whenever they saw an opportunity in the days of their manager Guus Hiddink, keeper Heurelho Gomes, Alex, Phillip Cocu and Mark van Bommel, they pounced. Especially in the Amsterdam Arena against Ajax; PSV remained unbeaten there for years.

In their own stadium Ajax always felt morally obliged to dominate play and steer the game: it's part of the club's culture in Amsterdam. Fine, PSV thought. We'll let them have the ball and let them dominate. Only, in reality, that attitude, that decision, was actually PSV being dominant. PSV allowed Ajax to retain possession without giving away a single chance.

As soon as they lost possession Ajax were caught with the gate wide open and vulnerable to counterattack. PSV used an extremely clever strategy. First with Ruud van Nistelrooy in the attack and later Mateja Kežman—he subsequently played for Chelsea—they always found a few opportunities to exploit, to Ajax's great frustration. The Amsterdammers remained ever faithful to their club's attacking ethos instead of adapting to the situation. PSV would not have known what to do if Ajax had allowed them to take the initiative occasionally. Yet that theory could never be tested since it was simply not in their repertoire. I still consider it a serious deficiency.

On the other hand, the club has produced strikers such as Marco van Basten, Patrick Kluivert and Zlatan Ibrahimović, capable of playing extraordinary, totally original soccer. Ajax's attacking style also created superb forwards such as Wim Kieft and John Bosman, goal-scoring machines who were especially strong in the air. Ajax would attack from the flank with crosses from the left or right wing.

Few teams still play that way. It requires a strong header of the ball up front who moves automatically to the nearest post when the cross comes in. Strikers like Kieft and Bosman are rare these days; they no longer fit in the system, pushed out by tactics such as playing a left-footed winger on the right and a right-footed winger on the left. These players never cross the ball, they look for a quick passing combination. That requires different qualities from a striker leading an attack. To measure a striker's success in terms of goals scored is not always fair since his role is often to serve wingers and attacking midfielders.

It's still true that even at the top the ability to adapt to opponents improves your chances. At Ajax they have little time for that approach. PSV had mastered the art and often employed that tactic. No surprise then that the club reached the Champions League semifinal in 2005.

PSV in 2016 play the same style as PSV did under Guus Hiddink. Give the other side a false sense of security, a feeling that it has space to play soccer, that it could even get a result, and then pounce. The difference is that today's PSV have fewer individual skills and they don't manage to hermetically seal the defense. The team run by their manager, Phillip Cocu, concede too many goals.

Of course, it's difficult for attacking teams like FC Barcelona and Ajax to play a waiting game. Breaking that ingrained pattern, that internationally generally accepted dogma, just isn't in the nature of players who always want to go forward. On the other hand, it's also about a certain tactical maturity. It would be interesting to see if Barcelona could do it. But in reality I wouldn't even want Barça to try. Maybe not even Ajax, although Ajax lack the quality to compete internationally without being able to adapt.

At AC Milan we had mastered the 4-4-2 formation so thoroughly that we could beat everyone. We were fortunate enough to be able to switch to different game patterns within our system. We had to, since pressing on the opposing side when in possession was harder then than it is today, given the old rule that allowed keepers to pick up a back pass. There was no point blindly chasing the ball; within seconds the goalie would have it in his hands. So we developed tactical tricks to tempt opponents to the touchlines and to pile the pressure on there. That also required adjustment.

Individual class

In my first year as a player at Chelsea, the team was not on the same level as Manchester United. As a player you did what you could to deal with the quality deficit, yet the difference in skill of individual players between United and Chelsea left us almost without a chance. United often let opposing sides think: we could win this—only to raise the pace and simply leave them standing.

I experienced that even more dramatically as a manager at Newcastle. I had already won the FA Cup with Chelsea, so during the final against United at Wembley on May 22, 1999, I thought Newcastle had an excellent chance, yet in the end we lost 2–0. United played their own game from start to finish. I watched it later when the final was aired by ESPN Classic in America, on their Classic Matches program. Newcastle were playing well, even dominating some phases of the game, but two moments of individual class by Paul Scholes and Teddy Sheringham were enough to finish us.

In the end it all depends on individual class. That was evident in 2015/16 at Barcelona when Messi was injured and unable to play for a while. The organization remained unchanged and, keeping the lessons already learned in mind, Neymar and Luis Suárez were brought in: two world-class players, two individualists, two goal scorers. Neymar is deadly in limited space and, in the absence of Messi, he effortlessly took over the Argentinian's role as the player who makes the difference, while Suárez was the fulcrum. As such, with the same forward pressure by the defenders and midfielders, with quick, short positional play and a high percentage of possession, Luis Enrique's team continued to win.

All this showed that FC Barcelona were not just a synonym for Messi, as was once the case. Moreover, Luis Enrique is clearly not a manager who remolds the whole team when a key player is absent, even if that player is the star of the team. No, he has a smarter approach: he keeps his carefully crafted system intact, even if it is based on individual class. He just doesn't let it depend on one specific player. If you have the resources to attract players of sufficient quality to the club, you can still excel even without your star.

At Barcelona the whole strategy is designed to allow individuals to make the difference. In the last year under Pep Guardiola, the 2011/12 season, the plan began to fall apart because Barcelona relied too heavily on Messi as their exceptional player. It took only a couple of defenders to mark out Messi and the team suddenly looked less spectacular. Reason enough subsequently to bring in Neymar and Suárez, mainly to take the heat off Messi as the sole decisive factor.

The truly great

My professional career began at Haarlem, an average side that sometimes looked up from below and occasionally down from above in the Dutch first division. When we played Ajax, with Johan Cruijff, you could do what you liked but in the end you didn't stand a chance against the amazing class of a player like that. In those games Cruijff was always the decisive factor.

After a brief intermission following his adventure in America, Cruijff returned to Ajax, his first love. He was thirty by then and many speculated that he would find it hard to play in the Eredivisie, the top level in Dutch soccer, the second tier in Europe. A taunted, vengeful Cruijff turned out to be the best in the world.

On December 6, 1981, when I was nineteen, we were holding our own at Ajax's old stadium at De Meer. Haarlem were playing well in fact. But not well enough. In the twenty-second minute, Cruijff began to dribble on the left, far outside the penalty box, moving toward the right. Not forward or back but across the width of the pitch, around twenty-five meters from our goal.

After a quick combination he eluded a couple of Haarlem players, avoided another tackle and ended up on the far right of the pitch. Then as if out of nothing—no one had seen a chance or an opening for a goal—he produced a truly incredible lob from around twenty-five or thirty meters that flew over the fingertips of our keeper, Edward Metgod. Bang in the net.

And there you are. An extraordinary goal and there's only one thing left to do: applaud. There are no tactics to deal with the individual class of a player of that caliber.

Balance in a team

Guus Hiddink came to Chelsea in the middle of the 2015/16 season to replace José Mourinho as interim coach. He began by establishing stability in defense. Building up logically, based on experienced players such as John Terry, Gary Cahill, Branislav Ivanović and Thibaut Courtois. To give a drifting team structure, start with the foundation, the defense. Hiddink began with an amazing record-breaking series of unbeaten games, although he drew too often for Chelsea to be able to have a big impact on the Premier League.

By contrast, Louis van Gaal started from the top when he took up his post at Manchester United, whereas his defense was too vulnerable to maintain the club's place among the Premier League leaders. Van Gaal brought in the strikers Radamel Falcao and Ángel Di María, only to let them go again a year later. They didn't fit in. Yet at Paris Saint-Germain, Di María was free once more to bring down the roof.

At United, the new strikers didn't get a chance to show what they could do, because behind them the team was in disarray. The whole edifice caved in at Old Trafford. Van Gaal made the same mistake by bringing in the forwards Anthony Martial and Memphis Depay, rather than the kind of defenders you need in the Premier League.

To construct a team based around forwards is to commit hara-kiri, especially in the Premier League. There you need a stable base.

As Sir Alex Ferguson's Manchester United did. His teams always had a strong back line as well as a phenomenal axis: in 2008, Edwin van der Sar, Rio Ferdinand, Nemanja Vidić, Paul Scholes and Wayne Rooney. Accompanying these he had players of the highest caliber, such as Cristiano Ronaldo, Ryan Giggs, Teddy Sheringham, Carlos Tévez, David Beckham and a host of top players.

These weren't sides that humiliated their opponents. In fact Manchester United often left it to the final quarter of an hour to strike: Ferguson's famous last fifteen minutes. They almost always scored just before the game was about to end, often in injury time. Many put it down to luck, but it was hardly a matter of chance, it was quality. They could accelerate the pace when they needed to and were almost always able to score since their opponents had no energy left and were unable to keep up. Up front, United would have a couple of real goal-getters, each one a killer who only needed the one chance, like Yorke, Cole, Solskjaer, Sheringham, Rooney, Ronaldo and Tévez—almost all of them capable of creating chances by themselves and making the most of them.

A contact sport

When I first started playing professionally I never wore shin pads. They became compulsory in August 1990 and I really disliked that.

They didn't feel comfortable, even though it was a time when players kicked a lot more readily than they do today. The television cameras picked up far less detail than they do now and players got away with much more in their eagerness to neutralize a particular opponent.

These days referees stop play for the slightest infringement. Less so in the Premier League perhaps, but certainly in Dutch competition. The ideal is a kind of glorified indoor soccer. That's due in no small part to the prevalence of artificial grass at almost half the eighteen top clubs. It's as though contact is prohibited, even though soccer is a contact sport.

In my day, soccer was a lot less gentle: an elbow in the face, boots with massive aluminium studs to stomp on your foot, shirt tugging, groin grabbing, hair pulling . . . you could expect anything and everything on the pitch. It wasn't acceptable, it was against the rules, but it happened. You had to protect yourself and you had to watch out.

Today it's all a lot less physical, despite the *mano-a-mano* duels and the frequent clashes in the Premier League. English referees are much more tolerant. Yet that often puts English clubs at a disadvantage when they play on the Continent. They are continually being penalized. In fact teams that compete internationally need two styles of play: one for the English league and one for European competition.

Great expectations

No club in the world has higher expectations than Real Madrid. This is the result of its amazingly successful history and its philosophy. Madrilenians want a combination of superb, attractive, attacking, winning soccer with lots of goals by absolute top players who are among the best in the world and can supply them with plenty of oohs and aahs. Madrilenians want entertainment. It's fine if the other side scores a couple of goals, as long as Real score six.

Since the situation in Spain and abroad dictates that this only ever happens occasionally—Real's arch rivals in both arenas being FC Barcelona—these expectations have an adverse effect. Time and again the club's ambitions are frustrated and one manager after another gets the boot. Even Carlo Ancelotti, who gave Real *La Décima*, their tenth European Cup, was sent packing because he could not lift the club above Barcelona in the Primera División.

At Barcelona the fans have also become accustomed to success. A mediocre result is immediate cause for alarm. The fans demand victory, every time, with spectacular skills and mouth-watering combinations, although the Catalan supporters are less prone to turn against their club, especially since Barcelona are Catalonia's flagship, the pride and joy of the northeastern autonomous region where the desire for independence from Spain is huge.

Fans of AC Milan were also spoiled by success and trophies for many years. For supporters it is difficult to admit that yesterday's superpower is now no longer. When you have been at the top for so long, the new situation can be difficult to swallow. Take a look at AC Milan–Cesena, and all you see is empty stands. Around 20,000 spectators turn up for a match like that. In my day the San Siro was always full. I see the pain of the fans in the grandstand when I visit. It grabs you. But the story is simple: the club doesn't have the financial muscle to attract top players. The budget determines the result and AC Milan have been eclipsed: internationally by many and in Italy by their rivals Juventus.

The same goes for Manchester United: always on top under Ferguson and public enemy number one for the fans of every other Premier League club. First, as the performances decline you get derision, later sympathy, eventually pity. What could be worse for a top club? Well, having a neighbor that's even wealthier and manages to snatch the crown away, like Manchester City. In fact Liverpool are in the same boat as Man United.

Arsenal sail their own independent course. Financial security is the bottom line, so the club doesn't spend extreme sums on great players to buy its way to the top. Which means in the end that it occasionally wins a trophy or two, but that it never gets to dominate the Premier League or Champions League and falls short of the main prize. Arsenal supporters have loyally backed that strategy for years, but a vocal and growing minority are trying to force change.

The European elite

If you want to compete with FC Barcelona, Real Madrid and Bayern Munich then you must have absolutely top players. Real Madrid have the resources to buy players of that level, so have Barcelona. Spain rules because Spain has the best players.

Manchester City, Manchester United and Chelsea can also afford whoever they want to buy. The more interesting question is: do the best players *want* to play at City? Is a Lionel Messi or a Ronaldo prepared to say goodbye to Spain and settle in England? Manchester City hope to change things by appointing Pep Guardiola as manager. Maybe he has prepared the way for Messi or Ronaldo to make that move.

I don't know if it will happen, but I'm curious to see how Guardiola gets on and who he signs. I believe he can win the Premier League, but the more important goal for City is to win the Champions League and secure his status. In fact I suspect that Guardiola was brought in by City precisely for that purpose. They have already been Premier League champions twice.

Bayern Munich brought him in to win the European Cup, but with his trademark tiki-taka soccer. It was a style of play that influential people like Karl-Heinz Rummenigge and Uli Hoeness considered sacrosanct. They wanted Bayern's version of that style to be the new world standard, in the same way Guardiola developed it at Barça.

He made a promising start at Bayern, capped by a sublime Champions League game in Manchester in the autumn of 2013 against City.

Unfortunately Guardiola had to deal with long-term injuries to Arjen Robben and Franck Ribéry, players who possess the individual class to be able to make the difference in a game along the flanks. The team's level was high—Robert Lewandowski is an exceptional finisher—but in the end a manager depends on the individual qualities and class of players to make the decisive difference when the prizes are being divvied up.

At Manchester City, Sergio Agüero is the closest the club has to a Messi or a Ronaldo. But whereas Messi and Ronaldo can do it alone, Agüero needs support and assistance. The Spaniard David Silva approaches the top level, but is prone to injury. Given the intensity of the English game and the number of matches, Silva often suffers from his apparent fragility. In England, the physical demands on a player's body are almost impossible to hold up against for an entire season. Guardiola will have to take account of that.

In Germany and Spain they play fewer games and the physical contact is less intense. It will be fascinating to see whether Guardiola is able to introduce tiki-taka at Manchester City, or if he maintains the English soccer culture. In my view the latter is a precondition for winning the Premier League.

The dead ball

Corners and free kicks remain strangely underappreciated. In fact there are a lot of advantages to be gained from dead balls. The English cult club Wimbledon really knew how to exploit this aspect of the game to the fullest. Many teams fail to use dead ball set pieces effectively, even though they can win a game. It all comes down to agreeing tactics and practice, practice, practice.

The wall

The wall is the keeper's responsibility. It is up to the goalie to say where the wall should be placed and how many players should stand in the way of a free kick. Generally I think walls are a good thing and as a manager I always liked my keeper to use one. I once had a keeper who decided not to and the ball ended up in the back of the net from a good distance. My only concession to a keeper who doesn't want a wall—in theory it blocks his view of the ball—is to take one or two players out of it to leave a gap.

Keepers who don't place a wall for a free kick often find an opposition wall looming up in front of them instead. The player taking the free kick will send a couple of players to stand in a line, because a wall helps a free-kick specialist aim. The idea is to aim between the second and third player in the wall.

I prefer to have tall players in the center of the wall rather than at the ends, which used to be the fashion. Shorter players can stand on either side. Almost all balls over the wall pass between the first and second, or between the second and third, in the line.

Most walls comprise four players. At the end there's usually a player who runs into position if the free kick is taken in two stages. Keepers may go for a five-player wall nearer the goal; for example, if the free kick is on the edge of the box. With five in the wall, you almost force the free-kick taker to direct the ball at the corner where the keeper is standing. If the free kick is on the edge of the penalty area then the distance between the wall and goal is usually too short for the ball to be chipped over the wall. Messi, Maradona and maybe Michel Platini could do it; there's probably no one else capable of arcing the ball sufficiently.

Free-kick specialists

Smart players fire the ball under the wall if they see the keeper telling the players in the wall to jump. A well-prepared free-kick specialist knows what a keeper wants from the defenders in a wall. By the same token, a keeper should know the free-kick specialist's preferences.

If the player is on target despite all the countermeasures then the only possible response is applause; well done to the specialist. Clearly he is exceptionally good, assuming the keeper stayed in place. Keepers often make the mistake of moving left or right before the strike, or even of diving—often out of uncertainty. It is an appalling error because keepers can generally count on the ball coming directly at them. Sometimes they don't even follow their own instructions.

Most free-kick takers prefer the ball to be placed a little back from the penalty area. Twenty meters is ideal. Pierre van Hooijdonk, a former Dutch international who played for Nottingham Forest, Celtic, Fenerbahçe, Benfica and Feyenoord, was the uncrowned king of free kicks at that distance: making himself the best in the world by practicing over and over again until he developed a perfect strike.

Pierre was quite happy to place the ball a few meters farther back from the goal, while other players often secretly try to place it slightly farther forward. They are only making it harder for themselves. With one or two extra meters, Van Hooijdonk was able to give the ball even more power and the added distance also gave the ball a chance to drop sufficiently to go in just below the bar.

The corner

Why do some players prefer to take short corners? Mainly to disorient the defense and draw defenders away from the goalmouth. The results

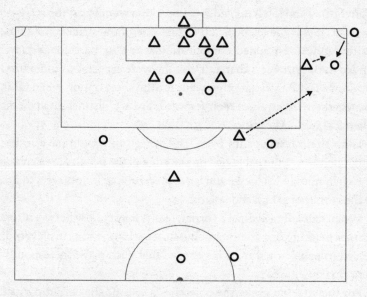

Short corners draw defenders away from the goal area.

--→ route of player
—→ route of the ball

of a short corner may differ, but the intention is to force two defenders to come out of the otherwise crowded penalty area. If only one defender comes out to deal with a short corner, the two corner-takers will have few problems getting past. Two defenders have to come out to a short corner.

If you also position a player on the edge of the penalty area, to receive a direct pass from the corner, then that will draw yet another defender out of the penalty area. The fewer defenders in the box, the easier it is for the attacking team to head the ball in.

Funnily enough, defenders often take the contrary viewpoint: the fewer the number of forwards in the box, the easier it is for the keeper to get the ball. And if the defending team places two strikers on the halfway line the attacking side has to withdraw yet more players from the area to cover the possibility of a quick counter should the keeper grab the ball and loft it upfield. FC Barcelona would post three strikers up front. It was the keeper's job to find one of the strikers for a quick counterattack. An added complication was that Barcelona's players tended to be rather less than tall, so they were especially vulnerable in the air. In fact Barcelona often went for the short option when taking corners themselves, since their forwards are at a distinct disadvantage when it comes to heading.

With three Catalans up front, the other side would have to keep four defenders at the back, one on the edge of the penalty area and one or two in midfield. That would leave just three or four players to head in the corner or take a shot at goal.

When defending against a corner, teams may choose between zonal or man-marking or a combination. Man-marking results in players dispersed in pairs; zonal marking means that each player is responsible for a particular area.

For the attacking side, the objective is to time the corner correctly to get the ball in front of goal, directly or curving, but out of reach of the keeper. Either way, the defenders need to be kept in place. If the ball swerves out and they get a chance to run, they can get the

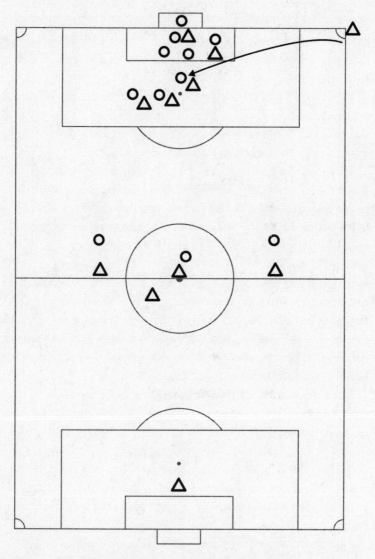

When defending against a corner, Barcelona keep three forwards around the halfway line, forcing the other side to leave at least four players at the back.

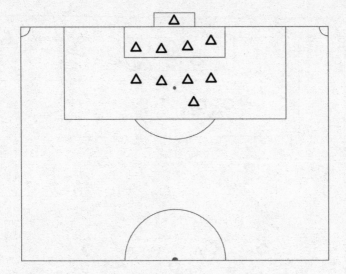

When defending against a corner with zonal marking, each player defends a specific area or zone.

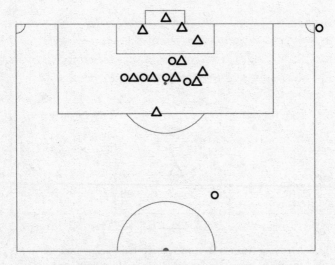

When defending against a corner with man-marking, each player marks a specific opponent.

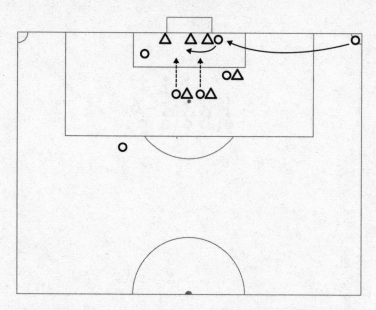

The ball is chipped to the near post and headed on to the approaching players.

purchase they need to jump higher. If they have to stay in their zone, it's far harder to jump high. That leaves the attacking side with the advantage, because then players can run in and jump higher.

An alternative way to deliver a corner is to chip the ball in an arc to the near post for it to be headed on to a couple of forwards running in blind. To touch the ball is to score, at least in most cases. You need a tall, strong player to head on, otherwise a defender or the keeper can easily get rid of the ball to the touchline and the whole question of heading on becomes academic. At AC Milan, this was our most productive variation.

Another smart corner tactic is to have five players running in while a sixth runs back and turns up on the edge of the penalty area. The sixth player often has a free shot at goal from there, around sixteen meters out. You can use that trick once, as a surprise. Once the other

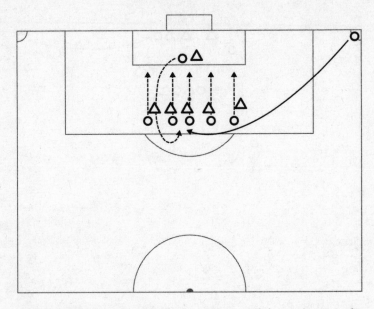

A surprise corner involves five players running in while a sixth runs in the opposite direction to receive the ball on the edge of the penalty area.

team knows it's part of your repertoire, it will post a defender between the penalty spot and the edge of the area as a precaution to stop it happening again.

Systems

Tactical formations

Everyone knows them, the diagrams of the team formations in the newspaper and on television before a game, and the endless discussions about which system the manager will choose: 4-4-2, 4-3-3, 5-3-2, 3-4-3, 4-3-2-1, 4-2-3-1, 4-2-2-1-1.

Note that if you add the numbers they always come to ten—keepers are never included when charting tactical formations. Yet today's keepers have to be able to play soccer too, especially since the rule preventing keepers from picking up back passes was introduced in 1992. Most managers see the keeper as the first link in the buildup of an attack from the back.

After all, there are eleven players in a team, not ten. The keeper plays an integral part in the team's tactics. But what are tactics? In short they are about exploiting the specific qualities of the player or players in your team who will be decisive in a game, and attacking the deficiencies of the opposing side. Tactics only work if they enable the individual to excel.

Tactics and systems are closely connected. For me, a system—whichever you choose—is a framework for defense and attack.

In defense, you use a system to organize and stick together so that the other side doesn't get through when it has possession. The point is: what to do when you don't have the ball? What to do to give the other side as little space as possible and limit its opportunity to attack?

When attacking, you stick to a system and a formation that will be able to create as much space as possible for your forwards to exploit their skills. At the same time, the task of the defenders is to

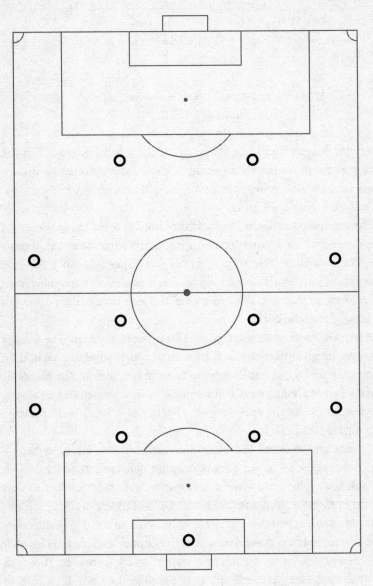

4-4-2 formation.

identify where the danger lies should the forwards or midfielders lose the ball.

Within those parameters you have to make it click between the players, so that they can sense what the others are going to do. In other words: before it happens. However paradoxical it may seem, it's not about what happens when you have the ball, but about what happens when you don't.

As we have seen, systems and plans of attack depend to a large extent on the qualities of the individual players. If the central defender is slow, the defense shouldn't be arrayed along the halfway line. With a fast yet technically limited striker, there's not much point trying to focus play in the other side's penalty area.

You need to start by drawing up an analysis of the strengths and weaknesses of your team before you can choose which formation to use: 4-4-2, 4-3-3 or some other variation. Then you look at the weaknesses of the other side's formation, or its individual players, such as someone who's not playing in his usual position.

To win the game, you need to have possession of the ball. But you don't need to have possession for long. You don't necessarily need more possession than the other side. That is a common misconception. Moreover, when you get the ball you don't need to keep possession: the main thing is to get as much advantage out of having the ball as you can.

4-4-2 game plan

A 4-4-2 formation is a system with a forward block of two central strikers. When in possession, the two strikers are the focus of the team's attack. It is easier to score with two strikers than with one. With two strikers it is also easier to force the opposing four-player defense further back, and to confuse the other side's buildup.

One of the strikers takes up position between the two left defenders and the other between the two on the right. That forces the keeper to bypass the back four in the buildup since the strikers can put them under immediate pressure. Many English clubs use this system with two strikers, as an attacking tactic as well as to confuse the other side's buildup.

In England, teams make prolific use of the long ball from the back to the two strikers. The best combination is a big, tall, strong striker alongside a short, lithe, nimble one. The tall striker goes for the long ball and heads it on as the shorter player goes deep or dives behind, or if the short striker remains in position, the taller striker plays it to the other's feet.

This maintains the pressure on the two central defenders, forcing them to play one-on-one at the back. It is especially difficult for central defenders because they prefer to have one defender dealing with the taller striker, while another takes up a free position behind to provide cover. With two strikers, the defense comes under pressure and the left or right back is forced to move toward the center to cover the back, as a result opening up the flank . . .

In a 4-4-2 formation, the left and right midfielders become wingers. When in possession, the team has four players up front. If the team loses the ball, the two outer midfielders drop back to a right and left back position to help cover the midfielders in the center. The two central midfielders take on a defensive role and seal up the defensive formation.

Once the team regains the ball it's easy to switch back to an attacking mode since the two strikers are ready up front. The speed at which a team switches between gaining the ball and losing it (defense) and losing the ball and regaining possession (attack) often has a crucial impact on the ability to obtain a result.

In my days at AC Milan under Arrigo Sacchi, we used to play 4-4-2. No comparison with today's 4-4-2, if only because keepers could pick up back passes. While we started with 4-3-3 our results were inconsistent, until an ankle injury sent Marco van Basten to the sidelines for a

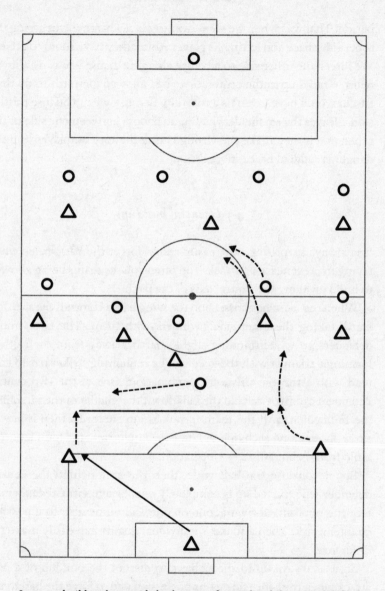

In a 4-3-3 buildup the outside backs move forward and the central defenders go wide. They form a triangular combination with the keeper to avoid the oncoming striker. One of the central defenders is then free to move into midfield, giving numerical superiority.

period. That was when we went over to 4-4-2. That involves giving the other side space and letting its players think they have room to attack. We forced the other side to advance along the flank; you can't allow a team to build up in the center. If we had allowed forwards to do that, Sacchi would have given us a roasting. Because when you lose possession it leaves the midfielders having to choose between one side or the other, and if they make the wrong choice they are outplayed and the danger is suddenly a lot more serious.

4-3-3 (central buildup)

It is always surprising how easily teams forget the basic rules when trying to prevent a 4-3-3 attack. Too often you see teams being allowed to build up along the central axis of the pitch.

When the team has possession the wing backs come all the way forward, taking the other side's wingers with them. The two central defenders go wide, standing slightly farther away from each other, forming a triangle with the keeper. The remaining striker has to contend with a three-against-one combination. One of the two central defenders can then dribble the ball down the middle of the pitch into the midfield area. If the team in possession succeeds, then it has an extra player along each line. A fantastic buildup and the foundation to build from behind in a 4-3-3 formation.

But if you lose the ball wide, then the area behind the central defender who moved up is completely open, leaving the defenders to face the opposing forwards one-on-one and vulnerable to a possible counterattack. Then a striker's individual quality can easily make the difference.

So it is always up to the strikers to disrupt the buildup of a new attack when the other side gains possession and to force the ball to the flank, ensuring the midfielder does not get into the position of having to defend against two opponents.

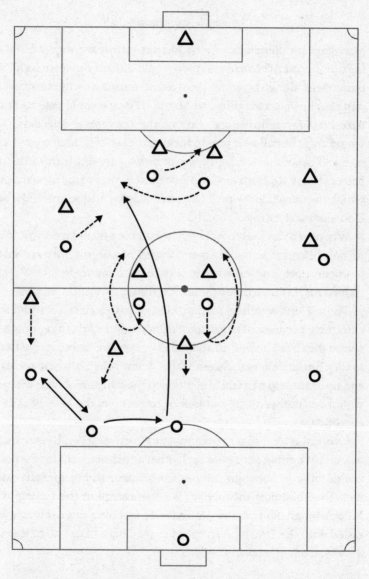

At AC Milan we often built up by sending a long high ball from the back to the striker, whose job was to keep the ball and pass it to the approaching midfielders as they escaped their markers.

Chipping as an attacking tactic

Managers at other clubs weren't just sitting idly by; they were study-ing our 4-4-2 at AC Milan and they would often try to force us to build our attacks along the wing. If we found ourselves without space, the wing backs Paolo Maldini and Mauro Tassotti would pass to Franco Baresi or Alessandro "Billy" Costacurta, the central defenders. They would chip the ball over the midfield to the strikers, Marco van Basten or me. Then either we kept the ball or we passed it back to the mid-fielders Frank Rijkaard or Carlo Ancelotti as they came forward, from which the attack developed. On either side we had sprinters: Roberto Donadoni and Angelo Colombo.

Whenever Van Basten or I lost the ball the other players would give us hell because the whole team would be surging forward at that moment, open and exposed to a potential counterattack. We often trained for this unorthodox kind of buildup.

Those chips were the hardest kind of passes since they had to be extremely accurate. The Italian defenders were breathing down our necks: they left Van Basten and me no space. We had to arrive exactly as the chip landed. Franco and "Billy" knew roughly where we would end up at the end of a run and scooped the ball precisely to where we would be. Truly amazing. It looked so easy, yet the level of skill was exceptional.

It was also vital that the combination between Van Basten and me worked. We could anticipate each other and never went for the ball, or ran deep, or left or right simultaneously. Our complementary move-ments were almost instinctive. We hammered in the timing at AC Milan's Milanello training ground over and over again. Having been raised with the Dutch preference for 4-3-3, both of us had to learn the 4-4-2 system.

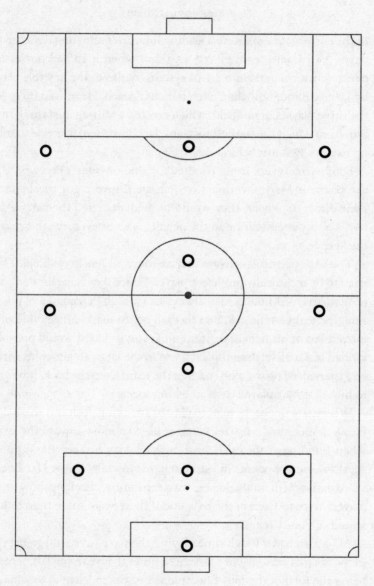

3-4-3 formation.

Ajax against Milan

In the early 1990s Ajax were a leading force in international soccer. On paper, Van Gaal's team played 4-3-3, but when it gained possession, effectively it changed into a 3-4-3 system thanks to the key role played by Danny Blind, now the Dutch national coach. He moved up to join the three players in midfield, which created a four-against-three situation from which the farthest forward, Jari Litmanen, was able to move up to a position just behind the striker.

Four strikers up front resulted in one-on-ones everywhere on the pitch. If Marc Overmars or Patrick Kluivert got the better of their direct opponent, they would immediately find themselves in a two-against-one situation in the penalty area or even eye-to-eye with the keeper.

The basic premise is always to have more players in midfield. These need to be technically proficient players, since they have limited space to maneuver. Although Ajax always had a high percentage of possession, the team would also lose the ball occasionally. Since Blind often moved out of his defensive position, Frank Rijkaard would provide a kind of residual defense. Rijkaard was in the latter stages of his career, an experienced player who coached the team from the back. It was due to him that Ajax played such attacking soccer.

Whereas wing backs tend to play in attacking positions these days, Frank de Boer and Michael Reiziger used to move toward the center when Blind went forward. That enabled Ajax to keep the distances short for the opponents in the attack. Meanwhile, Edgar Davids provided balance in midfield: he was constantly checking how many players were in front of the ball, and if there were more than four he would call one back.

AC Milan had a tough time playing their 4-4-2 system against Ajax in the 1994/95 season. They lost three times that year, the last occasion being the final of the 1995 Champions League in Vienna, to a Patrick Kluivert goal.

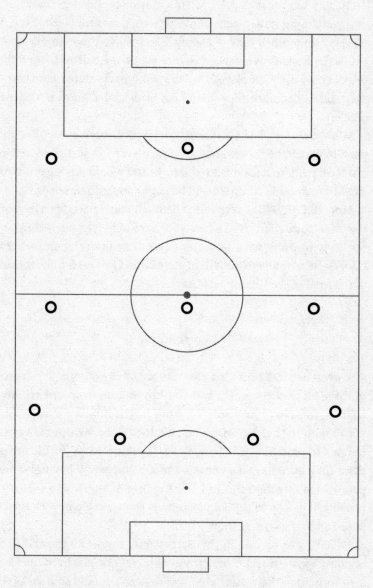

4-3-3 formation.

Ajax's wing backs had AC Milan's outside midfielders marked. The two remaining Italian central midfielders therefore faced three Ajax players, sometimes four if Danny Blind moved into midfield. As a result the Italians never had a chance to get the ball and found themselves completely outplayed. Milan's wing backs didn't dare come to their aid either since they were kept in place by Ajax's outside right and left.

With their 4-3-3 and 3-4-3 formation, Ajax created a situation on the pitch in which they always had an extra player. Because they were constantly having to decide who to attack, and would often get it wrong, AC Milan became confused and began to doubt themselves.

How did AC Milan respond? The team could have tried mirroring the Ajax formation. But when you have achieved such formidable results with your own 4-4-2-formula, it's difficult to change tack. Fabio Capello held rigidly to his Italian method and lost each time, including in the final of the Champions League.

4-3-3 game plan

The great advantage of a 4-3-3 formation is that you can play in groups of three all over the pitch, and you can link up from one trio to the next as you move forward. Working in trios makes it easy for the player with the ball because when it's done right there are always two options to pass forward. This leaves defenders in a difficult situation since they have to make choices and are constantly having to anticipate which direction the attack is heading in and where the trio are moving. The key to the combination is to pass the ball with the right pace and to the correct foot.

When I was playing in the Netherlands almost all the clubs relied on a 4-3-3 system and most games were won or lost in midfield. In a 4-3-3 formation the winger's job was to keep the field as wide as possible. The right and left wingers would stay close to the touchline, since that forced the other side's right and left backs to go equally wide, creating open spaces in the center.

Midfielders used the opportunity to dive into the space between the two backs and the two central defenders. To prevent this the two wing backs would regularly move to a more central position, which then opened up space along the flanks for the wingers to go forward along the touchline to deliver a cross.

The midfield in a 4-3-3 formation

There are three options for the midfield area in this system:

- A flat midfield with three players lined abreast: which rarely happens since a pass between any of these players makes the midfield redundant.
- A midfield in which the central midfielder is at the apex of a triangle pointing backward, so he is in front of the defense, playing as a number 6.
- A midfield in which the central midfielder is at the apex of a triangle pointing forward, in an attacking position near the striker, so he is then said to be playing as a number 10.

Among Dutch players, who refer to these midfield trios as triangles, the concept is a familiar one and well understood. In England, however, you don't talk about the apex of a triangle, pointing forward or back. In England you simply describe the team formation: 4-3-3 with the apex of a triangle toward the back is described as a 4-1-2-3 system; 4-3-3 with the apex pointing forward is a 4-2-1-3 system. So with the latter you have one attacking midfielder, and with the former two.

After Chelsea sent José Mourinho packing, Guus Hiddink tried organizing his midfield in a 4-1-2-3 system. To create an ideal midfield combination you need three different kinds of player: a controller, a sprinter and a creative forward who can score goals.

Hiddink had precisely the right combination with John Obi Mikel, Nemanja Matić and Cesc Fàbregas. Yet there was something wrong. Three excellent players, each with his own specific qualities, would surely fit into a 4-3-3 system? Not always. Obi Mikel plays defensively but lacks tackling skills, he doesn't take the ball away, and when the team gain or lose the ball, he doesn't switch roles quickly enough in depth. Matić is a sprinter, but often wide, with the ball at his feet, and doesn't play deep fast enough. Fàbregas is fantastic when it comes to attacking soccer, but in a defensive role he often makes mistakes.

When you're looking to buy a midfield, there's a lot that can go wrong. Combining the required qualities there is a delicate business: it may look right on paper, but that's no guarantee. You have to wait and see what happens in practice. Often these combinations gel together with one or two coincidental successes.

Take another example: Manchester United in the late 1990s. Sir Alex Ferguson had a well-oiled machine in midfield and his combination with one or two strikers worked with the precision of a Swiss watch. These talented and versatile players were also able to switch from a 4-4-2 formation to 4-3-3, with either one or two attacking midfielders. It worked because United's midfielders could play in different systems and in different situations.

Man Utd had fantastic strikers: Andy Cole, Dwight Yorke, Teddy Sheringham, Ole-Gunnar Solskjaer and Ruud van Nistelrooy. Along the axis there were Roy Keane, Paul Scholes, Nicky Butt, and later Michael Carrick and Darren Fletcher. On the wing were players such as Ryan Giggs, David Beckham and later Ronaldo. Their qualities could give United something extra whenever the game required it.

Sir Alex's teams always had an extra trick up their sleeve. I thought they were especially good when they played in Europe in the Champions League. They could switch their system effortlessly to a single striker with a supporting forward. It seemed like Sir Alex could send any eleven players onto the pitch and it would work out fine.

Which proves that in the end individual qualities are the decisive factor.

Rigid game

As a manager at Chelsea, Newcastle United and Feyenoord I always focused on the qualities of my players when working out a system. None of these clubs dictated a particular style of play. I think Ajax is the only club in the world that demands their manager employ a 4-3-3 formation. Every team at the club plays with that system, from the six-year-old youngsters to the first team. There is something to be said for giving the manager a guideline, but I have never known it so rigidly adhered to as at Ajax.

At Feyenoord I started by using 4-3-3, since I had Dirk Kuyt, a genuine striker. On the right I had the young Salomon Kalou, still a teenager at the time, a hugely talented Ivorian with an amazing ability to pass; quick, effective and with the knack of scoring. On the left I had the Belgian international Bart Goor, a diesel engine and a great striker of the ball who never stopped running back and forth. On paper he was a left winger, yet in reality he was a false winger who took every liberty when in possession.

In the Netherlands, Ajax have still held on to the 4-3-3 system, with the wingers sticking close to their positions rather than continually moving in to meet the advancing backs. Even when the club was playing in the Champions League or the Europa League, the recent manager, Frank de Boer, made no concessions. That generally resulted in a quick elimination for Ajax, since it is relatively easy to defend against this system.

Moreover, Ajax do not have the financial muscle to raise their talented youngsters to full maturity before they move elsewhere. And Ajax certainly don't have the resources to buy players of sufficient quality to play the old variation of the 4-3-3 theme which worked so well forty years ago. The world has caught up with Ajax and passed the club by: financially, physically and tactically. Physically, since Ajax field young players who have yet to mature. Tactically? That's simply a matter of obstinacy: the people at Ajax are living in the past.

In Amsterdam they like to point to Barcelona, but there is really no comparison. Barcelona can play 4-3-3 without having to take the opposing team into account. Their players are powerful individually— technically and tactically. At Ajax, that's beyond them.

Crazy or brilliant?

Wimbledon were known in the mid-1990s as the "Crazy Gang." But they weren't really crazy at all. The philosophy behind their 4-3-3 was extremely well thought out. They made clever use of the qualities at their disposal. I knew that from experience, because Chelsea played Wimbledon in the spring of 1997 in an FA Cup semifinal.

They did nothing without a reason in that team. It was certainly not a question of kick and run like mad, as many supposed. They built up from the keeper to the central defender, who passed the ball to the wing, slightly ahead of the approaching right back. With a tight diagonal ball forward, the winger sought out the striker Marcus Gayle along the touchline. He was a giant of a player and strong as an ox, who looked for confrontation and went into every challenge at full throttle, his objective being to force a throw-in deep in the opposing half or a corner. Then the three midfielders would move up to collect the loose ball.

They had a plan worked out for every situation. Wimbledon had specialized to such an extent that a throw-in or a corner was effectively a chance at goal. That meant all hands on deck. They were way ahead of their time. Now every team trains extensively for these standard situations because it is increasingly difficult to get through tightly organized defenses filled with top athletes. It was all superbly coordinated with players like Vinnie Jones, Øyvind Leonhardsen, Robbie Earle, Dean Holdsworth, and top scorers Efan Ekoku and Marcus

Gayle. That season, 1996/97, the Dons finished eighth in the Premier League and reached the semifinals of both the FA Cup and the League Cup, with the lowest budget in the whole division!

My strategy for Chelsea to get past Wimbledon to the FA Cup final was to throw our 3-5-2 system overboard and to work out a plan based on a 4-4-2 formation. I had to find a way to stop the long ball getting all the way forward, and if it did get forward then I needed a right and left back to help defend. I drummed it into my players that they had to do everything in their power to prevent corners, free kicks and throw-ins. Force them to play in the wings, I said, because they are far less skilled there than in their standard situations. It worked out brilliantly and Gayle hardly got a chance to cause his customary havoc.

New demands on the striker in 4-3-3

Soccer's evolution has led to a different kind of 4-3-3 from the formation that worked so well forty years ago, when Dutch players successfully developed the system at Feyenoord and Ajax and in the national side. Just take a look at Barcelona.

The attacking runs by their midfielders almost always go through the center, so that the other side's backs are forced to provide support in the center and leave their position on the wing exposed. That creates space for Jordi Alba and Dani Alves charging in from behind, alternating with Neymar and Messi playing from the left and right flanks.

Today the wing backs in a 4-3-3 system play a crucial role as attacking players, at first in the buildup and then in the actual attack. They are able to advance on the outside right and left because these days almost every team playing the 4-3-3 system has a left-footed forward on the right wing and a right-footed forward on the left wing. When the team has the ball, outside players gravitate naturally to the center. That allows the backs to dive into the open space on the flank, while two midfielders keep control behind these two advancing players. Ideally teams should also be able to switch play quickly from one side to the other, because the side where the ball isn't suddenly has oceans of space, all the defenders having moved to the side where the ball is.

When playing wide defenders who serve as attacking wingers, and outside players who move to the center to create a combination or go for goal themselves, strikers have to prove their worth.

Strikers have the toughest time in today's 4-3-3, while they used to have it easy. You used to wait for a pass from wide, make your run and then turn up just as in training at the near or far post to finish off the cross. Today, strikers are no longer able to run in at the head of the attack; they have to make space for other players in the team, especially as the wingers move in. But since there is hardly any space in front of goal, the striker often pulls back.

The modern 4-3-3 system creates new stars on the flanks, such as Messi, Neymar, Ronaldo and Robben, and it leaves great strikers in limbo, like Ruud van Nistelrooy in the Dutch team at the 2006 World Cup in Germany and Robert Lewandowski in his early years at Bayern Munich. They were among the leading players of the day, and yet they struggled in their position since it had become more important to make space for Robin van Persie and Arjen Robben, or Franck Ribéry and Arjen Robben, than to hone their own role as finisher.

In short, strikers have metamorphosed in the new 4-3-3. They are no longer purely attacking forwards. Even Zlatan Ibrahimović often falls back and gets involved in the midfield. In attacking teams that can produce an almost impossible combination. It is no coincidence that strikers find themselves under almost constant fire and often have to make way for midfielders who move easily and control the ball.

In the Dutch team at the 2006 World Cup in Germany, Arjen Robben and Robin van Persie were continually running in from the right and left flank and poor Van Nistelrooy had no idea where to go. It was enormously frustrating for him, and was exacerbated by the manager, Marco van Basten, who openly and repeatedly spoke about Van

Nistelrooy being unable to do his job in his position. After the World Cup, Van Nistelrooy retired from the Dutch squad.

In 2015 at FC Bayern, Pep Guardiola started by recalling Robert Lewandowski to the bench. Guardiola placed Thomas Müller, originally a midfielder, as the striker, with indifferent results—until Lewandowski suddenly scored five goals in a midweek home game against title contenders VfL Wolfsburg, then second in the Bundesliga. It was the sixth round and Lewandowski was on the bench. At the start of the second half, he was brought on instead of the midfielder Thiago Alcantara with the team 1–0 down at Munich's Allianz Arena. Between the fifty-first and sixtieth minutes Lewandowski scored five goals (final score 5–1), which earned him various records: fastest hat trick (three and a half minutes), fastest four goals (in under six minutes) and fastest five goals (within nine minutes) in the Bundesliga. And to think that before that he had been having an appalling time trying to recapture his place in the starting lineup, because he was unclear about what Guardiola wanted him to do and did not seem to have the qualities Guardiola expected of him as a striker.

Interestingly, neither Robben nor Ribéry played in that game against VfL Wolfsburg: the two wide players who constantly find their way into the center, Robben from the right with his left foot and Ribéry from the left with his right foot. Of course, it was no coincidence.

Strikers often experience this kind of problem in today's 4-3-3 system, whereby teams try to keep play in the opposing side's half. If you fall back into your own half using this system, or rely on the counter-attack, then it leaves the striker in a difficult role, although it is still possible for him to remain in position. Strikers need to be able to cover big distances to gain possession behind the opposing defense and they have to be able to keep the ball while outnumbered. In effect the striker is a target, the focus of play in depth.

That is yet another way of interpreting the striker's role. Normally, at least fifteen or twenty years ago, wide players were expected to

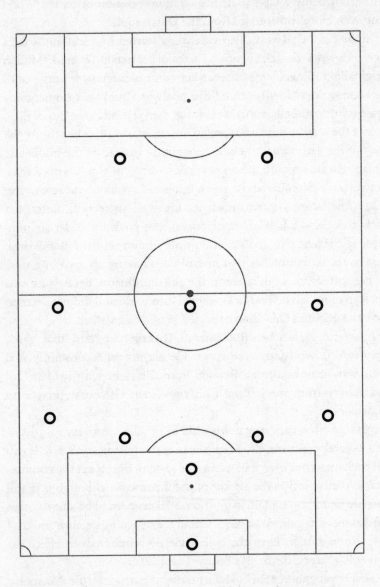

When the wing backs move forward, a 5-3-2 formation becomes 3-5-2.

support the striker. Today when the team loses possession, the wingers are practically forced into the role of right and left back since they have to chase their direct opponents (defensive midfielders) as they throw themselves into the attack while the actual right and left backs move into the center when a counterattack develops, often to the edge of the penalty area. Sometimes you see around five or six players form a defensive line, or a neat crescent.

3-5-2 game plan

When I arrived in England, Liverpool were using a 3-5-2 formation. That was due primarily to the presence of John Barnes in the team. Barnes was not especially skilled at tackling, but he was exceptionally good with the ball and had an amazing overview of the game. So what do you do as Liverpool manager? Give Barnes the opportunity to direct play. When defenders had the ball they immediately sought out Barnes, and of all the five midfielders it was Barnes who shaped the attack and had a free role to play as a striker too.

Juventus and the Italian national team, the *Squadra Azzurra*, used the same system to exploit Andrea Pirlo's qualities. Depending on who they were playing against, they sometimes adapted it to a 3-4-3 formation, purely to spare Pirlo when the team lost the ball and to protect him when they gained possession.

The latter was crucial since no team can afford to find itself paralyzed if a particular player is marked out of the game. When that happens, the team has to be able to make room for others to take the lead, or the players switch to another formation to deal with the vulnerability.

A 3-5-2 formation is perfect as you need plenty of players in midfield for your game plan. Inevitably, the formation will call for two players along the touchline who are able to run and who have no trouble dashing fifty or sixty meters back and forth time and again.

Depending on who has possession, these amazing sprinters effectively cover three different positions: wide defender, midfielder and forward. At Juventus they have the Swiss Stephan Lichtsteiner on the right. He must have five pairs of lungs.

Van Gaal, Brazil, 2014

To the horror of all Dutch purists, Louis van Gaal played a 5-3-2 system at the 2014 World Cup in Brazil, to support the weak defense with extra players. He even had one of the strikers (Robin van Persie) drop back half a line to seal the back completely. Van Gaal had the national side playing to its own merits.

With Robben able to cover every space in attack, the Netherlands may have abandoned their own historical 4-3-3 formation, but they did succeed in reaching third place in the tournament. As manager, you have to analyze the qualities of your players before you mold them into a tactical formation. In the World Cup qualifiers and in the competition games in Brazil, Van Gaal did an excellent job.

While the Dutch team played the defensive form of 5-3-2, the art is to quickly switch to the attacking form of 3-5-2 when you gain possession, by moving the two outer defenders up. Then you almost always have a numerical advantage in midfield, especially if the other team is playing 4-4-2. When losing possession, the two outer defenders move in to replace the midfielders dropping deep.

In response to the criticism in the media and in reply to the suggestion that he had stopped believing in attacking soccer, Van Gaal stated that he hadn't actually played a 5-3-2 formation, but a 3-5-2 system. No one believed him.

Whether the system is attacking or defensive depends on the team and the manager's game plan: how does the manager aim to win the game? Here too it was clear that a system is not in itself sacred; it stands or falls by the individual qualities of the players.

Van Gaal at Man Utd

Interestingly, after moving from the Dutch national side, Louis van Gaal introduced the 5-3-2 system to Old Trafford. In Brazil, with that bronze medal around his neck, Van Gaal had come to believe in the formation. That was surprising, since he had always held to a quite different philosophy: he had always stood for a 4-3-3 system, for attacking soccer, dominating in the opponents' half.

Van Gaal's new soccer vision was all the more unusual because he was projecting his new creed on one of England's most aggressive teams. Sir Alex Ferguson had developed a versatile style featuring calculated attacking soccer, a style that was a lot closer to Van Gaal's former vision epitomized at Ajax, Barcelona and Bayern.

Because Van Gaal felt that his defense was weak, yet continued to buy forwards instead of defenders, his system was described as negative, even though he often switched to four defenders during a game. The Dutch manager came under a lot of fire as a result and he won far too few games. Moreover, former stars such as Paul Scholes and Rio Ferdinand complained that his system was boring and soporific.

4-5-1 game plan

One of the most defensive tactics is a 4-5-1 formation. The four defenders are not expected to switch to an attacking role at any time, while two of the midfielders are principally concerned with maintaining the balance in defense. That leaves four players to go forward, though the attack mainly comprises the lone striker. If you have a quick striker, then the attack becomes a solo effort with support from one or at most two players. The remainder stay in position. If the striker is more of a ball player than a sprinter, then the whole formation has to move up to bridge the long distances and provide support. Without that, the other side has far too much space in which to counter the attack.

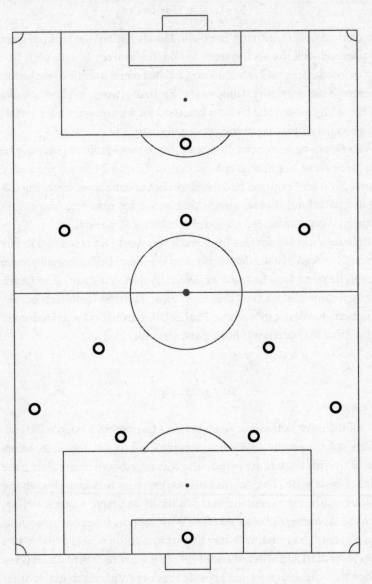

4-2-3-1 formation.

Leicester City's sensational triumph in the 2015/16 season was astonishing. Becoming champions of England is an amazing achievement. Claudio Ranieri's team played excellent counterattacking soccer because this style suited the qualities of the players perfectly.

Whenever they lost possession all the players went back to their defensive positions and only the lightning-quick striker, Jamie Vardy, remained up front. The result was a 4-5-1 formation; when the team regained possession this transformed into a 4-2-3-1. That works when the team understands what to do and everyone plays his part when the ball is lost. Vardy continually disturbed the other side's buildup, giving his teammates time to reassemble their tight, defensive lineup.

Not only were Leicester well organized, but the players were hard as nails in matches and possessed unbelievable energy, which they maintained for ninety minutes. Because they managed to work out the details of their strategy so well, they were able to exploit the qualities of their striker to the fullest, and those of their French-Algerian playmaker, Riyad Mahrez, and Malinese Frenchman N'Golo Kanté. And since the team were able to drop so deep there were always oceans of space in front of them that fast players and quick-switching midfielders were able to exploit. Week after week the ball found its way into the net, although everyone thought that this time their fairytale would come to an end.

Moreover, it was great to see that the tactics and the system were tailor-made, precisely to fit the team's players, just like at Wimbledon twenty years before. Had Leicester played a 4-3-3 formation it would have come to nothing and they would have lost more than half their games since playing without much space in the other team's half is not in their genes. And the defenders at the back were not the type of players who feel comfortable with wide-open spaces behind them. So Ranieri didn't even try.

In short: Leicester didn't adapt to the opposing side but to themselves. And then there's no point in listening to the critics who always start to complain once the honeymoon is over. Because Leicester City managed to challenge the top—the big money and the expensive players—so successfully, they began to find the major clubs ranged against them. And especially since they managed to achieve their success with a limited budget.

The ideal tactic against Leicester City is simple: use the same system they use. Force them to take the bait. Withdraw the team to a defensive position and think about attack only when you regain possession. It sounds simple, but can you do that if you're Manchester City, or Arsenal, or Chelsea, or Manchester United, or Liverpool, or Tottenham Hotspur? Which teams have the courage and the patience to play that way? Few, even though it would give them a chance to win. In fact you have no choice. This is top soccer, after all. Offer the initiative, and see what happens.

Leicester City aren't used to playing with the ball. They like to be the underdogs. If you let them have the ball they'll start to think they're actually pretty good and they'll soon tie themselves into knots. That's in every player's makeup; every player started out thinking he could do something special with the ball as an attacker.

That basic instinct is indelible, everyone has it. And that goes for Leicester City's players too. They have great qualities—after all, they're playing in the Premier League. And they also have the stamina to achieve results. But you really start to make things tough for them when you let them take the initiative.

Balance in midfield

When you play with three midfielders, the ideal combination is one player who moves back and forth, taking up a position near the opposing goal, another who reads the game and dictates the buildup and pace of an attack, and a third who deals with the dynamic of the game, taking the ball from opponents and delivering it to the playmaker or strikers. He should also be able to judge the other team's combinations.

This combination creates balance in midfield. That is essential since almost every game is decided in midfield, which is why many managers prefer to have four players here, or even five. Today, a 4-3-3 formation often transforms in defense to 4-5-1 as the wide men drop back to midfield. In England they call this 4-1-4-1. In the Netherlands the structure is based around a trio and most teams play with one player forward, namely 4-2-1-3, or one dropping back, 4-1-2-3.

For teams fielding four players in midfield, as in a 4-4-2 formation, the attacking mode transforms into 4-2-4. Often two midfielders shore up the attack, forcing the two remaining midfielders to stay in midfield in case the team loses possession.

If the midfield is diamond-shaped in a 4-4-2 formation, then one central midfielder is positioned just in front of the two central defenders and the other central midfielder is just behind the two central strikers: 4-1-2-1-2. The two outside midfielders play slightly less wide in this formation.

In any event, it is crucial that the midfielders are constantly thinking: what if? What if we lose the ball? Are we still in the right position? Know where your default position is, because soccer and analysis of opponents have become so sophisticated that a moment's distraction from what is or may be about to happen can be catastrophic if the team loses possession.

Third midfielder behind

When you play with three midfielders in a 4-3-3 formation with the third player behind, effectively 4-1-2-3, the two midfielders should be dynamic, moving forward and back. If one starts a run, the other should remain behind and wide to cover any eventuality if, say, the attack breaks down. Right and left midfielders should be intelligent players: they can't both join the attack. At least two players are needed to keep the width of the midfield covered. If only one remains the area is suddenly wide open: if the other side gains possession, its midfielders will sweep forward in a counterattack meeting virtually no resistance at all.

The right or left winger should always join the attack on goal, while his opposite number moves over to retrieve the ball if the cross is over-hit or if the ball is cleared.

Third midfielder forward

Playing with three midfielders in a 4-3-3 formation with one player forward, effectively a 4-2-1-3, leaves just two midfielders to cover the entire central line, largely to maintain defensive control if a striker or the midfielder in the forward position, the so-called number 10, loses possession. In fact the number 10's role is to play around the striker and create a nuisance, to chase and pressure the other team if it gains possession. He is also the link connecting the midfield to the attack.

These days a number 10's role is harder than it was twenty years ago because far more tasks have been added and the available space is more limited, forcing the player to act fast. Juan Mata is someone who feels at home in this position . . . although he doesn't score enough, for my liking.

Two Dutch players adopted this position to perfection: Dennis Bergkamp and Jari Litmanen at Ajax. They always emerged at the right place at the right time. Bergkamp's goals were spectacular: superbly crafted and almost works of art. People still remember them, like that amazing goal following an incredible run for Arsenal against Newcastle.

Rooney's position

Wayne Rooney is another player who knows how to play in the number 10 slot as a false striker. Rooney's managers have vacillated between the number 10 position, the striker position and as a wide forward on the left. Ferguson often used him in the latter. Rooney was never able to focus on one role. His position was often determined by his fellow players or his opponents.

I understand his managers, but the effect has not always been positive for Rooney, if only because the constant changes led to an endless discussion about his ideal position. As long as Rooney plays at the highest level, the media will always be wondering: is he a striker or a number 10? A superficial debate, since the discussion revolves purely around his goals. If he fails to score for three weeks then he's a number 10, and if he scores two goals as a number 10, then suddenly he belongs up there as a striker.

Probably Rooney will never be able to shake off this discussion during his playing career. All the messing about, with his position shifting from here to there, has prevented Rooney from developing into one of the world's truly great players.

Someone like Lampard

At Chelsea, Frank Lampard had an enormous impact off the ball. From his position in midfield he served less as a link to the strikers than as the finisher in the penalty area. He didn't think like a midfielder, more like a striker coming in from distance. He and the rest of the team had to be able to switch when they lost possession, so the team had to be well balanced. As a midfielder, a player like Lampard is always where the ball is. Which means that you need a midfielder to fill in the gap that he leaves. Without balance in midfield, you'll lose the game. This is the problem I have highlighted before with regard to the England squad.

Whenever Chelsea were the better side, it was relatively easy to solve that problem since they had sufficient players in midfield. But when playing against stronger teams, you have to be careful: if you can keep the balance intact then a player with individual qualities like Lampard can make all the difference. A manager who has a Lampard or someone like him in the team is constantly looking to put him in an ideal position. To achieve that, whatever the system the manager decides to use, you need the team—and if necessary players you bring in from outside—to support your Lampard and allow him to do his thing. It can make all the difference at that level.

Superior numbers in midfield

To achieve numerical superiority in midfield, you can move a defender up or drop a forward back. That creates space in the attack for players to come forward.

It is no surprise that Barça have the best midfield, which was even more the case when Xavi Hernández was still playing there and he formed a midfield trio with Andrés Iniesta and Sergio Busquets. A crucial aspect is the dynamic off the ball. How much work are they prepared to do for each other, to enable each other to play better? They have to keep moving all the time, and always be ready to take the ball.

Busquets was a defensive midfielder, Xavi the playmaker who passed balls left and right, and then there was Iniesta, the trio's attacking midfielder. He preferred to play forward, passing the ball, and turning up near the striker and in front of goal.

Shifting position

At Ajax in 1995, they always had one player more in midfield by moving the free defender Danny Blind up or dropping stopper Frank Rijkaard back. At Barcelona, Messi used to occupy the same position before Luis Suárez came in as striker. Messi would often drop back into midfield to ensure the numerical advantage.

Central defenders rarely leave their post so, with Blind and Messi, Ajax and Barcelona always had more players in midfield. Which, as we have seen, is where you win games.

In that case, in a defensive role, you have to base your strategy on the team's organization and keep the distances short, as Chelsea did in the Champions League semifinal in 2012. It is possible to compensate for having one less player in midfield as long as the team can anticipate where the ball is going from midfield into attack. It is crucial to keep a careful eye on who is advancing and to meet them, physically if necessary, by blocking them. You can't afford to have ball watchers in midfield. Midfielders need to have a wider view, continually surveying the game as a whole.

Johan Cruijff was a striker and gradually dropped back as his career advanced to be able to direct attacking play from midfield and to feed passes. He continued along the same line as a manager developing this in his teams. Cruijff realized the great advantage of having a striker who could drop back. A midfielder, or a striker in a midfield position, could quickly move into gaps.

I remember a discussion with Cruijff about an AC Milan–Ajax game in the early 2000s. Cruijff argued that Ajax should have started without a striker. "Fine," I said. "But it makes no difference for Milan. Milan won't change their defensive organization. The defense and midfield block stands squarely in the middle of the pitch supported on the outside by the backs and the wide players. If Ajax shifts to the left, the block shifts too; to the right, the same."

Double accordion

Leicester City's organization in 2015/16 was similar to that of AC Milan when I played there: a tight defensive block capable of moving flexibly to the side where the ball was. That kept distances short. It requires concentration and discipline from the players to be able to move continually like an accordion. In fact it is not just about moving from left to right and vice versa, but also forward or backward. For the other side, it's almost impossible to get through. You can't split that block up as long as they concentrate on remaining in position with respect to each other, always maintaining the same distance. The result is that the gaps are so small, it's almost always possible to deal with any situation.

For me, that defensive organization at Leicester City has a familiar ring to it. The manager, Claudio Ranieri, an Italian, has molded Leicester into a modern copy of AC Milan. From that perspective, we were twenty years ahead of our time at Milan.

Leicester City's attack starts in defense. Not all the defenders are equally fast. A player like Robert Huth is not particularly flexible either. He has the physique to stay on his feet for ninety minutes in the Premier League. But you can't play someone like Huth on the halfway line or with too much distance between himself and the keeper. So what to do? You place a block around your own penalty area. In addition you have two fast players in midfield able to take up defensive positions, three (or two) superquick, goal-hungry players in attacking positions in midfield and one (or two) quick strikers to surprise the other side with counterattacks.

Scylla and Charybdis

Years ago at Arsenal they played with a strong defensive lineup of four: Tony Adams, Martin Keown, Patrick Vieira and Emmanuel Petit. Behind them stood David Seaman, the keeper. Up front were the striker, Ian Wright, quick wingers such as Marc Overmars and Fredrik Ljungberg, and, of course, the stylists Dennis Bergkamp and Thierry Henry. Since Henry needed space to be able to rush forward, it was imperative that the defensive block didn't move forward too quickly. Arsenal's players might otherwise clog up their own position. As they got used to each other and learned to play as a team, they also began to play better in the other side's half. In the end they developed the ideal combination of two systems: playing in the opponents' half and counterattacking. The combination proved perfect and in 1998 it began to reap dividends: league titles, FA Cups and a place in the 2006 Champions League final against FC Barcelona in Paris.

Arsenal lost that final. That was when Arsène Wenger decided to develop his team and his style of play further. He seems to have taken Barcelona as his ideal. With Alexis Sánchez in the side, Arsenal do manage to emulate the Catalan style to some extent, and Wenger would clearly like to have someone like Sergio Agüero at the club too.

Each season you think and hope: this time Arsenal are finally going to do it, they'll get their trophy. You want them to succeed. Wenger has such an amazingly positive style of play and philosophy. Unfortunately, all he has managed to garner in the last ten years is the FA Cup and Community Shield, perhaps because Arsenal are caught between two options, steering a course between Barça and the old Arsenal— not a pure counterattacking side and not a pure attacking one either.

Finally

Tactics are a weapon in your game plan. But you need a system that suits your players and feels like second nature to them, one tailored to their specific qualities. Your tactics should also take into account the qualities that the other side brings to the game. To ignore that is to overestimate your own abilities and to underestimate the other team (unless you happen to be as good as Barça).

Nothing is sacred, no single system: it is the players who make the difference. Should I play on the halfway line with my defense if I don't have the pace at the back? No, of course not. Should I play two strikers even though I only have the one? No, then I have to ensure that the team combines to get the best out of the lone striker. And sometimes it may be crucial for the striker to give space to the winger, if the wide player is the one making the difference. Nothing is sacred.

Kickoff

The kickoff may seem insignificant, with the tap forward to a team-mate, who then ninety-nine times out of a hundred plays it back to the team's own half. Yet I always watch with interest. Often the side that kicks off uses the moment to signal its intentions: whether it's about to go for the jugular, or start by watching what the other team does; whether it plans to play a combination game, or intends to fight.

Sometimes you'll see three or four players ready to rush the defense after the back pass is sent flying into the other half. They want to put the other side under pressure from the start, so when the ball comes down, the defender has two or three players to deal with and the battle is on straight away. That is a clear signal: we're not afraid.

Some teams tap the ball around in their own half for a while, waiting to see how the other side will respond: what answer do its players have to us passing to each other like this? Are they going to put pressure on the ball, or are they going to wait and see too?

There are some teams that kick off by passing the ball back to the keeper, who holds on to the ball or kicks it all the way upfield. That leads immediately to tussles. If that is where your team's strength lies then that's the way to get started.

Patterns of play

When you start playing soccer as a kid you do what you feel like. Gradually you learn different patterns of play in training. These are incorporated into practice sessions, repeated time and again, over and over, and they become so ingrained that you never forget them, ever. These are the basic building blocks of the game. For me, learning the game as a youngster in the Netherlands, it was all about patterns of play in a 4-3-3 formation.

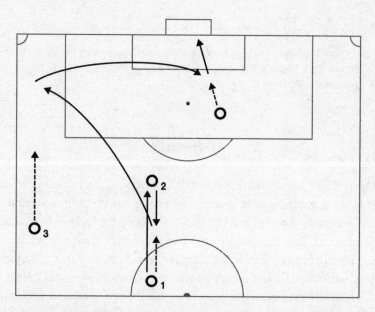

Pattern 1. Player 1 plays to player 2, who passes back; player 1 then passes to player 3, going deep. Player 3 passes to the striker.

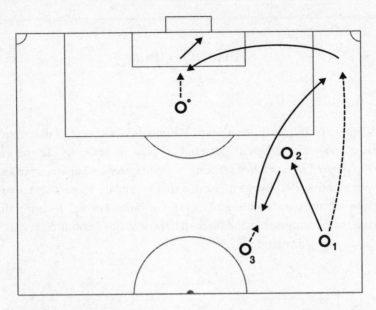

Pattern 2. Player 1 plays to player 2 and moves up. Player 2 passes to the approaching player 3, who passes deep to player 1 moving forward. Player 1 crosses to the striker.

Moving trios

The trio, the best-known and simplest pattern, is the basic ingredient of every combination in soccer: one player has the ball, a second is ready to receive a pass and the third is looking for space. These three elements encapsulate everything. The exercise consists of the following: pass and move, knock on and move, pass to third player and move. A variation is: pass and move, knock on and move, cross and finish.

These are patterns that you see at the highest level and with any number of variations. A key aspect of them is that players are continually moving, because that's always difficult to defend against, even in the zone. Against two players it is possible, but a third moving player,

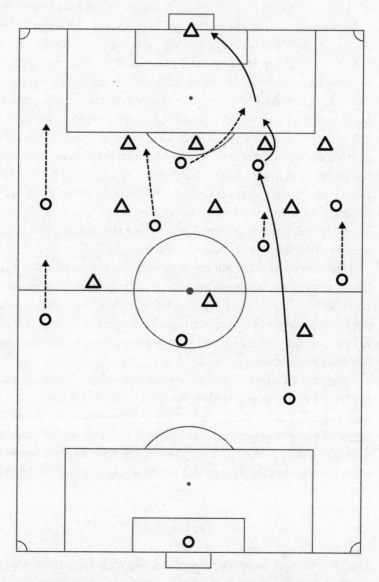

A long ball from the back to the striker deep in the opposite half. The entire team moves forward and traps the other side in their own half.

brought in to make the difference, is harder to defend against, especially since the third player isn't moving toward the second player passing the ball, but is always moving away, into free space.

You have to keep creating these patterns of moving trios, and two or three trios one after the other. In a good team with good players this comes naturally since regular training in their early years has made it second nature, and it is coupled with experience and quality.

These patterns work perfectly in a 4-4-2 or 5-3-2 formation. It is crucial that the two strikers always move in different directions. Number one passes to number two and number three runs off. That ball can be passed low, along the grass, or high, overhead, preferably chipped to allow the striker to chest it down and control it. Otherwise the risk of losing the ball is much greater. There should always be someone lying deep available for a pass, and preferably moving too.

If the two strikers remain standing together, it may look like a trio, but it's a static trio, while the trio should actually be moving around to break through the defense. It forces defenders to make a choice, which implies that they may choose wrongly. Nothing is easier for a defender than a forward who stands still, simply asking to be tackled or dealt a less than delicate tap.

Defenders in effect mirror the movements of the opposing attackers. If a ball reaches a striker, the two central defenders can't be standing still. One of them has to challenge the striker while the other covers in case the player breaks through. Where two central defenders face two strikers, one challenges the player with the ball while the other lets the second striker go and provides cover for the first defender.

The long ball

Long Ball United: everyone remembers Sam Allardyce's famous quote. Big Sam was West Ham United's manager when Louis van Gaal was in his first year at Manchester United. Van Gaal was always boasting about his team's combination game. He let anyone who would listen know how much possession his team had enjoyed and he considered it by definition unfair if Manchester United dropped points against teams that played according to an entirely different philosophy.

Man Utd had managed to snatch a point at West Ham in his first season following an old-fashioned kick-and-rush final offensive. Van Gaal reacted as if he had been bitten by a snake when Big Sam expressed his surprise after the game that United had played long-ball soccer. A few days later, Van Gaal produced a pile of statistics to show how wrong Allardyce had been. In vain. Especially when those very statistics revealed that while West Ham had played the ball forward more often, Manchester United had kicked the ball far longer.

I never understood why Van Gaal felt the need to respond. A long ball is a tactical weapon and therefore part of the game. There's much more to it than what the Dutch in general and Van Gaal in particular imagine. It is about far more than just kicking the ball forward blindly and leaving it to the strikers to work out what to do with it.

For Wimbledon, for instance, the long ball wasn't part of an all-or-nothing attack; it was a basic tactic which they practiced carefully and to which the whole team was attuned. The club even bought players to hone their game to perfection.

It is vital to have one or more players up front who know how to receive a long ball while facing forward, to control the ball and keep it while surrounded by opponents. If the forward can hang on to the ball, it gives midfielders the time to join the striker and to pass back and forth. Behind the midfielders, the defenders will move up too. It immediately places the other side under tremendous pressure in its own half.

It is crucial to coordinate this because losing the ball may otherwise open up huge gaps between the forwards and the midfield line, and between the midfielders and the defense. A team that knows how to exploit these gaps between the lines can counterattack against a long-ball team without much problem.

Some teams like to send the long ball to the center forward; others prefer strikers to move into the channels, the areas parallel to the touchline where the wingers roam. It's not always about keeping the ball deep in the other side's half. Sometimes you want a defender to head the ball out, because the midfielders will be able to pick it up as they run into position. In fact the possibility of winning a corner, a throw-in or a free kick may be even more valuable, and may even be the intention.

One advantage of sending the ball to the far corner is that it leaves you less vulnerable if you lose possession. If the other side win the ball, they're left building up all the way from the corner of their own half. They can only go in one direction, and that's easy to defend. If you lose the ball in the middle of the pitch, then the other side has the choice: they can build up to the left or the right, which forces your defenders to make a quick decision, and if they make the wrong choice, a path opens up for the other side.

The danger of the long-ball tactic is that you go straight for the striker when there may be a better solution elsewhere. With a big guy like West Ham's Andy Carroll the danger is all the greater since he is such a visible presence on the pitch and it's all the more tempting to pass to him with a long, high ball. All this requires a little soccer nous from teammates and a good deal of technique from the striker. Zlatan Ibrahimović is the complete striker par excellence: the perfect man to receive long balls. He has all the skills, under pressure, at the highest level.

You can deliver a long ball in two ways: straight or bending. A straight ball only works if there's plenty of space behind the defenders, and of course you need players moving up to support the striker. If the striker can head the ball on, then you need a second striker or you want the midfielders to take a chance and surge blindly through the defense to pick up the ball from the header and take it toward the opposing goal.

For a bending long ball you need a strong striker, tallish and with good timing and the ability to jump high to chest down the ball under pressure. Mark Hughes had exactly those qualities. Mark was not a big man, but he was solid and exceptionally strong. No one could take the ball off him. The nice thing about this approach to the game is that it's spectacular to watch—there's a lot of physical confrontation in the various battles.

At AC Milan we often faced teams that played long balls. No club wanted to take us on in midfield with pure soccer. With Frank Rijkaard, Carlo Ancelotti, Alberigo Evani and myself in the lineup, we were so strong that we could deal with anyone. So to get around that wall, opponents used to send in long balls.

Our defenders constantly found themselves in direct confrontation with a striker, a supporting forward or a winger. Even when they won these duels, it still took a while before they could start building up from the back again. It was an effective tactic to shake us off for a while. It stopped us from surprising the other side by switching to attack, while giving their players extra time to get the defense organized.

It drained our morale as well. That simple expedient of kicking the ball all the way upfield meant that the pressure we had been putting on had been for nothing. And a long ball meant that you had to sprint back forty or fifty meters. You had to refocus on building up a new attack from the back. And you needed plenty of patience.

In effect, a long ball can be an offensive or a defensive weapon. An essential ingredient is a willingness to get stuck in: players need to want and dare to confront opponents. You can forget it if you think you will leave the pitch after ninety minutes without a scratch.

It's surprising how few teams use long balls against Barcelona, relying on their soccer skills and on building up from the back. Do they imagine that they can play their way through an attacking lineup with the likes of Messi, Neymar and Suárez? In theory it's possible. But if Barça don't have the ball and they want to get it within six seconds, then the whole team will come crashing down on you. That tactic is possible thanks to the trio up front. It minimizes the meters that the team has to cover to regain possession. Barcelona challenge their opponents to build up from the back by giving defenders as little space as possible.

It is the keeper who decides whether the team should build up an attack or kicks the ball upfield. I'd say: "Kick the ball as far as you can, then we'll get to grips with Barcelona over there." After all, it's precisely what the Catalans don't want, just as we at AC Milan hated it. Physical confrontations are not their strong point, it's their skills with the ball that they rely on.

The long ball is perfectly suited to winning territory and relieving pressure. Although, of course, you need a bit of variation, otherwise it becomes easy to defend against.

In the late 1990s, Manchester United found the perfect balance between long-ball soccer and building up from the back with combination play. When the team was under pressure, Peter Schmeichel took no risks and sent the ball flying to the forwards waiting up front: Andy Cole, Dwight Yorke, Teddy Sheringham or Ole-Gunnar Solskjaer. Let them take on the defenders. After trying that a couple of times, the pressure on United soon began to evaporate. The other side would realize that there was no point chasing United and take a step back. And then Schmeichel would revert to building up from the back, via the right or left flank.

That occasional use of the long ball is not something you see often in contemporary top soccer. Teams often lack the cunning to use this tactic. Which has a lot to do with coaches who consider it beneath their dignity, like Louis van Gaal and even Sam Allardyce, who was keen to emphasize in his Long Ball United exchange with Van Gaal that this was not the way his West Ham played: they preferred to use their soccer skills.

Tiki-taka

Tiki-taka soccer was invented by Pep Guardiola at Barcelona. Invented is perhaps not the right word, since he actually embroidered the style of play that Johan Cruijff introduced and perfected at Barcelona, first as a player and later as a manager. Tiki-taka is based on trios; it is Dutch school plus, you might say. Guardiola gave it an extra dimension, especially by using the exceptional qualities of young guys from Barcelona's youth-training scheme such as Messi, Xavi, Iniesta and Busquets.

Everyone likes watching tiki-taka, but few can actually play it, certainly not at the same level as Barcelona, who stand alone in the world. A tiki-taka player should be technically and tactically proficient, good in confined spaces, able to launch a run or a combination under pressure, and be able to quickly change the pace of the ball. All those players learned these skills at La Masia, the club's training facility. Interestingly, these were all players who played along the middle of the pitch, while the guys along the flanks were acquisitions from other clubs, such as Ronaldinho, Neymar and Dani Alves, or brought back, like Jordi Alba.

Everything in tiki-taka is based on possession. When the other side gets the ball, it is up to the technical and attacking players—who, like all forwards, are naturally lazy—to regain possession. And, for that, Guardiola introduced his six-second rule: the whole team chases the other team for six seconds to regain the ball. The idea being that every player, however good, finds it hard to keep the ball under pressure or to choose where to pass. That is why Barcelona regain the ball nine times out of ten with these raids. If the sudden pressure fails to achieve the desired result, then the team moves back twenty or thirty meters, reassembles its formation and lets the other side come to it.

For Barça's forwards, it's worth piling on this pressure because they know that if they don't they'll soon have to make up dozens more meters. The choice between ten meters in six seconds or thirty meters later is quickly made. Especially for players like Messi, Neymar and Suárez, who like to save their energy for those occasional bursts of pure brilliance.

When you watch Bayern Munich, you can see how difficult tiki-taka is. The team often approaches Barça's level, but they depend too much on Ribéry and Robben. The one time they succeeded in front of a watching world was on October 2, 2013, when they played Manchester City at the Etihad and tiki-taka-ed them into the ground, returning to Germany with a 3–1 victory.

If Guardiola hopes to bring tiki-taka to the Premier League via Man City then he'd better not underestimate the importance of individual strength and confrontation in English soccer. It is highly unlikely that a side would be able to play soccer at that level for a year in England with all the clashes and personal tussles. Arsenal try, but you can see how their players regularly go through periods of poor performance. Suddenly they lack the energy to play at the same level or support their teammates in avoiding one-on-one duels. In the busy Premier League program it is especially difficult.

That was more than evident when Arsenal met Southampton and Newcastle United in 2015/16. Both teams let Arsenal have it and the games turned into aggressive spectacles that the referees did little to temper. Any other team in England would have fought back, but not Arsenal. The team lacks players of the caliber of Adams, Keown, Petit and Vieira, who were always the first to dent the other side's armor. The fantastic Arsenal of Wenger's first years in London had that ability.

Viewing English soccer from that perspective, I wonder whether Barcelona would survive in the Premier League. In European Cup games Barça have no problem, since they only have to play two legs and referees are far less tolerant than on English grounds. Technique always makes the difference in Europe. But for a whole season? In the Premier League in England? I doubt it.

High pressure and low pressure

Pressurizing is about applying pressure, checking, chasing away. Forwards apply pressure on defenders and vice versa. High pressure implies a concentrated attack in the opponents' half, low pressure is concentrated defense when the other side is ten or fifteen meters over the halfway line. Total pressure is what a team like Barcelona delivers, pressing directly wherever the other side wins the ball. This requires maximum concentration from every player, no one can afford to get outplayed because that could cost you a couple of goals. Applying pressure creates highly dangerous open spaces should anyone slip up.

As a manager you have to vary the pressure since applying it like this costs a lot of energy and is impossible to maintain for ninety minutes. High and low pressure also depend on the qualities of the players. If your team need to create space, like Leicester in 2015/16, then high pressure is not the answer. Let the other side come to you. That creates space automatically for when you regain the ball. And then Jamie Vardy can run into that space.

The ideal is for a team to be able to do both. Then you can vary things by occasionally surprising the other side with pressure in its own half. Ferguson's Man United mixed high and low pressure, but they also had a weapon for the final fifteen minutes: total pressure. They swept their opponents off the pitch, whoever they were. In 1999, they even won the European Cup with it against Bayern with two goals in injury time.

Smart defense

Jürgen Kohler, a German international in the 1980s and '90s, had a clever trick when defending against a long ball from the back. He would start by standing behind you; most forwards don't mind that

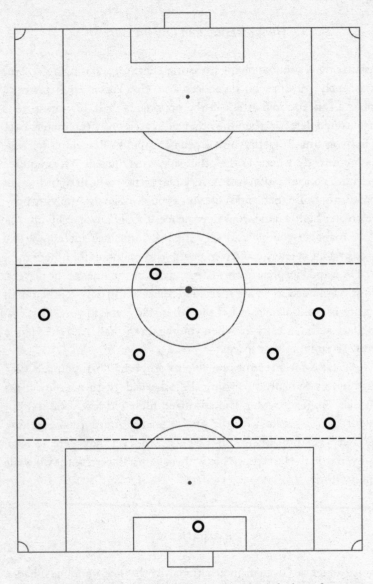

Low pressure involves facing and pinning the other side down from just past the halfway line. This encourages the other side to come forward and creates space for a counter.

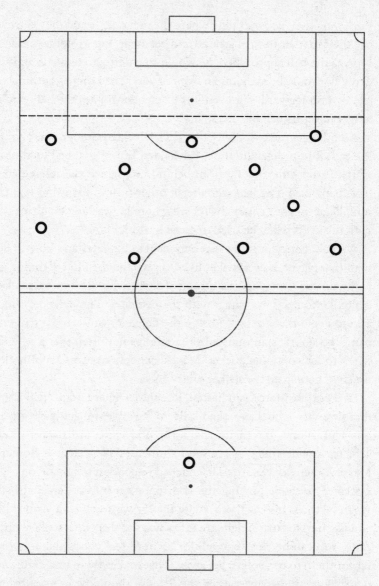

High pressure involves locking down the other side deep in their own half. This robs them of space to build an attack. When you retake the ball you're already close to the opposing goal; however, when you lose possession the other side can cause havoc in the open space behind your defense.

since then they know exactly where the defender is and they can even use their marker to turn around and get away. But in Kohler's case, as soon as the ball approached, he would step deftly to one side and suddenly he would be standing in front of you. Then there's nothing you can do as a forward; not even if the defender misses the ball: you no longer have the ball in your sights.

After he got me twice with that trick I decided enough was enough. Instead of him defending me, I defended him. I grabbed hold of his shirt to stop him moving from behind me, which the referee could have penalized if he had seen me; at other times I turned to half face him. That meant I could always see where he was and block his path with my arms when he tried to creep in front of me.

A smart defender knows an opponent's character and how to deal with that player; how a striker likes to play and the kind of things that really annoy him. Big and strong strikers who are not particularly agile like to keep in contact with the defender. The defender should aim to avoid that contact. Losing the defender can cause a striker to panic, because it's an unusual situation: it's not often that a defender dares to let go of the striker. Most defenders need to keep in close touch to anticipate the striker's next move.

Strikers like Marco van Basten, Ronaldo, Didier Drogba and Zlatan Ibrahimović, who have the skills to be able to get past anyone one-against-one, and then make a run and score, are always a headache for any defender, as are small, nimble strikers such as Romário, Messi, Agüero and Suárez. Defenders do their best to remain on top of a striker, without turning the confrontation into a personal battle when he turns his back, otherwise the forward will lean against him and use him to turn. There are other ways to deal with strikers physically. You can be close enough for them to feel you're there, but too far for them to use you to get away. That makes them uncertain. And if a striker still gets past, then the defense should be in place to provide cover.

Player without portfolio

At Feyenoord I played with Johan Cruijff in the year we won the Dutch league and the cup. He was a false striker, or rather a false no. 9. On paper, Cruijff—in his final year as a player and thirty-six at the time—was an outside left. But he rarely stayed in that position. He wandered all over the attacking lineup, behind the forwards and around the attacking midfield. Cruijff was unsurpassed playing between the lines. He practically invented that elusive role. And he played in that position on and off the ball. In that championship year he was both support and finisher. It was 1983/84: Cruijff was far ahead of his time. Players like that are common enough today, but then it was new, as were many other aspects of his career as a player and later as a manager.

To be able to play a free-roaming role, Cruijff needed someone ready and willing to clear up after him. Apart from guarding against losing possession, he needed a player to close the gaps and deal with incoming opponents. This role was filled by Stanley Brard, a standard left back whose position was now left half, behind Cruijff.

Brard knew exactly how to work with Cruijff on the pitch and how to compensate where he fell short. He always remained away from the ball when Cruijff made himself available and only got involved when the other side took the ball. You couldn't send Cruijff in too deep; it was Cruijff who made space for others to go deep. In fact it was impossible to defend against him, because his marker never dared follow him as he dropped back into midfield, for fear other players would go deep. Which left Cruijff free to roam between the midfield and the forwards and always be available. Remarkable, really, that the best player got the ball easier than anyone else.

As soon as Cruijff got the ball, the right midfielder, André Hoekstra, would automatically start on a run. Cruijff would then offer him the ball on a silver platter. For variation Hoekstra might make space with his run for yet another player, to whom Cruijff would then pass the ball.

Hoekstra was not perhaps the most spectacular player—his technique was not brilliant and his finishing less than deadly. Yet he had an uncanny ability to go deep at just the right moment and to quickly elude his marker. If you get your timing right then you have the time and space to do something interesting with the ball. But one-on-ones with the keeper weren't Hoekstra's strong point. He never managed to score in those situations. But if he found himself in trouble, with no time to over-think it, then he acted on instinct and shot on target.

Everyone had their doubts about Hoekstra, but without him our game was always below par. Then we really missed him. Moreover, Hoekstra was as strong as an ox; luckily, because the role Cruijff assigned to him and the style of play required plenty of stamina.

Although Brard and Hoekstra may not have been the best players, they were ideal to enable a team with someone like Cruijff at their hub to operate well. Cruijff, however, was the player who invariably made the difference for us.

Indispensable links

Players such as Brard and Hoekstra are perhaps comparable with the later well-known Dutch internationals Edgar Davids and Clarence Seedorf. These were key team players. Davids had an incredible drive going forward, while he was also conscientious in defense. He was an avid tackler and would then pass the ball to someone like the brilliant Zinedine Zidane when they were both at Juventus. Seedorf had many strings to his bow, not least because he was always in full control. His tremendous technique also enabled him to dominate play. Yet for me it was always as a team player rather than as an individual that he made the difference at the highest level.

Davids and Seedorf were crucial in completing the puzzle. You missed them as soon as they weren't there. Unique individual players are the type who, while they may not be the absolute best, are often the most useful in the team. And so too in a sense the most important.

Claude Makélélé was another of that ilk. Maybe not the most technical player, but the most important link in the Real Madrid team when they became known as *Los Galácticos*, with players such as Ronaldo, Zidane, Beckham, Figo, Raúl and Roberto Carlos. Makélélé had a similar role in the French national side and later at Chelsea. Jan Wouters was similarly crucial for Ajax, Bayern Munich and the Dutch team. Paul Scholes was another player of the same type who was also an extremely good player. Man United's Michael Carrick, not the most elegant player, maintained a perfect balance between attack and defense.

For me, Roy Keane was one of the best. He approached perfection. First and foremost, his principal purpose was to maintain balance in the side. Keane was a good player, an undisputed leader, he could tackle and could get a team that had fallen into a stupor back on its feet. When the game was going badly, he could motivate individual players and get everyone back on track. Someone like Keane is the ideal extension of a manager on the pitch. A rare quality.

Players like that, who can take matters into their own hands, are increasingly hard to find. Players tend not to think things through and that starts with the youngest kids, who everything is worked out for in advance, with a couple of coaches standing on the touchline barking orders at them. And in such a way that they are too scared to color outside the lines, and so lose all sense of initiative. That is the kiss of death for soccer, that and the lack of opportunity for children to play out in the street these days, unable to form their own teams and choose who to play with, instead sitting in front of a computer screen or playing on their phone.

Frank Rijkaard was quieter as a leader. He was on a par with Keane, with an extra weapon: he could score. Rijkaard played slightly farther forward than Keane and often hit the target. Carlo Ancelotti covered

Rijkaard and took over many of his defensive tasks. When he played, he was in command.

The best in today's generation is Sergio Busquets at FC Barcelona, although he doesn't have the leadership qualities of a player like Keane. Keane was Man Utd's standard bearer—no one could mistake him and everyone held him in awe. That isn't Busquets.

All these players were crucial for the balance of their team. They provided the yin and yang. Without them there was often no real connection between the players, and those with exceptional qualities were unable to make a difference.

By the way, you often can't have more than one of these players in a team. Ancelotti and Rijkaard complemented each other at AC Milan, but at Chelsea in 2015/16 Nemanja Matić and John Obi Mikel were too much of the same in one team.

Weakest links

Everyone wants to play with stars like Cruijff and Messi: they win games for you, collect trophies, and increase your market value. Some way below that top category there are other types of players, who let others clear up the defensive work and pretend to turn up just a fraction too late for almost everything.

I'm thinking of midfielders like Cesc Fàbregas and Wim Jonk. With players like that in a team people can get extremely irritated when the results disappoint, because they cut so many corners in defense. They let others do the work and arrive at the end to show off their skills. This was how Jonk and Fàbregas played at Ajax and Arsenal, but when they were transferred, to Internazionale and Barcelona respectively, they found they could no longer get away with it.

Players like that are constantly pretending to be busy, to be rushing into tackles and helping defend. Often spectators don't realize, but as a player, on the pitch, you can tell they're not doing anything. In fact they often let their immediate opponent go on purpose, and then walk away with a baffled expression and a gesture that suggests: "Oh, missed it by a hair's breadth."

But, being strong in their position, they stand where they are directly available for a pass when the team gets the ball back. And when they receive the ball then they start to play and use the free space to do something decisive. On the ball, players like Jonk and Fàbregas are obviously talented.

In fact Jonk, with his sharp eye and quick passing in depth, emerged as a playmaker from the back at Ajax, Internazionale and PSV. With the two former clubs he won the UEFA Cup. It was at Ajax that the Jonk–Bergkamp duo emerged: provider–finisher. Internazionale bought both, but in Italy Jonk and Bergkamp were never able to realize the potential they had shown. Their only decisive moment was in the UEFA Cup; in Serie A far more had been expected and demanded of them.

Dutch journalists explained that the lackluster performances Jonk and Bergkamp produced was the fault of Internazionale's own players, but in Italy they thought differently. Jonk returned to PSV in the Netherlands, and Bergkamp gave his career an enormous boost by joining Arsenal under the auspices of their French manager, Arsène Wenger.

Fàbregas's shortcomings only really came to light at Chelsea. At Arsenal and Barcelona he was surrounded by an incredible array of talent, which tended to cover up his failings. At Chelsea in 2015/16 this no longer applied, and as the results grew more disappointing the player's role became increasingly noticeable, because that is when you need people in your team who can tackle. Above all you can't afford to have someone in midfield who can't deliver the goods. On the ball, Fàbregas is fantastic, but at this level of soccer you need the full range of skills: at Arsenal and Barcelona he was okay, when Chelsea are in form, he gets away with it, but when they're not it begins to show.

When Chelsea played Paris Saint-Germain in the Champions

League, Terry was not in the team, and Diego Costa went off injured. You would have expected Fàbregas to step up and lead in a game like that, but it didn't happen. He just isn't that kind of player. Can you blame Fàbregas? Hardly. Chelsea bought him so that he could do his thing with the ball.

It's not always as easy as it seems to make the pieces of the puzzle fit.

Halftime

The atmosphere in the dressing room at halftime mainly depends on how the first half went. So too the manager's input. Often there are a few tactical points to consider, possible substitutions to be discussed and made, and sometimes the manager goes in for some theatricals, depending on the degree to which the team's performance met expectations, the halftime score and the effort made by the players. Legendary stories abound. Especially about disappointed managers kicking in doors, smashing massage tables in half, slinging cups of tea across the room and all kinds of nonsense to wake up the players and shake them out of their lethargy. Some are so angry, they refuse to even see the team.

Managers who throw a tantrum risk raising the issue of their expiration date. The first burst of anger makes an impression, but the effect soon begins to wear off. Foot-stamping managers are slightly comical too. You really have to be careful how you behave at halftime.

When I was manager at Chelsea I once sat and read the paper during halftime. It was an FA Cup tie against Liverpool in 1997. We were playing like amateurs and losing 2–0. From the corner of my eye I saw that the players had no idea where to look. No one took the initiative and there was a deathly silence. Just before the bell rang to signal the second half I made a slight tactical adjustment and I said to them calmly: "You have forty-five minutes to make up for that appalling display."

The trick worked brilliantly. We totally overwhelmed Liverpool and won 4–2, and went on to win the FA Cup—the club's first trophy in twenty-six years. I never read the paper again at halftime. If you want to motivate your players, you have to surprise them.

Positions

Keeper

When I started playing soccer at the age of eight, the goalkeeper was the odd one out. Keepers have always been different. They have different personalities from outfield players, they are solitary, focused on themselves, and in my day they weren't very good at playing the ball, otherwise why would your friends leave you to stand in goal? All that changed radically twenty-five years ago. On July 1, 1992, keepers who weren't good on the ball suddenly found themselves in trouble when a new rule meant they could no longer pick up a back pass. It also meant that defenders had to find ways to build an attack farther forward. The average number of goals soared in the aftermath of the new rule, and every keeper was busy practicing blasting balls upfield when defenders passed back. For a while the old-fashioned English kick-and-rush style of playing was back in vogue: belt the ball forward and let the forwards and the midfielders sort it out.

Soon keepers found themselves required to join in team training sessions, especially for positional exercises. They became faster and more confident with the ball. Gradually the goalkeeper emerged as the eleventh player. These days, keepers are more like roaming defenders and sometimes wander so far from goal that they risk being caught out with a long lob.

When the Netherlands were runners-up in the 1974 World Cup in West Germany, the man in goal may not have been the best keeper, but he was certainly the best ball-playing keeper. That's why Piet Schrijvers was on the bench that day and Jan Jongbloed stood in goal.

Johan Cruijff captained the Dutch side, which the Brazilians dubbed

"*Laranja Mecanica*"—the "Clockwork Orange." Later, when he was manager at Ajax, he chose another keeper with all-around skills, namely Stanley Menzo, who was good enough to have been a professional outfield player himself.

At Barcelona, Cruijff again chose a keeper confident on the ball, Carles Busquets, father of today's midfielder Sergio. He pulled the strangest stunts, dribbling past opponents or challenging them far outside the penalty area. He was not the most secure of keepers, but Cruijff refused to listen to his critics because Busquets was an excellent all-around player.

An extreme example is the Colombian René Higuita. He regularly joined in the game upfield and could often be seen wandering far from his penalty area. Higuita was a bit over the top. He would dribble past players and take the ball into the midfield area. His finest moment was at Wembley in 1995. Higuita could presumably have caught Jamie Redknapp's shot with ease, but instead he dived forward and "scorpion-kicked" the incoming ball off the goal line and over his head with the heels of his boots—an amazing trick that will be remembered and celebrated for years to come.

Top keepers

The Dane Peter Schmeichel came to Manchester United in 1991 and remained until mid-1999. The new back-pass rule seemed to have no effect on him. He is the most complete keeper I know and against whom I ever played—a huge personality, excelling in every aspect of goalkeeping.

Schmeichel was an imposing presence: he was a leader, a good goal-line keeper, strong in front of his goal and at corners, and reasonably skilled on the ball. Outfield players are always grateful to have a keeper like that in their team. He radiates such confidence that defenders rely on him blindly. With Schmeichel behind you there's no need to bring down that elusive forward. One-on-one, it was almost impossible to get past him. In fact he earned his club points and won many a game. At the European Championship in Sweden in 1992, he kept goal for Denmark. In the semifinal he held the Dutch firmly at bay, blocking their way to the final, which the Danes eventually won, making them European champions.

Schmeichel hated taking risks. If his team was under pressure he invariably went for a long clearance upfield. He never got his defenders into difficulties by forcing them to pass their way out of trouble. He demanded the same of his fellow players, and was ready with a selection of withering invective to keep them in line. Some of his outbursts have become legendary. Ask any of the guys he played with back then—many of them were literally afraid of him.

When I was in the Dutch squad, Hans van Breukelen was our goalie. He had played for Nottingham Forest under Brian Clough. Van Breukelen was not a natural; he trained and practiced incessantly until he made himself one of the best keepers to ever play for the Dutch national side. Van Breukelen was the closest to Schmeichel's level.

The best all-round keeper in professional soccer today is Manuel Neuer. His soccer intelligence is excellent. He sees situations developing and can anticipate events, both in defense and in the buildup to an attack. Yet he sometimes lacks confidence with the ball.

One of the most remarkable keepers is Rogério Ceni. He is not well-known in Europe, but he kept goal for many years for a leading Brazilian club, São Paulo. For a long time, Ceni was also high up in the top-scorer list, and not just because he took their penalties—he also took any free kicks near the opponents' penalty area. Ceni was a genuine specialist: he scored over 130 goals and far exceeded the Chilean José Luis Chilavert's record as top-scoring goalkeeper (sixty-two goals). Ceni retired in 2015 at the age of forty-two, an unusually ripe old age for a keeper, especially at that level.

Dino Zoff, who kept goal for Juventus and Italy, was remarkable for not being remarkable. A calculating keeper, he seemed to have to pick up balls only as they trickled in or to catch shots directed straight at him. He never made spectacular dives; he didn't like diving. Zoff's greatest quality was to be in the right place, since he could tell how the situation was going to develop two seconds before it happened. He sensed where the ball would be.

In fact keepers who dive are probably standing in the wrong place and have misjudged the situation or have organized the defense badly. Personally, I prefer boring keepers. If you know where the ball is going to be then you'll always be where you need to be on time and you won't need to perform spectacular tricks. No keeper can keep every shot out of course, but if you have a sense of where the ball is heading, you can anticipate. Coaching your defenders is a crucial part of this. Organize them properly and you'll have fewer problems yourself.

On the other hand there's Gianluigi Buffon of Juventus: a spectacular keeper. He is loud, marshals his defense and is in constant contact with his central defenders. A keeper who makes himself heard has presence. It helps if you're slightly crazy, because you'll occasionally have to dive at the feet of an oncoming forward, risking a sharp kick to the head, or studs in your cheek, or a ball smack in the stomach or in the groin, or a broken wrist or fingers. Buffon often tapes his hands to protect them and keep his fingers whole.

Keeper as coach

The keeper is a key element in the formation. A goal-line keeper doesn't feel comfortable with a defense that plays on the halfway line. A one-on-one specialist won't have a problem with this, happily covering the whole penalty area. Keepers of that sort tend to get nervous when five players suddenly gather round for a corner. A short keeper finds that equally problematic.

The goalkeeper tells the defenders what to do, the defenders coach the midfielders, who in turn steer the forwards. What keepers decide entirely for themselves is how to play corners and free kicks. The keeper has to feel comfortable. A manager may offer insights, but tactics are up to the keeper.

Players who stand by the goalposts are mainly there for when the ball is headed or fired in so close to the goal that the keeper doesn't have time to respond, especially if it goes into the top corner. So keepers have a choice: one player by the post or two, although some prefer to have no one else on the goal line because that makes it difficult to dive. From a keeper's perspective there's something to be said for each of these options. In the end he is the one who gets the blame if the ball goes in.

So the keeper decides, in consultation with the coach, whether the team will defend corners with zonal marking, man-marking or a combination of both. With zonal marking, players cover a particular area, intervening if the ball enters it. Man-marking involves defenders shadowing particular opponents in the penalty area. These are one-on-one duels. Who is stronger, or smarter? In a combination of zone and man-marking you may want to mark a notorious header of the ball, leaving the other defenders to focus on zones.

I'm not a great believer in zonal marking because in theory it forces players to stay in one place for a corner or a free kick. If, when the corner is taken, you stay in your zone, it makes it easier for forwards to avoid defenders. Plus it's hard to jump high when standing still. When you're running you can jump much higher. Italian teams tend to opt for man-marking, since they know how to hold on to an opponent and they are strong in one-on-ones.

When FC Barcelona defend against a corner, they often keep three players up front. That is both a defensive and an attacking ploy, especially since many of Barcelona's players are short. Which is why they go for an attacking short corner rather than a high ball.

Teams defending against Barcelona have a problem: no manager can afford to play with just three defenders. One-against-one would be suicide. So a fourth defender has to be brought in to close down the back.

To deal with the Catalan trio, you need to have someone cutting off the supply line too. In effect it takes six players to do the job, while there are at most four forwards in the penalty area and maybe one on the edge. This leaves the keeper space to see what's going on and to move wherever necessary.

But if corners are a team's speciality, as was the case with Wimbledon, then these are real opportunities to score: their corners, their free kicks and their throw-ins (more like quasi-corners) were deadly weapons.

A first header by a player stationed close to the near post is impossible to defend against: the ball can end up anywhere in the penalty area. The surprise is complete, although the attacking side also has no idea where the ball will go. So it sends three or four players surging into the area in the hope that the ball will ricochet off someone's head.

Hugo Sánchez, Real Madrid's Mexican striker in the late 1980s, always started by blocking the keeper's view, standing close while being careful not to foul. As soon as the corner was taken, he ran back quickly, and because many defenders and attackers tend to watch the ball at that moment, they lost sight of Sánchez. Whenever a ball went past the keeper, he was there to tap it in at the far post. This sneaky trick earned him any number of goals. I remember talking about it with Gary Lineker, who said that he had noticed it too and had often scored using that same Sánchez tactic.

A short corner, taken by two players, has the advantage of drawing one or two defenders out of the goalmouth, which creates more space for advancing forwards to meet the cross from the corner. A threatening run toward the near post may also draw the defender stationed there away from the goal, and may even get the keeper to come forward.

Defenders also train intensively to deal with these standard situations. The goalkeeping coach has acquired an increasingly important role here. Every situation is considered: a corner that lands by the near post or by the far post, a ball curving in, or curving out, or situations in which a tall player stands in front of the keeper, or when a striker lurks on the edge of the penalty area, or when the other team is packed with good headers of the ball.

Right back

These days at the back, most teams field converted midfielders who can sprint and have some idea about attacking soccer and what to do when they get to the other end of the pitch. They are key players: they have more possession than anyone else in the team. So they have to be able to play.

When I was young, I remember seeing Wim Suurbier surging up the pitch for Ajax, all the way from his right-back position to the outside right, at least if Sjaak Swart, outside right in their 4-3-3 system, wasn't glued to the touchline as usual and had moved into a central position. In the late 1960s and early '70s, Suurbier's sprints were sensational and there was no one like him in Europe. In Brazil, that style was common. Well-known practitioners included Carlos Alberto, Leandro and Cafu on the right, and Francisco Marinho, Júnior, Leonardo and Roberto Carlos on the left.

These days, entire soccer systems have been devised around players like Dani Alves and Jordi Alba to give them space to get involved as a defender, and even in an attacking role. Sometimes, indeed, the outside right will be a left-footed player who moves in precisely to make space for the emerging right back, while the same happens on the left, only the other way around. The outside player initiates this: the back's role is primarily to distract opponents.

The best examples are at Barcelona: Lionel Messi with Dani Alves (now at Juventus) on the right, and Neymar with Jordi Alba on the left. These modern backs roam the channels so that in the end you get a kind of one-against-two situation and opponents are forced to choose. If as a defender you wait for the decisive moment before choosing, then you're already too late.

In a 4-4-2 system, the left and right backs play a more defensive role, although they can move farther forward if the midfielders take over their task. At AC Milan, we played a similar combination with me as a right half, backed by Tassotti, with Ancelotti or Rijkaard beside me. We were a trio that could both defend and attack.

An amazing right back was Gary Neville. Not especially gifted technically or even the fastest, yet Sir Alex Ferguson leaned heavily on him. Neville had a fabled insight into the game and always chose exactly the right moment to support a given player, to go deep or to offer to take a pass. He knew precisely where danger loomed when the other side won the ball. Neville was always there on time, and he was ruthless.

I realize why Gary Neville never became a schoolboy hero, but that was perhaps his strength. He could annoy his opponents no end; he could make an entire team lose all sense of purpose while never allowing himself to be distracted once. He could have a whole team in the palm of his hand, by himself. The more I watched him, the more I admired him. It is not difficult to find right backs who are technically more proficient, but none has the character of a Gary Neville.

Left back

Paolo Maldini was the epitome of a left back. When I played with him at AC Milan he was still a teenager, only nineteen, although he had the substance and the physique of a mature player. An unusual attribute was his ability with both feet. Even now, I have no idea whether he was originally right-footed or left-footed. Maldini had the stamina to play the entire left flank and the intelligence to choose the right moment to join the attack.

Maldini's intelligence was not confined to Maldini the player: it was also a characteristic of Maldini the man. He had a unique perspective on the world, quite unlike most players. He wanted to see the world, although as a player he saw surprisingly little of it and hardly ever left Italy. I asked him once if he ever regretted that. "I had a good career. Naturally I would have liked to have played abroad, in England perhaps, but I don't regret it, Ruud. I won everything." It was a typical remark, especially for an Italian, because winning is everything in Italy. His list of trophies is astonishing. As a club player for AC Milan he won everything there is to win, not just once but two, even three times. Yet with Italy the main prize eluded him; he only managed to collect four consolation prizes: once runner-up in the European Championship and once in the World Cup, and once third place in the European Championship and once in the World Cup.

The German Andy Brehme was one of the better left backs in my day. Unusually, he was a right-footed player. It was with him that Internazionale's attacks usually began, and although he wasn't fast, he had an infallible instinct for when to turn up. His insight and his free kicks were often decisive. I found Brehme a formidable opponent and I faced him several times playing for AC Milan against Inter, and with the Netherlands against Germany. A man with great stamina.

Marcelo, Real Madrid's left back, has similar staying power and is an excellent individual player. As a left back he gets past opponents like a genuine winger. And he keeps going down that left side. If he's not playing, his absence is noticed in the Real Madrid attack. Ronaldo would certainly agree—Marcelo is the perfect foil for him.

Paris Saint-Germain's Maxwell may not be well-known, but if you list his employers—Ajax, Barcelona, Internazionale and PSG—then this Brazilian, who actually started as a midfielder, is enjoying a tremendous career. His technique with the ball is almost perfect, so pure, so aesthetically pleasing, and so calm; he's always a pleasure to watch. Faced with pace, he is less equipped to compete. Yet I'm glad that despite the evolution of top-level soccer toward strength and stamina,

In Amsterdam's DWS youth side. *Private collection*

Haarlem's nineteen-year-old Gullit vying with Johan Cruijff on his return
to De Meer stadium, Amsterdam, December 6, 1981. *Copyright © Hans Heus/
Hollandse Hoogte*

Training with Cruijff at Feyenoord. "Johan Cruijff opened my eyes to my own personal role in football." *Copyright © Nationaal Archief*

Playing for Feyenoord against PSV at De Kuip, Rotterdam, May 7, 1985.
Copyright © VI Images

Playing for PSV against Ajax's Frank Rijkaard. Eindhoven, March 29, 1987.

Copyright © C. Barton van Flymen/Hollandse Hoogte

Playing for AC Milan against Ascoli. Milan, October 4, 1987. *Copyright © VI Images*

With coach Rinus Michels at the 1988 European Championships.

Copyright © VI Images

Scoring to make it 1–0 in the European Championship final against Russia.
Munich, June 25, 1988. *Copyright © VI Images*

With the Cup. *Left to right:* Ruud Gullit, Berry van Aerle, Ronald Koeman, Gerald Vanenburg, Arnold Mühren and Jan Wouters. *Copyright © VI Images*

Milanello training complex. Frank Rijkaard, Marco van Basten and Ruud Gullit. Milan, March 15, 1990. *Copyright © Hans Heus/Hollandse Hoogte*

With "the best player ever," Diego Maradona, ahead of a game against Napoli. Milan, March 3, 1991.

Playing for Sampdoria against his old club AC Milan. Genoa, October 31, 1993.

Copyright © VI Images

With the FA Cup, Chelsea's first major trophy in twenty-six years, at Wembley, London, May 17, 1997. *Copyright © Camera Press Ltd/Hollandse Hoogte*

On the touchline as Feyenoord coach in the derby against Ajax. Rotterdam, April 17, 2005. *Copyright © VI Images*

With BBC *Match of the Day*'s presenter Gary Lineker and analysts Alan Shearer and Kevin Kilbane. *Private collection*

At SBS6 Champions League studio with Ronald de Boer.
Copyright © Jan Bijl

there is still a place for a player of beautiful, technical soccer that is pleasing to the eye.

From a manager's perspective, I'd post a Speedy Gonzales to oppose him, and I'd say: "Go for it, run rings around him. Our right half and right back will deal with him if he comes forward. Make him run a few meters and after you get the ball I'd be surprised if Maxwell will dare to take you on again or whether his manager will tell him to stay at the back."

As a manager I would always play Maxwell. With his background as a midfielder he has the insight to play an attacking role well. And left backs who aren't afraid to hold on to the ball under pressure and who know how to get out of difficulty with relative ease are rare— even in teams that play in the quarterfinals of the Champions League.

Central defender

While there are still right and left backs who know how to defend, these days they are selected and judged particularly for their attacking qualities. For players in the center of the back line, defense is the priority. Italians prefer a player in defense who knows how to defend; in the Netherlands they prefer someone confident on the ball. Yet it's easier to teach a defender how to pass. If defense isn't already in a player's repertoire, you'll never cram it in. The ability to defend is a quality you can improve, but you'll never really shine if you don't already have the talent.

I admired Tony Adams, with his enormous personality, and Claudio Gentile is as far as I know the only defender who could totally neutralize Diego Maradona. He played for Juventus and Italy and had the ability to concentrate on making it impossible for his opponent to play soccer for the entire game, to take part in any way. He stuck to his mark like a limpet and would have followed him all the way to the bathroom.

I used to play with Alessandro "Billy" Costacurta, a clinical defender and at the same time a ruthless man-marker whose baby-faced charm deluded people into thinking that there was no way he could be so nasty. He wasn't particularly tall but his efficiency really impressed me. He had the ability to get the maximum advantage with a minimum of risk. Costacurta was a good player, but his priority was to pass every ball without risk to a player wearing his colors. Many strikers underestimated him and thought he would be an easy target. Yet with him as an immediate opponent it was almost impossible to make a decisive pass.

One of the very best I ever saw was Pietro Vierchowod, my teammate at Sampdoria. That Van Basten only ever scored once in all our battles when Pietro was in defense says it all, in a period in which Van Basten was hailed as the world's player of the year three times.

Against Vierchowod, no striker ever had a good day. With his heavy, almost clumsy posture, Vierchowod surprised his opponents with a superquick first five meters and his unanticipated agility. He was not considered mean, but was hard as nails. He made sure he kept in shape: a true professional, only retiring in April 2000, still playing top soccer at forty-one.

Jürgen Kohler played professional soccer from 1983 to 2002, at Bayern Munich, Juventus and Borussia Dortmund. He was known as a shrewd center back, a stopper, someone to build a team on: a player who never took unnecessary risks, which only increased the reliance the rest of the team placed on him. He would never try to get around an opponent if there was any way of avoiding it. His motto was: why dribble if you can pass to someone else? In defense he was clever and cunning, not averse to pushing and tugging shirts and kicking a leg or two.

Players like these are less common today: John Terry, Martin Keown, Rio Ferdinand, Nemanja Vidić and Gary Cahill. They are essential because they provide a firm foundation for the side. They may slip up, but they never let you down. Their motto is: "Don't mess with me!"

Defenders like these are hard to find in the Netherlands, which is largely due to the priorities of today's scouts: the players at the back need to have soccer skills, to be able to play the ball. But it seems to me that's not all they need. After all, a man-marker's primary purpose is to defend by neutralizing the striker; he should not be taking risks, moving forward occasionally but mainly passing the ball to others who can launch an attack. A nice long ball from right to left or vice versa is a welcome addition, although if it isn't part of the package there's no harm done. You can learn a lot in training.

Sometimes defenders get overconfident. They think that they can play with the ball, they take irresponsible risks and then it all goes wrong. Risks are for the opposing side's half, never your own.

Often central defense will combine a pure defender with a *libero*, or sweeper. The latter is more versatile with the ball and is able to do more than just neutralize forwards. He is often the first link in the chain of a new attack, receiving the ball from the keeper, maintaining the team's formation, moving up to midfield or alternatively behind the other defenders to provide cover at the back. Sweepers are often leaders and the captain of their side.

Ideally both central defenders should be able to command all these facets of play.

Franco Baresi, the Italian sweeper and central defender, is the best I know. I had the privilege of playing with him at AC Milan. He possessed the whole range of qualities. He had the intelligence to play AC Milan's well-known accordion tactic: moving together vertically or horizontally as a team to win the ball back after losing possession. That required precision, because if anyone failed to keep up, a gap would immediately open through which the other side could penetrate. Looking from above you would have seen the whole team moving three meters to the right, four meters forward, five meters left, ten meters forward and so on.

Baresi was in charge and would lead the team with strict discipline. If you missed a step he would let you know in no uncertain manner, and it didn't matter who you were. He was also a good player. Two-footed, he could pass the ball long with great accuracy. In defense he was ruthless and Baresi's personality gave AC Milan what Schmeichel would later give to United: leadership.

At Chelsea, John Terry is another pillar of strength. Once you write his name on your team sheet you don't have to worry. In defense he stands his ground and he never does anything silly going forward. Moreover, he gives a team a sense of direction and maintains a tight defensive formation. With Terry in your side you also have an extra weapon for corners and free kicks. He is a fantastic header of the ball, so good that he'll beat the keeper in one-on-ones. That's how high he jumps and how good his timing is.

Javier Mascherano, the Argentinian, interprets the role of sweeper in his own way at FC Barcelona. Before coming to Spain, Mascherano played in midfield at Liverpool and for Argentina's national side. He's like a terrier who sinks his teeth in as soon as his side loses the ball, and when he has possession he shows he can play. Yet he knows that others at Barcelona can probably do that better so he quickly passes the ball on. He is constantly crowding his opponent and often stops passes because he has an instinct for where the ball is going.

His ability to anticipate a situation is uncanny. He is constantly watching, looking for the moment when his teammates lose the ball, ready to pounce immediately and to regain possession without delay. Losing possession is always a risk with creative players like Messi, Neymar and Suárez, who like to go on individual runs.

Often you'll see Mascherano setting off in a completely different direction from the rest of the team. Then you can be pretty sure that if Messi loses the ball here or there, the other side will eventually turn up in a counterattack in that zone. So that's where Mascherano goes. He'll change direction if Messi plays to Neymar and he begins an individual run. Then if the other side were to gain possession the ball would end up somewhere else. Mascherano can judge his opponents' lines of attack from defender to striker.

A sweeper is a perfect complement to the Barcelona style of play, which concentrates as much as possible in the opposing side's half. That is why Mascherano is able to play in this position. And why he takes charge when the team loses possession and presses the other side.

Carles Puyol preceded Mascherano as sweeper at Barça. Compared to the Argentinian, Puyol possessed more qualities as a defender and was a bigger personality. He was a leader and with his Catalan background he was a figurehead for the entire club.

The difference between a good and a poor defender is the difference between a defender who focuses on the ball and one who doesn't. A ball watcher can never be a good defender. Defenders who watch the ball are enjoying the spectacle, almost as if they want to applaud, only to be jolted out of their reverie when the ball reaches their immediate opponent. Well, then it's too late.

Good defenders think ahead: they are continually asking themselves: "What if . . .?" Players like Baresi, Puyol and Vierchowod focus on the possibility of losing the ball: what if we lose the ball there? Where should I be in that case? That's what I call defending and taking responsibility. Too many defenders only think ahead when they get the ball. You can't blame them—after all, the scouts spotted them and selected them on the basis of what they could do with the ball. To me, that's a big problem. You see these defenders move toward the ball, positioning themselves to pass it. On the face of it they meet expectations, but they forget their priorities when their defending leaves the formation disorganized.

The ideal central pair is complementary: they give each other directions, communicate with each other, and think like one person. You can see straight away if it works. Do they both run back to meet a deep ball, or does one go for the ball while the other covers the free space to anticipate forwards moving in deep? That should be automatic, for a complementary duo.

This understanding can develop. Look at Real Madrid with Sergio Ramos and the Portuguese Pepe. Pepe's qualities as a man-marker are well-known. When Ramos came from the right-back position to play in the center he had to get used to playing with Pepe, to the space, the coaching, the movement, everything in fact. As a right back, Ramos had gelled perfectly with Pepe as center back, but it turned out to be a totally different matter when Pepe moved into the sweeper position.

Ramos learned to play in the center, but at first he used to make mistakes. He was constantly having to fix situations and received a series of yellow and red cards as a result. "What if?" entered his head far too late. Today, the buildup on the ball is well prepared and now that he can anticipate better, and has experience in the role of sweeper, his confidence has risen and as a result he is rarely shown yellow or red cards any more. Having learned from experience, his tendency to commit fouls has almost disappeared. You can see him thinking: if we lose the ball here, then I should be there to prevent the counterattack.

As a central defender on the left in a 5-3-2 formation, Giorgio Chiellini is amazing in a three-player block. He plays at Juventus and for Italy, and he's a wonderful player. He never lets the side down. Never. That's not unusual in Italy, and yet he's particularly admired for that quality. A player like that must have something special. Chiellini gives his teammates a sense that they can attack all they like, he'll be there behind them—in fact not just as a central defender in a 5-3-2 setup: he plays the same role in a 4-4-2 or a 4-3-3 and even a 3-5-2 formation. You feel safe with him in the team; he avoids taking risks.

Risks are not part of the game for defenders. If you suspect that things are going wrong: get rid of the ball. Get rid of it! Then at least nothing has happened. I dislike players who take risks at the back. No players like that, and no managers. Maybe spectators do, but what's the point if you lose games as a result? I need the back line to provide security, so I can play freely as a midfielder or a striker, going forward without worrying about what's happening behind me. If a defender plays safe, then a forward can take risks. If Messi had to play with the handbrake on because Barcelona's defense kept slipping up, then he would never play at his best.

Midfielders

A team that controls the midfield controls the game. Almost all managers follow this golden rule. Which is why many soccer systems are designed to get as many players as possible in midfield. Louis van Gaal's great Ajax team of the 1990s achieved this by enabling the central defender Danny Blind to move up into midfield. FC Barcelona do something similar by allowing Messi to drop back from the front to midfield. It is crucial that the balance in midfield is maintained, filling in the positions according to the system (4-4-2 or 4-3-3).

With four in midfield you need players on the outside who can go deep; the two central positions are for the more defensive types. They shouldn't be standing next to each other, but diagonally aligned. The one standing farther back should be concerned with organizing the team while the other should be more creative and moving the game forward, perhaps even turning up in front of goal occasionally. An example of a defensive midfielder was Carlo Ancelotti, while Frank Rijkaard epitomized an attacking midfielder.

For a 4-3-3 system you need three different types who are attuned to each other and complement each other's qualities. Ideally there should be a defensive player, a creative midfielder and a player who will venture deep. Many teams get into trouble because they get this equation wrong or don't have the right players under contract. Then the problems begin.

On the left

Glenn Hoddle of Tottenham Hotspur, AS Monaco, Swindon Town and Chelsea would have been perfect on the left in midfield in a 4-3-3 formation, but in a 4-4-2 system he was placed in the center. The problem for Hoddle was that he was actually born in the wrong country, or at the wrong time—which explains his lack of recognition. In the Netherlands everyone loved Hoddle, but in England they considered him too technical, he couldn't run.

John Barnes, formerly of Liverpool, came into his own in a 4-4-2 system with his magical left foot, yet even more so in a 3-5-2 with the triangle pointing backward. He stood just in front of his defenders and from there he orchestrated the team's buildup. He was a playmaker, a smart player who had a good overview of the game.

Two stars, in my opinion, were the Spaniard Rafael Gordillo of Real Madrid and Davie Cooper of Glasgow Rangers. Cooper, who tragically died of a brain hemorrhage in March 1995 at the age of thirty-nine, was technically perfect, with a wonderful grasp of the game, and a gift for scoring goals. Gordillo had tremendous stamina and patrolled the left flank tirelessly in a 4-4-2 system: his socks were always around his ankles.

I was a great fan of these two players, Cooper and Gordillo, as I was of the French midfielder José Touré, who played for Nantes and AS Monaco. I first saw him at a youth tournament in Austria and was totally enthralled. Later, he had problems in his personal life and he got into difficulties. Another player I enjoyed watching intensely was the Spanish-Belgian Juan Lozano.

Different players fit different systems, even if their positions seem similar. That is due to the other surrounding positions. For example, Edgar Davids was always on the left in the 4-3-3 formation at Ajax and Juventus, although he tended to move more into the center. Edgar was inexhaustible and never stopped running, tackling and winning balls. Moreover he had amazing skills on the ball, although he preferred passing to someone such as Zinedine Zidane, in the interests of the team. That too is a great quality: knowing when to give way.

On the right

Frank Rijkaard and Carlo Ancelotti were the best to play in central midfield in 4-4-2 at Milan. They managed perfectly in those confined spaces, they were strong and knew how to win the ball. And their mind-set was always: "What if?" What if the striker gets in trouble, in midfield, to the right, to the left? How can we anticipate that? AC Milan had six players who always thought like that, so we were always covered if things went wrong up front or elsewhere.

Frank Rijkaard was a star. It took a lot of persuading on my part to convince the directors at Milan to bring him over from Real Zaragoza. They wanted to know everything about him, and they still weren't sure. I told Sacchi and the board hundreds of times: "Get him!" At AC Milan we were already a good team, but with Frank in the squad all the pieces of the puzzle came together and for two years we won everything there was to win.

Frank had the energy and the power to keep going in midfield, forward or back. Yet he was far more than just strong. He could play fantastic soccer in those confined spaces and even snatched a few goals here and there with ease. Surprisingly many, for a defensive player. Frank actually scored in the final of the European Cup against Benfica, in Vienna.

He developed further at Milan, and as a Dutch international too, going on to play a second stint at Ajax, by then a player who could make sure that his team won, sometimes with a goal, although often more with his presence and his qualities as a player and even as a motivator—especially in the youthful, successful Ajax of the mid-1990s.

An amazing defensive midfielder was the Frenchman Claude Makélélé of Chelsea and Real Madrid. On the pitch, he too was always wondering: "What if?" He had a keen eye for danger. At first sight, Makélélé did little more than win the ball and pass it to someone who could do something with it. But with his soccer nous and the position he chose on the pitch he was often the one who took the sting out of the counterattack. Like Davids, Makélélé sacrificed himself even though he was an excellent player of the ball, and at the highest level.

An entirely different type of midfielder was Bryan Robson, a player with tremendous dynamism and a real leader of his side. If anyone could head an attack it was Robson. He gave his team that extra spark. He combined the knack of taking the ball from anyone with good skills and an ability to score.

A beautiful player to watch is Manchester City's David Silva, a playmaker who I don't see as a pure midfielder, and equally not as a pure striker. He can do both and often also plays between the lines. He is difficult to defend against, yet he can also cause his own team defensive problems. So he is often posted out on the left, even though he plays best in the center.

Zinedine Zidane is the exception. A natural leader, with his presence rather than with eloquence: he was always about action rather than words. Every team he played in gave Zidane all the freedom he wanted. Many managers were even prepared to adjust their side just to enable Zidane to make the difference.

Zidane may not have said much on the pitch, but he saw everything. As he moved it seemed as if he was doing everything in third gear and yet he glided past opponents who were clearly operating in fifth. Like an elegant ballet dancer, and with a grandeur . . . watching Zidane was pure pleasure.

Another of Zidane's strengths was the way he used opponents to move or turn and get away, like a catapult, although he normally avoided physical contact. Few could get an opponent off balance as effectively as Zidane by feigning a step forward, or dodging to the left or right only to pass on the other side. He moved with such ease that it seemed so simple, despite requiring meticulous timing. When Zidane was on the ball he always made the difference for Bordeaux, Juventus, Real Madrid and the French national side.

Since Zidane never pretended to specialize in defense, at Real

Madrid they brought in Claude Makélélé. The two players were complementary: they were the supreme duo, a championship pairing.

Players like Zidane, Platini, Maradona, Cristiano Ronaldo and Messi think out of the box. These are players that we should nurture in soccer. Managers shouldn't discuss tactics with players like these: they should trust them and give them freedom. And listen. If you asked them, I suspect they would fill your mind with all sorts of philosophical ideas. Cherish them, because they are the exceptions that make soccer so amazing.

Although Diego Maradona originally emerged as a midfielder, he played in his own style and could never be pinned down to any particular position. Whatever system his team played, Maradona was not really part of it; he had his own system: 9-1. Everyone played around him and he was always the player who made the difference, the ultimate example being the Argentinian side that beat West Germany in 1986 in Mexico City to win the World Cup.

I regularly played with and against Maradona. I took part in various friendly matches in which he appeared on my side, but on most of the occasions we met, I was in the opposing team. He was a leader in every way. He could explode in anger if teammates failed to do what he wanted. One time, someone in Maradona's team was substituted— presumably on his orders—and he shouted abuse at him all the way to the bench. Maradona did everything to win. He was no less tough on himself. When he was injured, he just carried on, as in the 1990 World Cup in Italy, when he was kicked nonstop throughout the competition but succumbed only in the final against Germany. Players who were not prepared to risk a knock or two were bound to get into trouble with Maradona.

How good was he? AC Milan had the best defenders in the world, but no one could take the ball away from Maradona. Like Zidane, he used his opponent as a kind of catapult. If someone grabbed hold of him, he'd lean against them and use their strength to get away.

Physique and speed are more important now than they were twenty or thirty years ago. Yet Maradona would still have been a superstar today. In his day defenders could bring him down with impunity. He was constantly flying through the air after yet another dreadful tackle, although he also avoided just as many opponents by leaping high in the air. If Maradona had received the protection that referees give the likes of Messi today, we would have been able to enjoy a lot more of him.

Maradona was in my opinion the best soccer player ever. He was the whole deal, the player who understood everything about tactics, technique, insight, the lot. Sometimes he was such a genius that you thought: What is this . . . what's happening here? I experienced this playing against Maradona, and when I played with him too. I played in a benefit for him along with Gianfranco Zola, Gustavo Poyet and many other former stars; yet every ball went to Maradona. Naturally, almost. From respect. And because, after all, Maradona is Maradona.

Whenever we got together off the pitch we always had great fun. He's a fantastic guy and just wanted everyone to like him. That made him an easy target. People managed to manipulate him, to get him to do what they wanted and to use him. He fell for it time and again. But as a player Maradona was brilliant, the best player I ever saw.

When it comes to Pelé, I can't judge. I never saw him play live. There are astonishing images in film clips, but whether he was better than Maradona, I couldn't say. I believe all the superlatives about him, I know his trophy cabinet is full to bursting, including three World Cup titles with Brazil. But, unfortunately, I never saw him in action and so I can't really give an objective opinion.

So for the moment I'll stick to Maradona. Who knows, maybe in a couple of years I'll change my mind when Messi retires and I'll concede that he was actually better than his compatriot. Although I'll always maintain that in the age in which he played, Maradona faced far tougher opposition. He never had the protection that Messi enjoys today. It was open season all year round. If Maradona had played in today's environment he wouldn't have suffered such long and serious injuries as he did when he met the butcher of Bilbao, Andoni Goikoetxea.

In the center

While Michel Platini did not have a fixed place in midfield, he mainly played in the center. An amazing player and a prolific goal-scorer who rarely had to help in defense, he could always rely on players like Alain Giresse, Jean Tigana and Luis Fernández. This central trio maintained the team's sense of balance. They were all excellent players in their own right and knew exactly how to deal with any danger that threatened when Platini went forward. It was a question of pure soccer nous and self-sacrifice.

That's why some managers put players like Platini along the flank, where they can do the least damage if they lose the ball. The same happened to Platini's successor, Zinedine Zidane, toward the end of his career. Yet in Platini's heyday it had hardly been necessary since the speed at which teams switched to regain possession was far slower.

To exploit Platini's qualities to the fullest, the French coach, Michel Hidalgo, just looked at what he needed: which players to play alongside him, which tactics and which style of play suited Platini best? In the end, Hidalgo came up with *le carré magique*—the magic square: Giresse, Tigana and Bernard Genghini (1982 World Cup) and later Luis Fernández (1984 European Championship). In the 1984 European Championship in France, Platini scored nine goals in five games, a record that still stands, although these days more countries play more matches—for the 2016 European Championship, the number of countries was raised from sixteen to twenty-four.

There is hardly any place for an old-fashioned playmaker like Platini in top soccer today. It is increasingly difficult to maintain a place at the top of the international game with only that quality. The last to have succeeded, in my view, was Andrea Pirlo.

Now it's all about stamina, physical strength and quick adjustment on the pitch. While it may not be difficult to find these qualities gathered together, players like Platini and Pirlo would be able to thrive only in extremely technical teams. You can't afford to lose the ball today, otherwise even the best players can be overwhelmed. Which is why these playmaker types tend to find themselves on the wings, where losing the ball is less dangerous.

Dilemmas in midfield (1)

Steven Gerrard and Frank Lampard both played as attacking midfielders. They appeared together in the English national side and each successive coach faced the same question: how to ensure that these two superb midfielders could play together in such a way that they exploited their respective qualities to the fullest. That this never materialized is perhaps one of the biggest disappointments in contemporary English soccer.

Lampard has no fixed position, whatever the system, because he runs everywhere. In fact you have to create a position for him without wandering too far from your system or your tactics. So who do you place next to him and behind?

One way or another, Lampard and Gerrard failed to complement each other, even though they were both fantastic players. According to the English system, one should be on the outside in midfield and the other in the center. So one of them had to sacrifice his position. Both think forward, but if you play 4-4-1-1 you get a problem in the center if the ball is lost up front. At one time Lampard was even placed behind the striker, but his strength is to come up through midfield. That's why Chelsea's 4-3-3 was perfect for Lampard.

Unfortunately, England's coaches never really experimented with a 4-3-3 system with the triangle pointing backward in midfield. A solid midfielder like Paul Scholes would have been ideal in that combination. But even he was exiled to the sidelines, after which he announced his retirement from the national side, far too early in my opinion.

Gerrard was given a more defensive position in midfield at Liverpool. There he was more of a passer of the ball. Naturally he could do that easily enough, but it isn't the quality that people appreciated about him the most. Gerrard is too good a player to spend the match patrolling in front of defense. He should play farther forward, that's where his strength lies. Eventually, however, he agreed to take on the defensive role.

A number of England coaches found the Lampard–Gerrard question too hot to handle. In fact it was a relief when one of the two was injured, because no England coach ever had sufficient authority to be able to ride the storm that choosing either one over the other would have entailed—the English fans and press simply wouldn't have accepted it.

The qualities of the two players clashed. And still successive coaches refused to choose. If they chose one, they were against the other. If the coach had chosen Gerrard, there would have been hell to pay from Lampard's fans, reporters, coaches and his teammates at Chelsea. And vice versa.

I can tell you that for a manager, even a national coach, it is extremely frustrating to be saddled with a dilemma like this. You can never get it right. It's impossible. I always felt a bit sorry for the England coaches. And by the same token for Lampard and Gerrard, because they knew just as well: we can't play with each other and we can't play without each other.

Meanwhile, both press and public were enraged that Lampard failed to perform for England while he excelled in his Chelsea colors, and that the Gerrard who played for England was a different Gerrard to the one who played for Liverpool. "Why doesn't Lampard score?" people were constantly asking. I understood why. Frank could never be himself in the English side, where he lacked the players he needed around him. The same goes for Gerrard.

For a national coach it is a disaster: a generation of world-class players, and the best two can't play together. A situation like this Lampard and Gerrard quandary disproves the notion that two good players will always automatically be able to play well together, that they'll have a natural rapport because they're on the same level. Not always.

Between 2000 and 2014, Gerrard was capped 114 times, scoring twenty-one goals in all; at Liverpool he scored 120 times in 504 matches. Lampard played 106 times for England between 1999 and 2014 and scored twenty-nine goals; at Chelsea he netted 147 goals in 429 matches.

Successive coaches struggled with this dilemma in vain: Kevin Keegan (1999–2000), Sven-Göran Eriksson (2001–6), Steve McClaren (2006–7), Fabio Capello (2007–12) and Roy Hodgson (2012–14). None could come up with a solution; neither could I.

Dilemmas in midfield (2)

While it was a tragedy for those involved, the Gerrard–Lampard problem is also interesting. There are other similar cases. In the Dutch squad, the same issue occurred with Rafael van der Vaart and Wesley Sneijder. Successive attempts were made to find ways to enable the two to play together. Both were at their best as attacking midfielders. Van der Vaart made his debut appearance for the national team slightly earlier than Sneijder after they had both worked their way through Ajax's youth training scheme. In the end, managers and national coaches preferred Wesley Sneijder as midfield playmaker.

Both at Ajax (under Ronald Koeman) and in the Dutch squad (under Bert van Marwijk) it was the bad-tempered street fighter, Sneijder, who was preferred over the stylist, Van der Vaart. At Ajax, Van der Vaart was shifted from one position to the other, from forward to midfield, and was always second fiddle to Sneijder.

A difficult choice for a manager and a national coach, but they simply didn't gel. Van der Vaart and Van Marwijk never really got on as a result, although the former had been on excellent terms with the previous coach, Marco van Basten.

As a coach, if you have to choose, you will almost certainly lose a player. You need to realize that. But will it be just the one? What kind of person is that player? Will others allow themselves to be dragged into the controversy? If the player begins to share a few truths about the manager with friends in the game then you may have a problem, especially if it starts to snowball. It could result in a corrosive, negative atmosphere among the players in the dressing room. You can't afford to have that in the national squad. Happily, Van der Vaart isn't like that.

What should you do? Play both, like various English coaches did with Lampard and Gerrard? Even though it makes no sense technically or tactically? In the Dutch squad, Van der Vaart was even used as a defensive midfielder. No problem on the ball, but not the best solution in the defensive lineup. Sneijder eventually survived the crisis and is still in the Dutch side. Yet the discussion continued almost throughout both their international careers, and that is of course far too long.

It wasn't good for the players and it wasn't good for the Dutch squad. And I considered both Sneijder and Van der Vaart to be good players. Eventually Van Marwijk chose a system (4-3-3 with Sneijder at the triangle pointing forward) with Van der Vaart as a left winger. In that position he rarely achieved the kind of success he was used to at his clubs.

Van der Vaart played 109 international games between 2001 and 2013 and scored twenty-five goals. Sneijder has played 120 games from 2003 to date, and has bagged twenty-nine goals.

Barcelona's midfield

While two midfielders like Lampard and Gerrard or Van der Vaart and Sneijder were unable to play together, FC Barcelona's three top midfielders—Xavi, Iniesta and Busquets—play very successfully in combination for their club and for the Spanish national team. They form a complementary trio: Xavi as the brains, Iniesta as the attacker going forward and Busquets as the connection and player blocking the opposing side's lines of attack.

Although all three often leave the field with clean shorts, Busquets is the one who occasionally makes a sliding tackle. Iniesta's shorts are more likely to need a wash because opponents try to floor him. Xavi is too smart, avoiding sliding tackles and individual tussles.

Xavi is the foundation of the midfield; he never loses the ball and makes sure that it gets to the forwards. He has a sixth sense for when to extend play from midfield to the forwards, without the forwards incurring any particular risk of losing the ball in a one-on-one.

Iniesta thinks ahead; he is an attacker, from the left, and takes more of a risk. His genius is to be able to deliver a final pass to one of the three forwards. Despite the extra risks he takes here and there, he hardly ever loses possession and he certainly can't be got off the ball. He turns so easily and is so quick on his feet that he's impossible to defend against. He always knows which way to turn, as if he has an extra pair of eyes in the back of his head.

Iniesta is not the kind of player to run great distances, or to even try—which does not really matter at Barcelona. Whenever the team loses possession it immediately applies pressure—that keeps distances short and players only have to move a couple of meters.

This style of play requires absolute concentration and continual focus on where the ball is and whether it has been lost. That means keeping a constant eye open and remaining alert to who's standing where, both opponents and your own teammates, so you know which player to mark if your side loses the ball. And, as with Xavi, you always have to play to Iniesta's feet. If you look for either of these two by playing the ball in the air—neither is taller than 5 feet 7 inches—you might as well just hand it over.

Standing behind these two is Sergio Busquets. While he sometimes comes up to the penalty area for corners and free kicks, Busquets's principal task is to maintain balance in the formation; he is Barcelona's "What if . . .?" guy. In fact Busquets is also solid as a rock on the ball. Yet he always gives every ball away, not to the opposition, but to Xavi or Iniesta.

You see: if the three players in midfield never lose the ball, they never have to do the work of regaining possession. In the buildup from the back, everyone always searches for Xavi, who creates more depth in the attack. This ensures that the other side has less time to reorganize. Sometimes Busquets and Xavi switch, yet they never get in each other's way and complement each other almost without fault.

Conflict with the coach (1)

Messi's role has changed as the seasons have passed, at least after the arrival of Luis Enrique as manager and later of the striker Luis Suárez. Under Guardiola, Messi's role was that of striker. Occasionally he dropped back to give himself or other players space. Today he plays from wide on the right: in other words, he starts off in that position, from which he searches for free space, automatically opening up room for the advancing right back.

This pattern ensures that Barcelona always have four players in midfield and allows the two strikers, Neymar and Suárez, to move freely along the entire line of advance. That creates space for other members of the team who are continually cutting into the forwards. They can do that blindfolded since Messi, once he has the ball in midfield, almost never loses possession. Moreover, from there he can place the ball wherever he wants with meticulous precision. It couldn't be easier. Start running. Messi will decide where to deliver his pass.

It took Luis Enrique two seasons to work out this system. No surprise that stories began to leak out in the first months of Enrique's tenure that he was locked in conflict with Messi, something Pep Guardiola had never dared do after all the successes they had enjoyed together.

One of Guardiola's successors, the Argentinian Gerardo Martino—who had come to Barça on Messi's recommendation and was a good friend of Messi's father—refused to get to grips with his star player and treated him with kid gloves, allowing Messi too much say and far too much influence. If a player gets to dictate what happens in a team, the club is on a downward slope. There can be no suggestion of parity between manager and player. The hierarchy that divides them should be maintained at all costs. You can't even be friends or visit each other's houses.

When Martino left and Luis Enrique took over, Messi began to take on the new manager by leaking the occasional dressing-room secret. This went too far and the club seemed ready to dismiss Luis Enrique, but eventually the manager won the battle of wills, with the support of Barcelona's board. And rightly so. Kudos to Luis Enrique for sticking to his guns and managing to persuade Messi that he should give up his ambition to play as a striker, in the interests of the team and hence in the interests of FC Barcelona.

In fact the change in the club's attacking lineup came suddenly. When he arrived from Liverpool, Luis Suárez still had to sit out his three-month suspension following the incident during the Uruguay vs Italy game at the World Cup in Brazil, when he bit Giorgio Chiellini. Once he was eligible for selection for Barcelona, Suárez played on the right wing for around three months. In late 2014/early 2015, after half a season in Catalonia, Suárez suddenly appeared as a striker, the position he had played in all his career at FC Groningen, Ajax and Liverpool.

Argentina's Messi, the world's best player, had made way for the Uruguayan Suárez.

Luis Enrique had finally managed to persuade Messi to give up his place as striker in the team's interests—and by implication in Messi's own self-interest. All the competitions subsequently won are proof that Messi's sacrifice was the right move to make, with the Champions League title as the ultimate trophy. On the pitch Messi and Suárez are now generous to a fault, always looking around to combine and obviously enjoying every minute. The same goes for Neymar. You often see the three of them creasing up with laughter.

Messi is far less concerned now about scoring three, four or five goals or about competing with Ronaldo to be top scorer in Spain and Europe. He no longer cares. Last season Messi even let Suárez and Neymar take a few penalties and free kicks. These small examples say a lot about the way the players relate and play together. Each member of the super trio knows he needs the others and that, as a trio, the whole is greater than the sum of its parts.

That Messi agreed to accept this evolution is very much to his credit. One of the greatest players of all time placed his ego to one side in the interests of the team. It makes the Argentinian even better and more complete than he was. Although I hope he'll always continue to dribble at helpless defenders.

Now that Messi has raised his profile as a team player, he has also emerged as far more of a leader of this Barcelona side. Together with Iniesta, he is the real heart of the current team, having started as a kind of guardian angel intervening at critical moments. Today almost every member of the team is capable of saving the day if necessary.

The best evidence of the change is the period in which Messi was out with an injury. It turned out that Barcelona could also win without Messi. Suárez, and especially Neymar, made the difference in those weeks. When Messi returned his teammates immediately passed the ball to him. Partly out of respect, because they all know that he and no one else is the heart of FC Barcelona.

His compatriot Martino made him the leader, let him train less and if the team needed to put the other side under pressure Messi was excused. That is not how a soccer team works. Fortunately, the board stepped in and brought Martino's reign to an end and so too the privileges his star player had enjoyed. Luis Enrique took on the tough assignment of bringing the player into line, which he succeeded in doing. Meanwhile Messi has matured of his own accord into the role of generally accepted leader.

Conflict with the coach (2)

As a manager, I had to deal with a similar situation. You have to be able to persuade players you are right. Sometimes you manage it, and sometimes you don't. If you can't manage it and you don't tackle the problem, then it's time to go. I faced a dilemma like that at Chelsea.

The problem involved Dennis Wise, who played in central midfield. Wise had come from Wimbledon and still thought he was part of the Crazy Gang—as Wimbledon were known rather disparagingly. Wise suspected that as a foreign coach I wanted to fill Chelsea with foreign players. I thought Wise had great potential, one of my better players, but not in the way he reckoned.

An away game against Leicester City was the last straw for me. We were 1-0 down and Wise was going wild on the pitch. Tackling, running, flying, swearing and shouting, he was playing his own game entirely and at halftime I left him in the dressing room. Eventually we won the game, after which Wise just avoided me.

Two days later I heard from a mutual golfing friend that Wise had been complaining about me and objecting that I wanted to fill the side with foreigners. My friend knew better and had told him: "Dennis, it's not true, believe me. I see Ruud often. You're wrong, that's not the way it is. If I were you I'd just call him." Which is precisely what Wise did.

So I invited him to a meal and I told him: "Dennis, you're one of my best players, but all you do is charge about and make trouble, getting yellow and red cards one after the other. I don't need that. You're too good to play like this. I need you on the field, not off it. You should be playing football. If you play as well as I think you can, you'll be my captain and my best player. Will you do that for me?"

Dennis looked amazed and said: "Yes."

So I continued: "Okay, no more yellow and red cards and nothing stupid. Take the captaincy and play as well as you can. I promise you, they'll be asking you to join the England squad before too long."

"Yeah," he said. "Sure they will."

But that's exactly what happened.

It is extremely difficult to win a fight like that with a player in such a mind-set. You have to try though, and not walk away, because the player waiting to come out of that cocoon could be brilliant if you manage to get across to him what it is that you see and what it is you want.

Wingers

Ajax's Sjaak Swart, Johan Cruijff's support in the golden years, stayed close to the touchline: wingers had to have chalk on their boots. You hardly see players like Sjaak Swart these days. The outside right and left of yesteryear have become completely different players.

David Beckham was more than a right half and false outside right. He was a player who added a unique quality to a team with his passes and crosses. Beckham didn't need to get past his opponent to be able to feed a dangerous ball to the striker. He could also perform on the inside, to make space for Dennis Irwin or Gary Neville. You had to play the ball to Beckham's feet, not deep. That's why he was always offering to take the ball in combinations.

Chris Waddle played deeper on the right than Beckham, but he also rarely reached the back line. As a left-footed player on the right, Waddle instinctively veered to the center. He and his manager Raymond Goethals at Olympique Marseille were twenty-five years ahead of their time. Waddle always gave us a major headache at AC Milan. Pep Guardiola is one of the champions of playing a left-footed winger on the right and a right-footed winger on the left. He put his theory into practice at Bayern Munich with Arjen Robben and Franck Ribéry.

You would imagine that players of this caliber would invite more pressure by moving into the center, while forwards actually need space to be able to attack. That it nevertheless makes sense to move in is due to their speed; once they start dribbling they can pass their

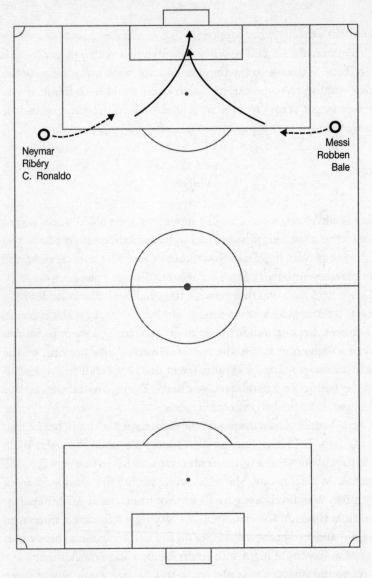

Neymar
Ribéry
C. Ronaldo

Messi
Robben
Bale

A right-footed forward on the left and a left-footed forward on the right are both able to move in from the side and shoot with their stronger foot. Here the forward rarely moves all the way to the touchline. In this formation, crosses are delivered from the touchline by wing backs.

opponent's weak leg and earn themselves that extra half meter to shoot at goal.

The reason why Arjen Robben and Lionel Messi often score with the same kind of run—moving in from the wing and shooting—is simple: because they're running at full speed and still in control. Defenders think they've got them, but they never have. Players like Robben and Messi run with small strides, so they actually shoot faster. Just when a defender is unable to block the shot because they're on the wrong leg or their legs are apart, that's when they shoot.

Robben and Messi have such an instinct for the game that they know exactly when to squeeze the trigger. For defenders who shadow them there's always a critical moment when they're vulnerable to the individual quality of a Robben or a Messi, who anticipate those moments and with their amazing insight are able to shoot at exactly the right time. That's why their trick succeeds over and over again.

The opposing side's manager might try to prevent an attack by using a left-footed defender in the right-back position and vice versa. But I've never seen that done, since managers don't think about their backs from a defensive perspective, more for their attacking qualities, so that a right-footed player on the right and a left-footed player on the left makes more sense. Their job is to push forward when they can and to make well-timed runs behind (so as not to close up space for the forwards) as the attacking players, such as Robben, Ribéry and Messi, move in.

Steve McManaman was a technical dribbler along the right. He could pass on the outside just as easily as the inside, and could cross the ball. Sometimes players manage to get past an opponent beautifully, only to stumble. Some do the first thing that comes into their head: they cross, or take a shot at goal. Players who behave unpredictably cause problems for the rest of the team, since they have no automatic responses.

Ryan Giggs was a left half and a false outside left. Giggs had speed, and he could pass his opponents—it was almost serpentine the way he wound his way around them—with a good run toward goal as he moved inside. If he moved outside, nine times out of ten he would send in an accurate cross. No surprise that he was known as one of Britain's finest players. Unfortunately, he never qualified with Wales for a major international tournament.

My position in AC Milan's 4-4-2 system was half right midfielder and half outside right. I hated playing a pure outside right in a 4-3-3 formation, if only because it makes you rely on others and you're left waiting for the ball if the other players forget about you or can't reach you, generally through no fault of your own. An outside right in a 4-3-3 formation in those days—today only Ajax play this system—was not allowed to roam about; you were completely dependent, which is a horrible feeling, especially for someone like me who likes to be in control.

Sometimes when no one gives you the ball it's as if you're standing on an island. When that happened I never enjoyed the game. I remember the group match against West Germany at the 1992 European Championship. The coach, Rinus Michels, posted me as an outside right. We won 3–1 and went on to face the Danes in the semifinal. I was glad we won, but the game had been awful. For an hour and a half I had chased after Michael Frontzeck, their left back. His assignment had been to keep me as far away from goal as possible. When he had the ball, he was practically an outside left and me a right back.

I felt more at ease on the right in a 4-4-2 formation. From there I could happily create my own space, because I wasn't the sort of player who could take on two opponents in limited space. I didn't need to be that deep. I could go inside or outside, I could use my energy and exploit my pace. Perfect.

Strikers

Whole books have been written about strikers. They come in all shapes and sizes, yet in the end the common denominator is: a striker needs to score, has to score. Strikers live to score goals. Even the forwards whose job is to help others score—even they want a goal or two as well, to restore their confidence.

The Brazilian Ronaldo was a phenomenon because he could run at full speed—he was amazingly fast—and still have total control of his body and the ball: a rare combination. He could conjure up a surprise move to force a goal from nothing. It was all about speed and control for him. He was no goal-getter.

Paolo Rossi or Romário or Ruud van Nistelrooy were. They lived in the penalty box, constantly focused on the goal. Romário hated running, whether on the pitch or off, whether in training or in a game. Romário was always tired. At the same time, he had an assassin's mentality, like a feline predator lying in wait and all of a sudden pouncing. That was Romário. Paolo Rossi too.

Romário's and Rossi's goals helped their countries win the world title: Brazil in 1994 in the USA, and Italy in 1982 in Spain. Players like these need a team that plays in the opponents' half. Then the goal-getter doesn't need to do so much work, or to run as much.

Dennis Bergkamp's managers always gave him free rein. You don't put a player like Bergkamp in defense and you don't tell him to make sliding tackles—you can't expect that of him. Anyway, he never played like that: Dennis always came off the pitch without a mark on his shorts. Arsène Wenger and the rest of the Arsenal squad gave him the opportunity to show what he could do: exploiting his individual class to make a difference with goals and assists.

Thierry Henry was also a player who needed space to excel. While he was officially a striker, he invariably dropped back to the left, somewhere between left half and outside left. That forced the rest of the team to adjust. Arsenal's other players understood that they needed to keep that position free for Henry while the attack started on the other flank—the right—aiming eventually to get the ball to where Henry would arrive to finish with a shot at goal. Perfecting this involved hours of training, and even then there was no telling how Arsenal's opponents would respond. What would the central defenders do when they saw Henry pull away from the center and move into a left-half position? If they stayed put, which most usually did, then Arsenal would have to find some other way to tear the two of them apart and create gaps to pass and dribble through toward goal. Variation was essential, otherwise they would be too easy to defend against. An attack must contain an element of surprise.

Barcelona's style of play gave Henry less time and space and made life difficult for him when he first arrived. After Arsenal's vertical soccer, he had to adjust to Catalan combination soccer, the tiki-taka style of Pep Guardiola's team. With Lionel Messi in the lineup, Henry was no longer the undisputed star of the side. Moreover, the team's performance was more important in Catalonia than individual talent. That was Guardiola's philosophy. Even Messi had to shift back into position after the six-second scramble for the ball, according to Guardiola's six-second rule.

At Barcelona, Henry had to remain on the wing, which reduced his room for maneuver even more. At first he found it difficult to adjust, but fortunately he was surrounded by an amazing amount of talent. Many of his teammates knew how to send a ball inside through the defense so that all Henry had to do was run on to it.

Eventually, Henry mastered the Barcelona style of playing. Quite an achievement if you consider his specific qualities and you compare those to Barça's style of soccer. It was not without reason that many thought Henry would fail in Catalonia. It didn't happen, thanks to his intelligence. He had to give up some of his status, to think a little about how he could adjust, but he managed to change as a player— remarkable at his age. In Catalonia it was not about Henry, but about Messi, Samuel Eto'o and others.

Yet I preferred Thierry Henry in his dominant role, with those fantastic runs at Arsenal.

Thierry Henry and Cristiano Ronaldo like to roam: they are strikers who step away from the spearhead of the attack, only to reemerge again suddenly; players who have learned to drop back to create space for themselves, because their body and technique prevent them playing at their best in the crowded penalty area.

Once they accelerate they have enough control over their body and sufficient ball technique to get past opponents without any trouble as they head toward goal. And they can round off a run themselves because they always have just enough time to get past the keeper with a premeditated plan. To describe how it happens takes a hundred times longer.

Messi drops just as quickly from his striker position, although he does so mainly as a tactical move to make space for other players to come in. There is no one better than Messi in crowded spaces, and no better finisher, though he can also score at speed, because he has total control over his body. Specifically, he has an especially low center of gravity, allowing him to keep his balance more easily.

By contrast, the classic finisher hangs around the box. Strikers such as Didier Drogba, Ruud van Nistelrooy, Luis Suárez and Pippo Inzaghi like to pop up behind the defense. That rips the opposing team apart lengthwise. That is the kind of striker needed by teams that want to retain possession. The opposing defense has to give up space at some point, and then the striker's job is to penetrate deep and to be ready for the pass at exactly the right moment. These players are often offside, but if the interaction with the rest of the team is good, the pass comes through just in time. Then the striker can make a run and score.

Gary Lineker was a thoroughbred finisher. He always gave the impression that he didn't really like playing soccer, he just had this thing about scoring goals. It made him a unique phenomenon. He scored with such ease. He was lightning quick as he began his run, impossible to catch. He also had a low center of gravity, so that he always kept his balance as he turned. The strong, massive English central defenders found him difficult to handle. Lineker spun around them.

While Ronaldinho was a striker at Paris Saint-Germain, at Barcelona he played as an outside left. As a relative novice in that position he gave the term an entirely new meaning. He interpreted the position in the way Cristiano Ronaldo plays at Real Madrid today. With his runs and goals, Ronaldinho became a sensation.

The Mexican player Hugo Sánchez formed a deadly striker duo with a Spaniard, Emilio Butragueño, at Real Madrid. Sánchez was a short, technically proficient player who accelerated as if he had been released from a catapult. A clever player and extremely irritating, the way he stepped on your heels or your toes, forever badgering and bullying and trying to manipulate the referee.

Mark Hughes was a unique forward at Manchester United and Chelsea, in a class of his own. If I were to compare him to a player in today's game I'd choose Zlatan Ibrahimović, strong as an ox and always ready to receive the ball. With a Hughes or a Zlatan in your team you only need to tell your players one thing: "Play to him. All the time." When players like that are in possession, no one gets the ball. They don't let anyone near. Of all the leading players, they hold on to the ball more than anyone else.

Marco van Basten is one of the most complete strikers I have ever known and certainly the best I've ever played with. And it was so easy for him. He could make his own goals: he excelled where there was no room to move, his headers were strong, he didn't shy away from one-on-ones, and he was technically skilled, quick, and a cool, clinical finisher. I often stood and watched on the pitch and thought: what's that Bassie up to now, never seen anything like it, incredible.

Marco needed just half a meter to get the ball in. It was beautiful to see: an elegant striker. At the same time, he could be really nasty on the pitch, hard and unkind. Above all, he was an absolute egoist. If he hadn't scored, but a teammate had, he would shout: "Hey, let me have the ball, give me the ball, give it here!" I often heard him ranting on. Brilliant, a real phenomenon.

Strikers in national teams

You may have a good keeper and nine top players in your national team, but without a top striker you'll never win a major competition. If you have a good keeper and nine top players and you do have a top striker, then you have a chance of becoming European or world champions. Alongside the Dutch team of 1974, the Brazilian squad of 1982 were the best that ever played in a World Cup without actually becoming world champions: a collection of incomparable Brazilians were eliminated by a good team with a world-class striker.

Júnior, Leandro, Toninho Cerezo, Falcão, Zico, Sócrates and Éder are Brazilian names that still conjure up an amazing image, even today. They were sent packing by Paolo Rossi, a scrawny Italian striker with a pale sunken face. A player who epitomized the Italian school of striker. If you get only one chance in a game, you have to make it count. Failure isn't an option. Brazil gave Rossi three chances. Three goals later, Brazil, the best side at the 1982 World Cup, were on their way home and Italy went on to beat Poland and Germany to become world champions.

Brazilians are by definition technical soccer players, but without a super striker they have never become world champions. In 1982, the unknown Serginho failed in the role. Whenever Brazil had a super striker, they always won tournaments: he is the one who pulls the trigger for the great players who make up the team. Pelé was one, and with him Brazil became world champions three times: 1958, 1962 and 1970. With Romário they won the 1994 World Cup in the United States, while Ronaldo made the Brazilians world champions at the 2002 World Cup in South Korea and Japan.

At the last World Cup in 2014, playing at home, the Brazilian squad once again lacked a world-class striker, and once again they failed to perform. Like Ronaldo in France in 1998, Neymar was much too young and inexperienced to carry the burden. He is also more of a wing forward. Without a clever finisher, who pays little heed to Brazilian soccer culture and lives only to score goals, almost all Brazilians play to the feet. However, even winning teams don't always have the ball at their feet.

A team needs depth. And you need a healthy mix to get results. Unfortunately, the Brazilians realized this too late and pulled the wool over their own eyes with a series of irrelevant victories in international friendlies. They had Ramires, yet he never played in the World Cup of 2014. A bit of luck saw Brazil through to the semifinals. There the side was demolished by Germany (7–1), after which the Netherlands did the same with a 3–0 victory in the battle for third place.

In Brazil they understand that they desperately need a world-class striker. Only they have yet to find the right player, judging from the list of international top scorers. Jonas scores like there's no tomorrow, but that's with Benfica, and he's already thirty-two. Then there's Alex Teixeira Santos, who played brilliantly for Shakhtar Donetsk. Past tense, because in January 2016 his manager sent him to China on a lucrative million-dollar contract—the kiss of death for this Brazilian striker's development in the sport. And after them comes Neymar. He is more of a player than a goal-getter and there's not much space for his kind of striker in today's game.

Portugal have a similar problem. You would think that the Portuguese had a superb striker in the form of Ronaldo. Only he doesn't always play in that position. He likes to get involved and to make runs in the channels. That puts him farther away from goal and makes it more likely that he'll lose the ball on the way than if he stationed himself in the penalty area. A few years ago Nuno Gomes and Pauleta were still playing in forward positions. They would have made a perfect combination with Ronaldo. Portugal are a very good team, but without a striker to support Ronaldo and simultaneously draw attention from him and distract the other side, Portugal and Ronaldo may not always fulfil their potential. And time presses: Ronaldo isn't getting any younger.

England have long had an excellent striker in the shape of Wayne Rooney, but he's also getting on. In his heyday other problems prevented him from raising England's game, such as the dilemma over Gerrard and Lampard. Rooney usually played as well as expected; it's not by accident that he's one of England's all-time top scorers with fifty-three goals. Harry Kane and Jamie Vardy, both English goal-getters in the style of Gary Lineker, are set to follow in Rooney's footsteps.

The Netherlands had two strikers—Patrick Kluivert and Ruud van Nistelrooy—who both played at the highest level and were known around the world: two amazing players who only ever played together in the Dutch national team. It never really clicked on the pitch, especially since loyalty to the 4-3-3 principle was more important than adapting the system to Kluivert and Van Nistelrooy's qualities.

That they played for top clubs such as Ajax, AC Milan and FC Barcelona (Kluivert) and PSV, Manchester United and Real Madrid (Van Nistelrooy) was no reason for the Netherlands' coaches to consider reshaping the team around one or both of them. In fact they were rivals, though any other country would have given anything to have had either of them as their striker.

Johan Cruijff was the best Dutch player ever, and Kluivert the second-best striker—after Marco van Basten—a superb, complete player. Van Nistelrooy was a late developer, less complete as a player, yet more of a goal-getter. He was devastating in the penalty area, totally focused on scoring goals. Nothing else mattered to him.

Kluivert and Van Nistelrooy were both born on July 1, 1976. In a sense, they followed each other in the Netherlands team. Kluivert made his debut in 1994 at age eighteen, and was capped for the last time at the age of twenty-seven in the run-up to the 2004 European Championship in Portugal. Van Nistelrooy was twenty-two when he played his first international, in 1999, after which he waited out the next two years while he recovered from knee injuries. He played his last international in 2011, at thirty-four. While Kluivert and Van Nistelrooy are exactly the same age, they only played together for the Netherlands for around three or four years.

At the 2006 World Cup in Germany, Ruud van Nistelrooy failed to make his mark because Arjen Robben and Robin van Persie continually moved into the center. That tactic left Van Nistelrooy standing empty-handed. Passing back and forth was not his style: he was a finisher, the final touch. He was wandering about as if he had lost the way, and never received any crosses from the wing during the entire World Cup. In which case there's no point fielding a goal-getter like Van Nistelrooy, whose place is as close to the opposing goal as possible. That is where he showed his devastating qualities as a finisher. Playing to serve other players was not Van Nistelrooy's style. He served by getting goals.

Today, filling the striker position is a problem for the Netherlands. A string of good strikers have worn the orange shirt in recent decades, including guys like Van Basten, Van Nistelrooy and Van Persie, as the most obvious examples: top international players who played for major clubs such as AC Milan, Real Madrid and Manchester United at the pinnacle of European soccer.

These days the pool of goal-scoring strikers is not large. In the Dutch league, Luuk de Jong is successful; at the international level, Arjen Robben is the only Dutch forward still playing at his absolute peak in Europe.

Second half

How the first half went often determines how the second forty-five minutes start. If you're ahead, you won't want to launch into an immediate attack—you'll be better off taking a wary stance. Substitutions and tactical adjustments may change the complexion of the game.

A team is a mechanism and if one element doesn't function—because a player has a cold, for example, or is out of shape or is thinking about something else—then that puts a spoke in its wheel. Take the right measure and you may solve the problem; then the whole game changes after halftime.

Form is something intangible—it may have disappeared in the first half only to reappear suddenly in the second. Or vice versa.

No player wants to play badly, but sometimes it just isn't working. If you feel out of form you can deal with it by just doing your job and playing more simply. Sometimes players try to force their way back into form by trying difficult runs, only they often achieve the opposite effect since the chances of succeeding are zero. In fact they make it even worse for themselves.

That players aren't robots—despite being judged as such—is often evident in the different way they play in the first and second halves.

Soccer cultures

Every top club in Europe has as many as four or more different nationalities in the same team. England is perhaps the ultimate example: Arsenal were the first to field a team without a single Brit. Yet despite the internationalization of club soccer, traditional national soccer cultures have continued to flourish.

England and big money

The champions of Europe between 1975 and 1985 were English clubs such as Liverpool, Nottingham Forest, Aston Villa, Everton, Arsenal, Ipswich Town, West Ham United and Tottenham Hotspur. They won the big European prizes (European Cup, European Cup Winners Cup and UEFA Cup).

Throughout those years, the players of these successful English clubs were very often locals, as was the case on the Continent: players from the actual city or the region. English clubs had the advantage of being able to draw on soccer talent from Scotland, Wales, Ireland and Northern Ireland. But foreign imports like the Argentinians Osvaldo Ardiles and Ricky Villa at Tottenham Hotspur and the Dutchmen Frans Thijssen and Arnold Mühren at Ipswich Town were rare.

After 1985, the Italians, Spaniards, Germans and Dutch took over the reins in European club soccer. In an attempt to regain their lost hegemony, England began to attract more foreign players in the 1990s to play in the Premier League. People like Eric Cantona, David Ginola, Faustino Asprilla, Peter Schmeichel, Jürgen Klinsmann and the Swede

Anders Limpar—the first to make the move—soon realized that they had to work hard to keep up with the pace of the British game, despite their surfeit of skills. Technically they were far superior and so the English fans looked on them as superhuman. Later, the Netherlands provided players like Dennis Bergkamp, Glenn Helder and Marc Overmars. And I came to Chelsea in 1995.

The flood of foreign players is now irreversible, especially since the Premier League quickly made a sensational leap forward in finance and marketing. But the advent of foreign players has affected the emergence of native English talent. There has been less space for young English players, who have been largely unable to bridge the gulf dividing them from their foreign counterparts.

There was also no limit to the number of foreign players per team, selection or club. The main consideration was to maintain the global status of the Premier League as the best and most sensational competition in the world, and especially to be able to sign increasingly lucrative contracts. It was a vicious circle, with the end still nowhere in sight. Meanwhile the twenty Premier League clubs get to share around £1.4 billion. The whole world watches Premier League games every week.

As the level of club soccer has risen and the money involved has increased, huge sums have been invested: gradually you see talented youngsters break through and get a fair chance at clubs like Tottenham Hotspur, Everton and even Manchester United, although at United they splash out hundreds of millions in the transfer market.

In the end, the pressure to win games weighs heaviest of all in the Premier League. Especially for managers. Their future depends on where the club stands in the league and not on how much talent it has nurtured, as it seems to be in the Netherlands, to judge from the team selections in the Dutch top division. In fact English youngsters are regularly lent out for a brief spell at clubs on the Continent.

I hope that the English national side will in the end benefit from the improved training academies. Gradually, a new, young squad is competing with Europe's top players—although when I ask people outside England about the rising stars ready to follow Steven Gerrard, John Terry and Frank Lampard, then, apart from Wayne Rooney, it often remains surprisingly quiet.

Obviously, the huge ambitions of clubs such as Manchester City, Chelsea, Arsenal, Manchester United, Tottenham Hotspur and Liverpool with all their foreign acquisitions stifle the development of homegrown players. More disturbing is the signing of mid-range foreign players who contribute nothing to the Premier League and are little better than most English players. There should always be room for exceptions, not for mediocrity.

Unfortunately, that is the impact money has on club directors. Each Premier League club receives over €100 million in its bank account each year, and no one dares save the cash. They buy players just for the sake of it, and put them up for transfer a year later with the same ease.

For top English clubs, income from Europe, even from the Champions League, is an attractive extra and no more than that, compared to the enormous, structural income from domestic and foreign broadcasting rights and sponsorship contracts. Moreover, clubs like Chelsea and Manchester City have megawealthy owners who can afford occasional spending sprees of a few hundred million euros and fill up the gaping holes in their budgets with a smile.

Yet it is curious that despite their astonishing wealth, English clubs do not attract the world's best players. Lionel Messi, Ronaldo and Neymar don't play in the Premier League. In fact if Barcelona or Real Madrid want, they can easily entice top players from England, as they did with Luis Suárez from Liverpool and Gareth Bale from Tottenham Hotspur.

Mature players from Bayern Munich aren't attracted by England either. Like Bastian Schweinsteiger, they cross the Channel only after they have passed their prime. Bayern Munich is the smartest club of all. They buy their players from other clubs in the Bundesliga and win the championship almost every year, and so too their Champions League place. They have to be in the European competition to balance their books.

While Bayern Munich can plan to capture the German title four years out of every five, the competition for the English league title is wide open every year. That is a major difference with the other leading competitions in Europe. While Bayern are almost always champions in Germany, in Italy it is Juventus, in France it is Paris Saint-Germain, in Spain it is FC Barcelona or Real Madrid, and in the Netherlands it is PSV or Ajax.

Chelsea, Manchester City and Manchester United may have shared the spoils in the last ten years, but in 2016 the title went to Leicester City, with Arsenal and Tottenham Hotspur close behind. That makes the Premier League all the more attractive to soccer fans around the world. If you switch to the Premier League, there are plenty of clubs to watch; if you switch to the Primera División—probably the best competition in the world—you'll probably only stick around for FC Barcelona and Real Madrid.

Other clubs simply don't come into the running. In England, broadcasting rights are distributed among the clubs in the top division, while Barcelona and Real manage their own television rights. That earns them many times more than any of the other clubs in the Primera División, which has completely distorted the Spanish competition. Only Atlético Madrid have any hope of keeping up with that illustrious duo. Italy has a similar problem.

To make the competition more attractive it might be advisable to sell the broadcasting rights as a package. In the end, there is nothing exciting about the French competition. Paris Saint-Germain win the French league each year by around twenty points.

Meanwhile, transfer prices for English players are rising exponentially following an adjustment to the rules. Each club must have at least eight homegrown players in the first selection of twenty-five: players from home or abroad who have been registered with the union in England or Wales for at least thirty-six months before the calendar year in which they turned twenty-one. Not many of these can keep up with the pace of the Premier League. That scarcity feeds the rising prices. Once an English club has its minimum of eight homegrown players, it can start to look abroad for new opportunities.

On the Continent, top-level players are available for a lot less money. For an eighteen-year-old English player you may pay millions of pounds, whereas the Algerian Riyad Mahrez, who plays for Leicester City, cost the club a mere £500,000 when he came from Le Havre in France. After he emerged as one of the Premier League's successes of the year, his example has inevitably prompted managers and directors of Premier League clubs to attract even more foreign players, which means that ever more young players in their own academies find it hard to win a place and miss the boat.

Jamie Vardy is the exception. His story defies rational explanation and he is one in a million: purchased for peanuts from one of the lower divisions, he developed in a couple of years into an absolute sensation at Leicester City.

National soccer cultures

In different countries people grow up with different soccer cultures that tie in closely with the mentality of their country and the sort of soccer which suits that mentality.

It is not easy to succeed in Europe playing the English style of soccer, since English clubs like to play an open, attacking game. For teams with a strong defense and a sharp, fast striker they present an opportunity which is easily exploited. English clubs like to make a game of it, while their European opponents lie in wait for a chance to snatch victory.

In the Netherlands, fans want soccer full of initiative, crafted, attacking and attractive. Sometimes that is even more important than winning. Their system is 4-3-3.

In England, fans want to see a contest with physical contact and the ball kicked forward, where it makes the most difference. There is no way forward faster than a long ball. The style of play is based on a 4-4-2 system, although with the advent of foreign coaches many clubs have adopted a 4-2-3-1 formation.

In Italy it's all about winning from a defensive position. Three points are more important than tactics and style. It's not about entertainment. Their systems are: 5-3-2, 4-4-2 or 4-4-1-1.

In Spain, they prefer elegant, attacking soccer with technical combinations and plenty of positional changes. Winning in this way is the objective. And the system best suited to it is 4-3-3.

But variety is the spice of life. And so too in soccer: as a player, if you are transferred to a club in another country you get a chance to discover that country's philosophy and traditions and the particular way in which soccer is played there. Soon you get to realize that there is more than one way to skin a cat.

In the Netherlands, winning has to be accompanied by attractive soccer, otherwise there's no end to the complaining. Attractive soccer and looking for positive solutions are key.

In Italy they don't care how you win, whether you play attractive or negative soccer. It's the result that counts, because winning is paramount—that's dogma. Aesthetics are extra, all depending on whether the other team leaves room for attractive soccer. Many clubs from other European countries have trouble dealing with Italian teams. Italy's national side is also tough to beat since Italians are not worried about playing well, just about winning.

In 2006, a World Cup year, a defender, Fabio Cannavaro, was acclaimed European Footballer of the Year and World Footballer of the Year. It's unusual for a defender to gain both accolades. It tells you something about the Italian culture. It is purely about survival: first defend, then attack. Not always entertaining, but certainly effective. Italians base their game on a solid foundation, grounded in defense.

In the soccer cultures of Italy, Spain and Germany, teams focus on not losing, basing their strategy on a well-organized defense. Not conceding goals means never losing, getting a draw at the very least. Clubs often post an international player up front who can make the difference, such as Antoine Griezmann at Atlético Madrid, Gonzalo Higuaín at Juventus and Pierre-Emerick Aubameyang at Borussia Dortmund, who demolished a hapless Tottenham Hotspur, then second in the Premier League in the 2015/16 Europa League round of 16.

Germans invariably have the right mentality, the strength and the stamina to play 120 minutes without breaking a sweat. Since 2000, they have concentrated increasingly on developing technical players.

Spaniards are technically proficient, elegant players, who put technique first and a winning mentality second. Add their speed and efficiency and you can put Primera División players in any competition in the world and they'll never be out of their depth.

In England, competing is more important than looking good, the Dutch ideal. English fans like to see a contest; the English find the Dutch preference for aesthetic soccer boring. Many also consider the Dutch 4-3-3 system a cowardly tactic, because then you have only the one striker, while English teams play with two strikers in their 4-4-2 formation.

These generalizations do not always apply in every situation, depending on the team's intention: what is a team planning to do with its one, two or three forwards, what position do they take when they are in possession and where do they stand when they lose the ball? It's not the system but the game plan that counts.

Spain

To play attractive soccer and to win: that is the ideal to which clubs strive in Spain above all, especially clubs like FC Barcelona and Real Madrid. If the combination of these two ingredients falls short, the result can be deadly for a manager at the Santiago Bernabéu.

As it was for Rafael Benítez, who decided in 2015 that he wanted Real to make more use of defensive players like the midfielder Casemiro: players who played with discipline. A wave of protest against his defensive strategy followed and forced Benítez to switch his approach and to play his best players when Real Madrid met Barcelona at home: he fielded all his stars. They were annihilated, 4–0. He had proved his point, but was compelled to resign soon after.

Real Madrid and FC Barcelona treat their managers to the world's finest players, or they pour money into their coffers to enable them to acquire top players of their own choosing. A huge advantage for Barcelona and Real Madrid is that there isn't a player who wouldn't give anything to be able to play for either of these clubs.

Germany

Among Germany's top teams and the German national side, continuing success has raised the benchmark ever higher. Especially for clubs like Bayern Munich, Borussia Dortmund and the German *Mannschaft*: the national squad. They are used to winning; it has become a habit. Their formula is 100 percent commitment and never give up.

Naturally, if you always win you can play attractive soccer. Yet until recently this was never a priority for German players, especially not in major international tournaments. Germany would often wobble at the start of a European Championship or a World Cup, only to improve as the tournament progressed and then eventually to win.

But since the technical revolution of 2000, all that has changed—as in the last World Cup in Brazil in 2014, when Germany started with a sublime victory over Portugal, beating them 4–0. Today's Germany doesn't fit in the historical mold, and we all remember the sensational 7–1 triumph in the semifinal at Belo Horizonte against the host nation.

Germany's soccer has become increasingly attractive as the selectors have been able to draw on an ever wider variety of cultural backgrounds, through second- and third-generation immigrant workers from Turkey and Africa. The German football association also began to play a role around 2000, by encouraging clubs to focus more on technique in general and technically talented players in particular.

France

With their multicultural background, *Les Bleus* enjoyed tremendous success in the 1990s. The team that became world champions at home in 1998 contained a remarkable number of African influences, including Zinedine Zidane, Thierry Henry, Patrick Vieira, Lilian Thuram and Marcel Desailly. Unusually perhaps, not one of these French internationals played for a French club. Most had matured in Italy, Spain and England and brought the level of excellence of those competitions to the national squad.

The French midfield, with Zidane as playmaker, Didier Deschamps for balance and Emmanuel Petit for pace, were a perfect combination. Christian Karembeu would often move in among them; he was a key attacking midfielder at Real Madrid. In defense they had Laurent Blanc and Marcel Desailly in the center. The left back, Bixente Lizarazu, had amazing energy, playing the entire left flank.

Teams this good come in waves. Before Zidane's French team conquered the world, France had won nothing in ten years. Prior to that dearth, in the mid-1980s, the French had an even more balanced midfield, with Michel Platini, Alain Giresse, Jean Tigana and Luis Fernández.

Both teams played a combination of 4-3-3 and 4-4-2. In 1998, Zidane played as a forward, roaming free on the left; in 1986, at the European Championship in France, Platini played in a free role in midfield, an old-fashioned playmaker, the number 10 which is so rare these days; now all eleven players have an assigned position when the team loses possession.

Zidane and Platini would both move back in formation, to take up their tactical position rather than to retake the ball. It gave them the possibility to peak at the moment it mattered. Their technical prowess gave the team an extra impetus. That, along with the tremendous quality of the players surrounding the two superstars, made those two French teams a joy to watch: for aficionados, fans and spectators. And they won too.

Belgium

These waves of teams in international soccer depend on the number of new players coming in at any one time. You would imagine that the chances of that happening in large countries like Germany, England, France, Italy and Spain were greater: after all, the pool of potential players is larger. But the theory is disproved by the success of smaller countries like the Netherlands, Denmark and Belgium.

The Belgians have a generation of talent to whet the appetite. Eden Hazard, Vincent Kompany, Kevin De Bruyne, Axel Witsel, Thomas Vermaelen, Jan Vertonghen, Marouane Fellaini, Nacer Chadli, Dries Mertens, Moussa Dembélé, Toby Alderweireld and keepers such as Thibaut Courtois and Simon Mignolet. Not to mention the luxury problem of which striker to choose: Romelu Lukaku, Kevin Mirallas, Divock Origi, Yannick Carrasco or Christian Benteke. For their football association it's all about setting the right policy. That is partially true, but there is also an element of chance: the coincidence of a generation of good players.

For a small country to win big prizes, it needs a bit more than a generation of talented players—it needs one or two world-class stars. The Netherlands won the European Championship in 1988 with Marco van Basten, and Denmark did the same in 1992 with Peter Schmeichel and Brian Laudrup.

For the Belgians, the 2014 World Cup in Brazil came a little too soon, but with Hazard, Dembélé and Chadli they now have players who can make a difference at the highest level. That Belgium's domestic competition is not the toughest matters little in today's international soccer world. The concentration of big money in a handful of leading competitions in England, Spain, Germany and Italy draws the best players to those countries. Each week the best face the best, raising the standard even higher and ensuring that everyone gets better.

The Netherlands

A country with a collection of players of the same generation playing at the peak of international club soccer has a chance of creating a national team that can compete seriously in major tournaments. The Netherlands is currently in the trough of the wave and does not have a role of major importance among the international powers, although the Dutch team reached the World Cup final in 2010 in South Africa and four years later the semifinal in Brazil.

There are not many players in Europe's top teams with a Dutch passport. PSV performed extremely well in the Champions League last season. Yet I consider it an exception rather than the rule: it is no guarantee of a place at the championship ball. In the foreign teams that reached the quarterfinals of the Champions League, the only Dutch player capable of making a difference in a game was Arjen Robben (Bayern Munich). But Robben won't be young forever. His contemporaries Wesley Sneijder, Robin van Persie and Rafael van der Vaart are no longer in contention.

Brazil and Argentina

Whereas Argentinians play to win, for Brazilians it's about the playing, about moves and skills. They lack the nasty, tricky aspect of the game. They are completely different on the pitch: frivolous, playful, often technically brilliant yet tactically sloppy. Brazilians often abandon discipline just when they need to be disciplined and not try to solve everything with soccer skills—in central defense for example. But once they get going, they are amazing. Top Brazilian players are often proficient in every aspect of their position. Brazilians adapt easily when they join leading European clubs because they have great basic skills.

The most complete Brazilian team I can remember—Garrincha and Pelé were before my time—is the one Italy eliminated at the World Cup in 1982. This, along with the Dutch side of 1974, is considered the best team never to have become world champions—which was for one reason: it had no world-class striker. If it had possessed a Pelé, or a Romário, Bebeto or Ronaldo, then Brazil would have become champions in 1982 too. The last Brazil side to become world champions, in 2002 in Japan and South Korea, was full of European experience. That team had discipline and routine and was able to let Ronaldo, Ronaldinho and Rivaldo do their thing.

Romário drove his managers crazy. He resented having to train: a manager's nightmare—it is impossible to justify this to the rest of the team. Yet, on the pitch, Romário made the difference, silencing his critics at PSV, Barcelona and Brazil. If Romário failed to score, then the rumors began. So he made sure he scored. He was incomparable in the penalty area, a real phenomenon, stalking his prey like a leopard ready to pounce.

As Barcelona's manager, Johan Cruijff recognized his quality and brought Romário from PSV. He gave the Brazilian the freedom to play exclusively around the box, saving his energy for the decisive moment. Cruijff had trouble with him later. Romário made up his own rules, regularly returning late from Brazil after international games, or summer and winter breaks. This made his position in the team untenable. Yet whenever he played, he scored—although, of course, you have to be on the pitch to be able to score.

There's often something not quite right about Brazilians. Some Brazilian strikers struggle when they lose the ball. They forget to take up their defensive position because they're still thinking about the chance they just missed or the ball they didn't get at the crucial moment.

Argentinians switch directly and apply themselves, whether they are Sergio Agüero, Gonzalo Higuaín or Carlos Tévez. For me it is not surprising that it's two Argentinians who are generally considered the best soccer players ever: Diego Maradona and Lionel Messi—although I can name a lot more amazing Brazilian players than Argentinian ones. Which puts the difference in a nutshell.

Germans are the Argentinians of Europe in my opinion, especially now they have added the technique of those from a non-German background to their arsenal. The German skill-set is more or less complete, since they already had physical strength, stamina, the right mentality and tactical insight. Today's German players are in many ways close to perfection as soccer players.

In fact there is something astonishingly similar about the Germans and the Argentinians. When they play each other, the game often disappoints, as in the World Cup final between Germany and Argentina in 2014. Both teams were so good that they hardly made any mistakes. It was no coincidence that the decisive goal was an extraordinary effort by Mario Götze. Only something on that level could make the difference. It seemed beforehand that Messi would decide the final, but his performance declined as the tournament progressed. At the World Cup he paid the price for an incredibly long and arduous season.

In the last two world championships, the Netherlands reached the final in 2010 and the semifinal in 2014. That last result was a fluke, more a question of luck than quality. The Netherlands didn't even qualify for the 2016 European Championship.

Tactically, the Dutch understand everything. That's not the point. The reason why the Dutch fall short is the lack of physical strength (defense) and technique (getting away from the opponent). Physical contact is practically taboo in the Dutch competition, so that confrontation is not part of the game. Everything is about position, with one or two touches. Yet the tactic lacks depth; far too much of the game is about passing wide, back and forth: they should ask players not to turn away or to get past an opponent in an individual move.

The Dutch youth-training program has a lot to answer for. Until recently, the occasional exception—Wesley Sneijder, Robin van Persie, Arjen Robben—has masked the trend. Sneijder made the 2010 World Cup for the Dutch and Robben the 2014 World Cup. Now they are older and make less of an impact, the Dutch team has declined.

Exceptional players need nurturing. You wouldn't expect Ronaldinho, Messi and Ronaldo just to keep passing. You need to encourage these players to show their amazing skills. Isn't the Netherlands the country that places a premium on individual freedom? Then why not encourage young talented players who like to bend the rules every now and then . . .?

Meanwhile, the Dutch team is slipping down the ladder of international soccer. Even the second-tier teams can beat us, as the Netherlands' failure to qualify for the European Championship of 2016 showed, eliminated by Iceland, the Czechs and Turkey. We have become complacent and convinced ourselves that everything is fine the way it is. But if you don't develop, you deteriorate. The competition is always improving. Dutch football allowed other football associations and foreign clubs to look behind the scenes. These associations and clubs copied our programs, added a more physical approach and mentality, and then left us standing.

And the Dutch know-it-alls? They still ask: "Why should I do this? Why do that?" Of course, that critical "why" and "yes, but" are a part of our mentality, and have brought us far. But you have to move on. At some point you have to show something for your effort. As a small country, surrounded by big countries, we know we have to offer something special. We don't have it at the moment on the soccer pitch.

Meanwhile, we don't even have any real defenders. There are two reasons. First, because referees don't allow physical confrontation, and second because the emphasis in defense is on technical skills. Since the focus is on keeping possession, that is the type of player scouts look for—players who concentrate on keeping the ball. But what I want to know is, when the other side has the ball, can that defender actually defend?

Daley Blind, not originally a central defender but placed there by the manager Louis van Gaal, is a good example: a fantastic player on the ball, but physically vulnerable as a defender. By contrast, Jaap Stam was a true defender, who also knew when and how to play the ball to his teammates.

Youth programs

Youth-training programs reflect a country's soccer culture. Go to any game in England, Spain or Italy and you'll see venom, aggression, everywhere and all the time, from amateur to youth soccer—it is ingrained and second nature.

For Spaniards, Italians and English, friendly soccer doesn't really exist. It's not in their vocabulary, because playing is all about winning. That is the priority. And it is part of their DNA, far more than friendly soccer. Practice games are a different matter, but then the competitive element is just as important. In the Netherlands that mentality is simply absent.

The Netherlands

Now my son, Maxime, plays in the B1 team at AFC, a local amateur club, against teams from Ajax, PSV, AZ and Feyenoord, so I'm on the touchline at Dutch youth matches every week. It's remarkable, no less than at the top of Dutch soccer, that the mentality is rarely about winning: there is no sense of making every effort to win and the world collapsing if you lose.

That absence of a winning mentality is as much the result of the coaching, training and scouting as it is of referees who don't allow that mentality to find expression. I don't mean that youngsters should be allowed to go wild and kick and hit other players or go berserk at the ref or an opponent. No, I mean showing a measure of desire. I just don't see it, or not any more. And you need to have that desire if you want to play at the highest level, just as players like Nigel de Jong, Jaap Stam and Mark van Bommel had.

"We need to train kids. Train footballers," I hear them saying. But soccer is about more than controlling the ball and position. Confrontation should also be a part of training.

Link the training to rewards. Make sure the kids always play for something. And if they lose when practicing finishing or passing, for instance, there should be some kind of symbolic punishment. So the losers should run an extra lap, or do ten extra push-ups, bring the balls to the pitch for a week and other minor jobs that even the youngest player hates doing. At the same time you should reward youngsters who win or do something well.

Today talent is not exploited to its full potential in the Netherlands. In fact an essential element of the game is lacking: combat, passion, winning mentality. All you see at youth complexes are clones. Too much of the same. Admittedly it is also the result of kids being unable to play in the street any more. That was where we learned the game, choosing teams, taking the initiative, playing as well as you could until you found a way to win. The fault lies just as much in computer games and cell phones.

Let the kids in the training programs choose their own teams, or set up a position play and make one player touch the ball three times; see how they get on with that. These days most position play is with one or two touches. I want to see how midfielders respond when they have to touch the ball three times and actually have to think about what to do next. Think about keeping the ball, about turning without losing it while opponents try to take it away. That teaches players to act faster, to choose a position, turn from an opponent, physically defend themselves in a tussle.

There are thousands of potential variations, but you hardly see any of them on the pitch in the Netherlands. What you see is passing, passing and more passing. Passing over and over and still not getting anywhere. And it's so boring and predictable . . .

Spain

At FC Barcelona the training program is at such a high level—the second team plays two steps removed from the highest professional level—that, indeed, youth players are occasionally selected to play in the first team. Every Spaniard will point this out with pride, but if you look carefully you'll see that hardly any new talent has pushed through in the last two years. Only Sergi Roberto is able to press his nose to the glass occasionally, but then only in games that can no longer be lost or where the chances of defeat in the first place are zero. As to extra quality that can make a difference at Barcelona's level? Since Lionel Messi, Andrés Iniesta and Sergio Busquets, I haven't seen any exceptional talent emerge from the club's training program at the Nou Camp.

England

Looking at England in the same critical vein, I notice that far too little attention is paid to the development of young technical players: players who are able to decide a game with their insight and their technical skills.

Look at the central midfielders in the major clubs. You hardly ever see an English player in the role of playmaker. They get bogged down in the action. Yet soccer is more than confrontation and one-on-ones. As long as technical development remains a second or third priority, the English shouldn't complain that top foreign players form the backbone, the axis, of the Premier League's more successful teams.

Consider the leading teams. The keepers? At Manchester City, Chelsea, Liverpool, Arsenal, Tottenham Hotspur and Manchester United they are all from abroad. And don't forget that England has a reputation for producing keepers, with historic figures like Gordon Banks, Peter Shilton, Ray Clemence and David Seaman.

Draw up similar lists of defending and attacking midfielders and strikers, and you come to the same conclusion. There are some English central defenders around, but English players are seriously under-represented in crucial positions in the Premier League's top clubs. It is in the youth programs that you have to address that problem.

However difficult it may be: make a gentlemen's agreement to establish a quota for a minimum number of homegrown players on the pitch. If you only need to have them in the squad, as now, you don't need to play them . . . Naturally I understand that it will be difficult to realize, but if you were to keep an agreement like that in place for three years, I think you would see a considerable number of English players breaking through within a few years and playing at a higher level than the surfeit of mediocre foreign players who do little or nothing to benefit English soccer. Unfortunately, the upper tier of the English game has little patience for young players. They have to be able to play from the start, which is unrealistic. In fact the top tier has little patience for newly acquired, inexperienced players: perform immediately or leave.

Take Manchester United, where a plague of injuries forced the coach, Louis van Gaal, to dig into his own youth program. Suddenly young, competent English players were making their debut: Marcus Rashford, Jesse Lingard, Cameron Borthwick-Jackson. Did Van Gaal play these youngsters because he wanted to promote Manchester United's own future and by extension that of English soccer? Maybe he did, but it was more than that. Van Gaal has always preferred working with young, malleable players. That is his genius. He finds experienced, tried and tested players difficult. At Barcelona he clashed with Rivaldo and Figo, and at Bayern with Ribéry, Luca Toni and Mark van Bommel, and his relationship with Ángel Di María at Manchester United was nothing short of poor.

Yet the question remains of whether young players can win games. I think so, as long as they are surrounded by experienced players who know the ropes. It didn't work out as expected at Manchester United because often there were too many young players and the pressure in the Premier League is huge. English games are more intense than those anywhere else in the world.

That's why clubs that have to win straight away, like Chelsea and Manchester City, despite their amazing youth programs and academies that operate with astonishing success only buy players who have already arrived. Sometimes it's as if they aren't training youngsters for their own team but for other clubs. A pity, because I'd love to see someone like Ruben Loftus-Cheek playing more for Chelsea.

Patience is a virtue that you rarely find at Stamford Bridge or the Etihad—even though paying out heaps of cash for experienced players is no more a necessity for success: just look at Leicester City and Tottenham Hotspur at the top of the Premier League in 2015/16.

Enabling young talent to break through

The problem with training young talent in the Netherlands is that young players rarely get the help and guidance they need from mature teammates, simply because top Dutch players leave the country too early and experienced players are no longer attracted to top Dutch clubs.

The Mexican Andrés Guardado is an exception. After his career ran aground in Spain at Deportivo La Coruña and Valencia, and in Germany at Bayer Leverkusen, he reinvented himself in spectacular fashion at PSV and has elevated the players and even the coaches along the way. He ensured that PSV managed to survive the winter in the 2015/16 Champions League season for the first time in nine years.

In addition there is Dirk Kuyt (formerly of Liverpool) at Feyenoord and Ron Vlaar (formerly Aston Villa) at AZ. Much of the time when you watch Dutch Eredivisie clubs you are actually watching glorified youth teams. Because players like Guardado and Kuyt are rare, most youngsters lack the necessary support as they turn professional. They have to work it out for themselves, which is not always a smooth process. Not a bad thing in itself, but it takes longer and there is a real danger some will lose their way in the process.

At the same time, I remain convinced that many Dutch players join foreign clubs far too soon. Leaving the Netherlands too early can easily kill a career. Far better to grow to maturity in the Dutch competition, even if it is weaker these days than it was twenty years ago. Young kids hardly get a chance to play when they join Manchester City, Barcelona, Chelsea or Manchester United, and they spend their crucial teenage years stagnating for two or three seasons at their giant club, effectively accumulating twice as many years in lost ground. Nathan Aké, Jeffrey Bruma and Karim Rekik are examples.

What about Marco van Ginkel, who chose Chelsea, only to find his way by all kinds of digressions, via AC Milan and Stoke City, on loan to PSV and back in the Netherlands? Jeffrey Bruma and Nacer Barazite followed a similar route only to return years later than planned by a roundabout path back to the Dutch second tier.

Nathan Aké was the victim of his own premature transfer. At Chelsea they kept him waiting for far too long. It was not until 2016 that he was able to book real minutes on the pitch at the highest level with Watford. "But at Chelsea he trained with all the top players," people say. Great, but training is not the real thing. You only really get tested when three points are at stake. That is incomparably more significant than winning in training.

It is different for Georginio Wijnaldum, Jordy Clasie and Erik Pieters, all three of whom moved to England with experience at club level and having played for the Netherlands. Their story shows that you should only leave the Netherlands once you have achieved maturity. I've never seen a Dutch teenager ready for the Premier League.

I understand the urge—after all, money is a big motivator. You never know if that bus is ever coming past again. While I can't look into everyone's bank account, I can say that there is no justification in soccer terms to transfer a teenager to a foreign club.

That young English players come to the Netherlands is another matter. It makes sense. They don't get a chance to play in the Premier League, but in Dutch clubs with all those young players, they can make real progress and rejoin at a higher level when they return to England.

While Dutch professional club soccer suffers from a major lack of funding and a hemorrhage of young players to foreign clubs, a third plague is the advent of artificial grass. No fewer than eight of the eighteen professional clubs in the top division play on a synthetic surface.

Proponents of artificial turf claim that the country is ten years ahead of the rest of the world, while in fact the Dutch are really ten years behind as long as real grass is the preferred surface under UEFA and FIFA. Quite apart from the stagnation in players' development, it also changes the game and distorts the competition; players respond differently on synthetic surfaces. Tackling is slower, so games tend to resemble indoor soccer matches. These pitches need to be watered; otherwise they become rough and cause injuries. But water makes the surface extremely slippery so that long, deep balls race away at the speed of a rocket. To prevent that, players tend to play short-ball combination soccer over short distances, as you do indoors.

Two major teams that introduced artificial grass in England, Luton Town and Queens Park Rangers, have now switched back from plastic to proper pitches, with real grass.

Technique, physique and tactics

Technique should be every player's first priority. Tactical insight into the various systems comes from actually playing in them in practice. You learn to adapt. For individual players, technical development has to be paramount, from the moment you start playing. That's why you have to let youngsters between six and twelve get on with it, let them try and work it out, a few comments here and there, occasional individual tips or pieces of advice, and for the rest let them find out for themselves. Tactics are for later—at least for those who have mastered the techniques, otherwise they become more difficult.

In the Netherlands we have tended to stagnate in terms of functional technique, maybe even regressed in youth soccer. It's all very well to learn tricks and keepy-uppy the ball a thousand times, but in games it's about basic techniques: taking the ball, controlling it and passing at the right pace with the correct foot. Unfortunately we're far too engrossed in positional play in the Netherlands. It looks good, but without sufficient basic technique and without being physically aggressive you'll never make it in the race for international soccer at the highest level.

Among the truly top-class players it is evident that there is a balanced combination of technique, tactics and physical aggression. Messi is short but strong, has superb technique and can play in any system, whether at FC Barcelona or for the Argentinian national side. Luis Suárez is as strong as an ox and has an unorthodox technique, but it's no coincidence that he invariably emerges from any situation with the ball.

Zlatan Ibrahimović is another player who received practically everything as a gift from Mother Nature. His strength is crucial for a striker and he also possesses an incredible array of technical skills. Despite his strength, it is technique that is his priority. Messi and Ibrahimović are physical opposites, yet what they both have is a unique technique.

The physique of the average professional soccer player at the top of the game has changed over the last thirty years. Whereas you once had to be big and strong, these days players are often short, lithe and explosive, especially in midfield. The strength of these short players is palpable. The game has changed too. As has the approach of referees.

Players receive far more protection: the whistle blows for the tiniest infringement. Meanwhile, players know that cameras are pointing at them so that it's impossible to give an opponent a quick going over. Whereas it used to be open season on forwards, especially in countries such as Italy and Spain, now the cameras provide protection. That protection has created space for a new kind of player.

A good example is Andrés Iniesta. When you see him turn away from opponents without a scratch . . . fantastic, although when I used to try that, and especially against someone like Marco van Basten, I'd get a vicious kick to the ankle. These days you can turn without worrying. In my view, it's a major change in soccer which has crept in without fanfare.

It is a positive development, because I'm not a supporter of the nastier ways of physically stopping an opponent. What I do think—especially in the Netherlands—is that it should be more macho, like in England. There the ref doesn't blow the whistle at every physical confrontation.

Referees and soccer culture

To an extent, the referee determines the level at which a game is played, and so too the level and the development of the individual players. In the Netherlands, referees award penalties as if physical contact were taboo. Dutch clubs venturing into European competition soon find their players scattered like bowling pins and are swept out of the European tournaments.

Body check

If you referee a game like an indoor soccer referee, you'll get indoor soccer on grass—or on that horrendous plastic turf. That does nothing for players' development and in this way you lose touch with the top even more. That process is now under way in the Netherlands, once a leading country at European club level. By permitting a little more physical contact, referees would help clubs and players be more effective in international competitions.

Meanwhile, at Stamford Bridge he scored the winning goal against Barcelona, the equalizer in the eighty-eighth minute of the final at the Allianz Arena and the winning penalty in the decisive shootout.

Going berserk can be a tactical weapon: to waste time, to win over the fans, to influence the referee, to disturb the other side's rhythm or to get an opponent a yellow card, or have him sent off. The latter especially is unfair. But then these kinds of professional tricks are all part of how you win games. English and Dutch fans cry shame; in Southern Europe they pat you on the shoulder.

To blame the referee in every case is unreasonable, because referees are often sent onto the pitch with all kinds of instructions. They carry out their orders because otherwise they won't climb the ladder and won't get to referee the top games. This repressive policy gives them little scope to interpret situations that arise on the pitch in their own way—a personal touch can have a certain charm and players often appreciate it all the more. Better to have a referee with personality than a robot who may also make all kinds of mistakes.

Healthy common sense

These days, referees are more emphatically present than they used to be, although that is also a question of image. Everything looks bigger on television. And there may be as many as six or even ten cameras around the ground so that everything can be seen from all angles. The pitch has no secrets anymore, which detracts a little from the game's charm: players, managers and fans feel aggrieved more easily, and complain more readily that a decision is unfair, all of which does not make life any easier for referees.

How referees respond often shows which country they come from. For me the most important thing is to be able to talk to them normally. They shouldn't be afraid of dialogue. This is often more problematic in Southern Europe than in Western Europe. It is above all crucial that referees use their common sense.

They do things differently in England. There, physical clashes a
part of the game—although English referees often err in the opposi
direction, and the way players are allowed to carry on in one-on-on
is also extreme—their tackles often leave you shaking when you se
the replay. When English clubs come to Europe they are constantly
penalized because Continental referees are far less tolerant than their
British colleagues.

When foreign players first line up for the kickoff in the Premier
League, they love the magnificent surroundings and the fast pace, but
they are shocked by the game's physicality.

When Didier Drogba came to Chelsea from Olympique Marseille
he was amazed, even though he's a big guy and very strong. Having
learned his trade in the French league he dropped to the ground at the
slightest contact, but no English referee blew his whistle, which led to
theatrical protests from Drogba. John Terry, Chelsea's captain, soon
called him to one side with an urgent request to stop his exaggerated
dives and his theatrics: "Or else you'll come to nothing, my friend,
here in the Premier League."

Drogba took that wise lesson to heart and instead of falling to the
ground, he kept going to meet the next challenge, with the result that he
became one of the most popular foreign players in the Premiership. I
think the only one to become equally popular was Eric Cantona. The
extent to which Drogba developed, controlling his skills and reading
games, was evident in the season in which Chelsea won the Champions
League. In the Premier League, Drogba played a physical game, but in
European matches he transformed himself back into the French Drogba.

Whenever his team was in trouble, or he wanted to gain some
advantage, he opened up his box of tricks and you could see the European referees falling for them each time. In the semifinal against
Barcelona and in the final in Munich against Bayern in 2012, Drogba
was lying on the ground more than he was standing. And the referees
kept on blowing their whistle. An English ref would never have
allowed him that kind of opportunity to influence a game.

Unfortunately, that is often lacking. If you're refereeing a Champions League final and you're about to make a decision that will kill the game, then stop and count to ten: what are your priorities? A good example is the 2006 Champions League final at the Stade de France between Barcelona and Arsenal. The Norwegian referee, Terje Hauge, saw Arsenal's keeper, Jens Lehmann, bring down Samuel Eto'o outside the penalty area. He didn't wait to see what would happen next—instead he blew his whistle, sent Lehmann off and Barcelona got a free kick just outside the area. Doubtless a technically perfect decision.

Only he missed the fact that Ludovic Giuly, following through in that same run, got the ball and scored a simple goal. Had Hauge given the advantage and awarded Barcelona's goal, then Lehmann would not have had to be sent off and a yellow card would have sufficed. That's what I would expect from a ref with common sense, rather than his spoiling a match in the eighteenth minute that millions in and outside Europe had sat down to watch. Hauge could have taken a wise decision without trampling over the rules and everyone would have felt that justice had been done. I realize that you can't bend the rules, because that's a slippery slope, but common sense should prevail.

How to treat a referee

Southern European referees are often proud, which means there's no point in offending them. Never shout at a Southern European or gesticulate wildly as you try to explain that the decision was mistaken. As long as you don't disrespect an official in public they won't be offended by a normal remark. Referees are used to complaints, but don't even think about cursing. Southern European referees appreciate humility, so make yourself a little smaller, bow a little and keep your hands folded.

That's how Italian players approach the ref, while they can also carp and criticize like their life depended on it. Spanish referees are similar. In England players immediately launch into "You f*** this" and "You f*** that." English referees shrug it off. But never try to use language like that against a Spanish or Italian ref.

The English have an antipathy toward diving. If you only give someone a vicious kick, an English referee will tell you to "Play on" and signal a circle to say: he played the ball, not the player. If you lie down and make a theatrical show of being injured then you'll get an instant yellow card, because you're cheating the referee as well as the opponent, and refs don't like that.

All this relates to the cultural differences between Western and Southern Europe. If you enter the penalty area, look for an opponent to touch you and then start rolling on the ground to win a penalty, then the Brits will call you a cheat, but an Italian will say: *"Furbo"*— "Well done."

It is interesting to see how players adapt to each other's culture. In the Premier League, Spaniards, Italians and Germans tend to dive less than they usually do. By contrast, English players soon learn how to dive when they play on the Continent in the Champions League or the Europa League.

Influencing referees

Referees are under enormous pressure and are often nervous too. Players, managers, fans, media and television audiences—everyone is watching. There is nowhere for the referee to hide, as players do when they have an off-day. And everyone knows that a referee never sees everything, because refs are people too . . . but if you really don't want the ref to see everything you have to manipulate and influence him. Few could do so as successfully as Roy Keane.

I hardly ever complained to the referee if he had made a mistake. Before the kickoff I would have a relaxed chat, making sure the ref felt comfortable, saying that I hoped it would be a good game. A smile and a bit of eye contact: it's all part of influencing the referee. The referees' guild appreciated my explicit support. Of course, I hoped that in the process the officials might favor my team a little more if necessary.

There was one Italian referee, Rosario Lo Bello, who I found insufferable. He always gave us a hard time at AC Milan. Really. Against Verona he showed us four red cards: Marco van Basten, Frank Rijkaard, "Billy" Costacurta and the manager, Arrigo Sacchi. We only asked him: "What are you doing, ref?" We all felt that something wasn't right.

Later, it was revealed that Lo Bello had a real aversion to AC Milan. After that he never refereed us again. Until then he had regularly officiated at some of our most difficult games. Not that it made any difference, because we were never given an easy fixture when Lo Bello was due to officiate. It was just that he made things even tougher than necessary.

For me, the golden rule for a referee remains: the less you notice him, the better—not like those overinsistent officials, constantly blowing their whistles to get into the picture without a thought of steering the game to a successful conclusion. On the other hand, players can be pretty annoying too. Some don't even know the rules of the game, or break them deliberately. Then you deserve to be penalized, in my opinion.

Measured response is not every coach's greatest asset. Managers like Sir Alex Ferguson, Arsène Wenger and especially José Mourinho begin to manipulate referees a week before the game: "We never get penalties from that official," or "So-and-so in the other side is always diving" and similar helpful suggestions for the referee. Sometimes it works, but it may just as easily backfire. Which goes equally for players who can't stop complaining.

Remember: referees watch *Match of the Day* too when they get home and can see how players provoke other players and dramatize, and try to pull the wool over their colleagues' eyes. It was all going well for Chelsea's Diego Costa, for example, until he appeared to be about to bite an opponent in a game against Everton, only to draw back at the last second. Yet that was enough for the referee to send him off—it was a foregone conclusion. Naturally a player will contest a decision like that, and quite rightly. In doubtful situations referees have to follow their conscience.

It would make life easier for officials if they didn't have to worry all the time about being ridiculed in the eyes of the entire country.

Italians and Argentinians are past masters when it comes to manipulating referees. When you get a corner against them, they hold you tight and the referee does nothing. If you, as a foreign player, grab hold of anyone it's an immediate foul and a penalty. In Italy they fire these clever tricks at you from the minute you arrive, and there's really no sense of embarrassment: gesticulating at the referee, a push, a pinch, a stomp on your foot, a boot to your ankle, shirt pulling, and so on. It's all *furbo*.

Clubs are equally culpable. A relatively innocent ruse is messing with the kickoff time. AC Milan's and Napoli's games were always scheduled for exactly the same time: a Sunday afternoon at two thirty. It was standard for the Neapolitans to start a couple of minutes later: they simply delayed the kickoff. Either someone was still in the bathroom or he had the wrong boots on, or the wrong shirt. Maybe someone was still in the dressing room getting his bandages tied. They used every trick in the book. It seemed quite funny to me, I understood their reasoning. And the comedy was all part of the show.

When we won, it made no difference. If not, it would mean waiting a tense couple of minutes for the result to come through from Napoli. After all, a lot can happen in those final moments!

In Spain they know a ploy or two as well. I remember going with AC Milan in November 1987 to Espanyol in Barcelona for a second-round UEFA Cup match. It had rained all day but the pitch at Estadi de Sarrià was nevertheless reasonably playable. After warming up, we went back to the dressing room, where we waited for the signal to come out for the kickoff. When we got to the pitch, it was soaking wet. "What happened?"

In the intervening minutes Espanyol's personnel had doused the grass with a water cannon. It made playing skilled soccer that much harder. After warming up I had put my studs on: they turned out to be the wrong ones for water ballet. We were slipping and sliding, especially me with my long legs. We had to make up a 2–0 deficit from the first game, and now there was no chance of that. A nice piece of gamesmanship by Espanyol, and it got them to the next round. In retrospect I can see the funny side. If you're not strong, then be smart.

These days, stunts like that are forbidden and UEFA exercises far more control. At the time, clubs would organize matches themselves; now it's UEFA that does the administration, or it's all done under its auspices, and official observers are present to supervise. It's not the club but UEFA that runs the stadium on match nights, and that works a lot better. There's no room these days for funny business.

To dive or not to dive?

Diving is so difficult to combat simply because it is such an effective ploy. In the 2015/16 season the Belgian Christian Benteke deliberately fell in the final minutes when the score stood at 1–1 away to Crystal Palace. He got a penalty and took it himself: 2–1 for Liverpool. Jamie Vardy did something similar at Arsenal—Leicester City and also won a penalty. While Benteke tripped over thin air, at least Vardy managed to find an opponent's leg to stumble over and there was some contact. He looked for a touch and he found it.

Smart as it may be, it is also shortsighted. Vardy—Leicester City lost the game, by the way—and Benteke were lambasted by the television pundits and in the press. English fans don't like that sort of thing and for weeks both players were reminded of the error of their ways whenever they visited other clubs with a chorus of whistles each time they touched the ball. Which was also a pertinent reminder for the referee in charge, because his colleagues had been made to look foolish.

While English soccer fans never tire of reminding me of the way foreign players like to dive, now we know that Vardy, Rooney and Ashley Young are all proficient divers.

And yet—not every dive is a dive. That's because there are players in professional soccer who are so good and have such brilliant skills that they know exactly what they are doing. Naturally they make mistakes, but there's usually some idea behind their attempt.

For example, I dribble and pass my opponent, who makes a sliding tackle; I avoid the tackle, jump over the player sliding in, otherwise I'll break my ankles. Every movement of my body is totally under control—we don't train every day for nothing—and I know how I'm going to land. The only trouble is that my contact with the ball is based on not having to contend with a sliding tackle. So I'm no longer running at the same pace as the ball. In fact I probably won't catch up with the ball at all.

What should I do? So I drop to the ground, otherwise I'll lose my advantage over the player I just passed. In effect, it's a dive. But what else can I do? Should I protect my ankles, or take a trip to hospital? It's an easy choice. Simply put: to keep your advantage and avoid a nasty injury you drop to the ground.

A dive? It depends. The sliding tackle was itself an infringement: I avoided the collision by jumping, so no actual foul was committed, and so it's my dive that gets punished . . . Whether the player touches me or not, either way I have lost the ball and so the other player's foul has achieved its purpose. But a referee who has never played at that level doesn't see things like that; neither do fans nor the media. Which leads to misunderstandings and arguments.

That is one example, but there are dozens more. Unfair? Yes, but it's an illusion to imagine that you can ban diving.

Soccer isn't fair

That refereeing mistakes are one of soccer's charms is not something you should ever say to an American, who generally prefers watching traditional American sports. Americans consider soccer the most unfair sport there is. In the United States they like to analyze sports rationally, so they love collecting facts and figures. Meanwhile, we find faults and flaws part of the appeal. And soccer is a succession of errors. If no one makes a mistake nothing ever happens. That unfair advantage prevails is one of the reasons soccer is so attractive.

Clearly: soccer isn't fair. If you care too much about errors and unfairness, then maybe soccer isn't the game for you. You need to accept that sometimes the decision goes in your favor and sometimes it doesn't.

Quite apart from the different interpretations you get, even with a video referee, I take soccer as it comes. That's how I approached the game as a player. Referees never had trouble from me. I never lost my temper or went into a tantrum to insist that I was right and they were wrong. Of course there were times when I said: "Didn't you see that? Incredible." But in the end you play within the parameters set by the referee, and a little unfairness is par for the course.

Americans find it hard to understand; the English get it straight away. If I say a foul deserved a red card, they say: "He gave a yellow card, what are you talking about?" Then if I ask: "What would have happened in Europe?" they reply: "Well, then it would have been red."

Some claim that Ajax, Feyenoord, PSV, Manchester United, Liverpool, Real Madrid, Barcelona, Bayern Munich, Juventus and other major clubs often have the referee on their side. It's possible that some officials may experience a certain unconscious intimidation when faced by the reputation, the surroundings and the ambience of a top European club. You have to be immune to it as a referee, but this can be hard to put into practice. Nevertheless I don't believe that any professional referee ever goes to a top club intending to give that club an advantage.

Moreover, before you start complaining, don't forget that an attacking side will always have more chance of not being penalized than a defending side simply because of where the action is taking place.

Everything to win

I never had any training in how to survive the last fifteen minutes of a game, or how to go hell for leather to force a draw or a victory.

Survival is often a matter of improvisation and may not involve much discussion. Forcing a result generally implies parking as many tall and physically strong players in the opponents' penalty area as possible, then pumping the ball into the box and hoping it lands on someone's head, foot, leg, stomach . . . anywhere but his hands.

When Manchester United wanted to force a result back in Sir Alex Ferguson's day, they didn't play long balls, but raised the pressure. Sometimes it was so intense that the only answer a keeper had was to kick the ball upfield. That meant that the opposing team's strikers would have to sprint back into position. At that moment, the team doing the pressing is at its most vulnerable.

It stands to reason: all the players are helping to score that last-minute equalizer or winner, and many forget everything they've ever learned and—with the best of intentions—their task. It makes them even more ripe to concede another goal than to score. On the other hand, strikers who come and help in defense can be a dangerous liability. In addition, the more players in the penalty box, the greater the risk that the ball will go in.

(Un)sporting solutions

An effective way to break the rhythm of a team chasing a goal at full throttle is to simulate a foul. No matter how insignificant the infringement, you need to fall to the ground and act as if it's a major injury.

That means staying down. Have the doctor come onto the pitch. In the final stages it is essential to break the other side's momentum. That requires shrewdness. There is no other way. In other sports there are regular opportunities to break a team's momentum by asking for time-out.

I can hear the soccer purists complaining: "Yes, but that's not fair." Why not? You're not doing anything that's forbidden, or not in the rules. If you get kicked, you may fall and you may be injured. Tragedy or comedy, that's up to the doctor. At the highest level you have to use tricks like this if you want to win. The referee's job is to set the limits. I see the charm in that.

In England, fair play is key and the English find this kind of theatrics revolting. For Brits, it smacks of cheating. They have less trouble accepting a vicious kick than a player rolling around on the ground. In Italy and Spain they do both, but the Argentinians take it to another level. You often see it in the Champions League and Europa League, in which many Argentinians play. If you don't join in their attempts to upset a game to force a victory then don't be surprised if they come down on you like a ton of bricks.

Louis van Gaal's Manchester United lost an opportunity to beat Chelsea and draw against Sunderland this way in the 2015/16 season. The team came under intense pressure but did absolutely nothing to disturb the other side's attacking momentum. Not De Gea, not Rooney, not Blind, not Carrick, not Smalling, and none of the Dutch— British coaching staff raised a finger to help. Chelsea and Sunderland were allowed to pile on the pressure and as a result United gave away two expensive goals. That turned out to be the week in which Manchester United lost the opportunity to contend for fourth position in the Premier League—and so lost the chance of a place in the preliminary round of the Champions League.

If you are defending a lead in the final minutes and you get a free kick, don't kick the ball into the penalty area. Of course that's where you can score, but scoring isn't the objective now: the aim is to guarantee three points. You can do that most effectively in the opponents' half by kicking the ball into one of the corners. If you have a free kick, send the ball into the corner. There it's far easier to waste time, to trap the other side in the corner and hope the ball rolls over the touchline.

If you have possession you may be able to force a throw-in, or a corner or free kick. You can also dribble the ball to the corner—anything to use up time before the final whistle. Often that causes desperation and infractions that may lead to a yellow or even a red card. Meanwhile, time marches inexorably on and the points are increasingly secure. However frustrating, inelegant, unsporting it may seem, this is part of the game, and has been within the rules for a hundred years.

As a manager it is maddening if your players refuse to acknowledge these rules and you concede a goal in the final moments because someone in the team decided he ought to act differently. On the bench or standing on the touchline, there's little a manager can do except substitute players. Or possibly offer a suggestion here and there if the game comes to a standstill. During play hardly anyone hears what you say amid all the noise.

The most sublime example of naivety in the dying moments of a game happened on November 17, 1993. David Ginola, a gifted French forward, had come on as a substitute in the last World Cup qualifying game between France and Bulgaria. The score was 1–1 and it was in the ninetieth minute: France had one foot on the plane to the World Cup.

Instead of keeping possession and playing near the corner flag, Ginola slung the ball forward in search of a totally superfluous 2–1. The pass was far too long and a Bulgarian defender picked up the ball, quickly passed to Lubos Penev, who then sent a long ball to Emil Kostadinov, who was now in position. With a shot cannoned from an impossible angle at goal the striker and captain of Bulgaria propelled his country to the World Cup in the United States, ten seconds before time. As a result players like Marcel Desailly and Eric Cantona missed the World Cup.

Injury treatment

The manager is the club's figurehead. It is up to the manager to appear a couple of times a week to say a few words to the media. Managers also oversee all the processes within a club and take ultimate responsibility. That is why they sometimes have to take tough action to keep everyone in line. And that includes medical staff, such as the doctor and physical therapists.

Internal differences are rarely aired in public. Not until recently. In the 2015/16 season, in a game against Swansea City, a much-discussed clash occurred between José Mourinho and the doctor Eva Carneiro, who was rudely rebuked, in her account, for treating an injured Eden Hazard on the pitch.

Carneiro followed the referee's instruction to go onto the pitch to attend to Eden Hazard, which under the laws of the game meant he had to be brought to the touchline before he could go back on. Mourinho was furious. Carneiro's intervention had left his team playing with nine against eleven—the keeper, Thibaut Courtois, had been shown a red card earlier in the game.

Without wanting to excuse José Mourinho's conduct, I can understand his position. After all, it's one thing to slow down the other side, relieve the pressure or break the momentum by faking an injury if you have eleven players on the pitch. With ten players it's possible to carry on playing, but if there are only ten on the pitch and you take another player off, leaving only nine to continue, then you have a serious tactical problem, and that is exactly what happened here.

In the end, Chelsea kept Swansea at bay, there were no more goals and the score remained 2–2. But this is all about the moment, and Mourinho recognized the implication of that moment, though Carneiro was not at fault. Unfortunately, his reaction did not make pleasant listening. Chelsea were not in a good place, stories were leaking from the dressing room and Mourinho vented his anger in public. The manner in which he dealt with the incident ensured that it would come to play a role in his eventual resignation from Chelsea.

A coin caused me to lose the championship with AC Milan. That is the impact a single detail can have on the result of an entire competition. In 1989/90, the battle for first place was between Napoli and us. Four games before the end, Napoli were playing Atalanta Bergamo and the score was 0–0: they couldn't break through the defensive wall. Fifteen minutes before the end, the Brazilian midfielder Alemão fell to the ground. He had apparently been struck on the head by a coin. The doctor came over and gesticulating wildly told him: "Stay down, stay down, stay. Don't get up." Then he shouted for a stretcher and Alemão was carried off.

The final score of 0–0 was later turned into an obligatory 2–0 for Napoli after a group of Atalanta fans had been identified by the Italian football association as having been responsible. At the end of the season we were left two points short and Napoli were champions.

Secrets and spies

Unlike in England and Italy, the training grounds of the top Dutch clubs are freely accessible for supporters and the media. Almost all the training sessions are open to the public. In the Netherlands they preach transparency and people kick up a fuss if teams train behind closed doors. Even the national team: "What about the old guys who stand along the touchline, then? You want to deprive them of their morning walk and their cup of coffee?"

It's all rather nice, but amateurish too: because professional soccer is bigger than that and it involves keeping certain things secret. It makes no sense to tell your opponents and the whole world more than they already know. With all the analysis in today's professional game, managers know practically everything about their opponents, their tactics, lines of attack, the buildup, their favorite corner for penalties, different corner and free-kick variations and much more besides.

If you want to surprise your opponent with a new tactic or formation, then you'll have to practice it with the doors closed. And as a manager you can't tell everyone about it at the press conference before the game either. Your opponents are following every move you make.

At AC Milan we knew absolutely everything about our opponents and they hardly ever managed to surprise us. The club sent out spies not just to watch games, but to training sessions too. If the public weren't admitted they had to find some other way of discovering what the club was planning. I think I prefer not to know how they did that.

Closed training facilities are the answer to this kind of espionage. That gives managers the opportunity to train undisturbed, without every incident being reported and exaggerated in the press. I was once involved in an altercation with Fabio Capello, my manager at AC Milan. I was really angry and ready to hit him; luckily Frank Rijkaard stopped me. It takes a lot to get me that angry. And, for me, Capello had gone too far. Yet that argument was never made public at the time, because we all recognized that it was against the club's interests.

Years later, Clarence Seedorf asked me about it—he was playing at Real Madrid and Capello had told them himself in the dressing room. He used what had happened to show how the club's interests were paramount and no one should ever leak stories to the press.

In every club, there are bound to be arguments between players. Often you never see or hear about them, but if the training ground were open to the public it would be on Twitter in no time and then on all the news sites, and then you'd have another fire to put out. These things distract from what it's really all about at a professional club: getting a result in the next game.

That's why major clubs around the world such as FC Barcelona,

Real Madrid, Chelsea, Manchester United, Bayern Munich, AC Milan, Juventus and many others invite the media in regularly, once a week. The day before a game, they are free to film the players as they kick the ball around for fifteen minutes.

It's amusing to see the press try to infiltrate closed training sessions of national teams with their cameras—especially in the Netherlands. In England and Italy the media don't see it as quite the same challenge. Their patriotism grows stronger as the international game approaches, although if things go wrong for the team then the criticism can be unforgiving.

Of course, the media's job is to try to inform the public and anything secret is simply asking to be investigated. But national coaches have entirely different concerns. They don't want the opponents learning more than they already know. They want to surprise the other side. That may be the deciding factor that determines the result of the game.

I regularly speak to managers, but they'll never talk about their tactics and their approach to the next game, or who's playing where. Why would anyone give away their tactics? That knowledge is exclusively for the managers and the players. And even if the eleven names on the teamsheet are known, you can still surprise your opponent by positional changes and tactical tweaks.

For example, PSV suffered an abysmal 3–1 defeat at home to FC Utrecht in the quarterfinals of the Dutch KNVB Cup. Three days later, Phillip Cocu took his team to Utrecht for a league fixture. To change his team after the previous defeat he switched the right back, Joshua Brenet, for his regular right back, Santiago Arias, a Colombian. Somehow the press got hold of it in advance. It was deemed a logical move. A back for a back, you'd think, which is what FC Utrecht's manager, Erik ten Hag, thought too.

Cocu kept his lips sealed. He had given Arias a totally different role, not as a right back but as a deep midfielder on the right. Within twenty minutes the game was decided with a goal by Arias and an assist to make it 2–0. Ten Hag and FC Utrecht were completely overwhelmed and never recovered. In short: if you're going to adjust your tactics, then be certain it counts quickly and make sure of your result before the other side's manager finds a way to deal with your surprise by substituting or changing a position.

Ideally a manager should be able to work between games in an undisturbed environment. At Feyenoord, my old club, the opposite is true. There the coach, Giovanni van Bronckhorst, has to hope first of all that his players don't get run over. Feyenoord's players have to cross a four-lane motorway to get to their training ground. It lies in a delightfully sheltered site, behind a dyke, protected from the wind, although anyone can watch what's going on at the training ground from the dyke. And that's just not the way things are done any more.

Milanello, AC Milan's training complex, was harder to get into than Fort Knox. Even members of your family couldn't get in without going through reception. Guests were received in a separate area altogether and only in exceptional cases could they watch part of a training session. On a tactical training day, no one was allowed at Milanello.

The coach gets involved

As a coach you're always looking for ways to surprise your opponents by exploiting their weaknesses and emphasizing your own strengths. If you have a striker who can head the ball then you have to think of ways to feed him as many high balls as possible. If the other side has a left back who doesn't know how to build an attack then you want that player to be the one who has to start the buildup, and so you mark the right back and the central defenders. Then the left back has to receive the ball, and you let the weakest link wander about a little and eventually the same old mistake will follow, as always.

These tactics need to be discussed in advance, along with the moves your own team will make from the moment you regain possession from the left back's mistake. That's the way a manager gets a grip on the game. Often the effectiveness of your tactics depends on the response of the other side's manager.

If the other side manages to surprise you then you have to assess the situation with lightning speed. What is the danger if I don't change my formation? Can I correct the situation with a slight adjustment or a positional change? Does their tactical move create an advantage for me somewhere else? How long should I wait before taking action?

A minute can be too long, and a half-hour too short. In other words, it's not always a rational decision—sometimes it's a gut reaction. At the same time, your team's confidence is at stake, and their trust in you as manager and your tactics. It is a complex combination of factors that you have to take into account.

So you have to give yourself time. Sometimes you think: okay, it's looking reasonably solid, we can carry on like this. Yet I never hesitated to make changes if I thought we would concede a goal if we stuck to the same pattern: a quick substitution of a player who is underperforming can sometimes be called for.

However, most quick substitutions follow an injury or a red card.

Red card

A red card tests the manager's ability both to improvise and to prepare in advance. Do you have a viable emergency scenario? If you're left with ten players, you often need to make a tactical adjustment. Many managers take off a striker or an offensive midfielder and bring on a defender or a defensive midfielder between the lines.

In January 2016, the Arsenal defender Per Mertesacker was shown a red card in the eighteenth minute in a game against Chelsea. Four minutes later, the striker Olivier Giroud was taken off in favor of the defender Gabriel Paulista, Theo Walcott moved into the striker's position and Arsenal continued to play without a winger. Wenger's first thought was: I need to get my defense sorted. That was more important than the fact that the target man, Giroud, was having a good game. Up front, Wenger went for Walcott's pace, thinking that if Chelsea played a more attacking style more space would open up at the back—which didn't happen incidentally.

Wenger's choice is the standard solution, but what strikes me about this situation is that managers rarely deal with being one player down with a simple positional change. The response is usually to substitute a defender. Arsenal started that game with four midfielders and Chelsea with three. So why not let one of the midfielders—Flamini for example—drop back a line into defense and try to keep your strength in place, in this case the Giroud–Walcott combination.

A week later, Ronald Koeman faced a similar dilemma when Southampton played West Ham United and the defensive midfielder Victor Wanyama was sent off around the fifty-fifth minute. He kept on his target man, Graziano Pellè, and brought off Sadio Mané. The score was 1–0 for Southampton. Pellè can keep the ball up front, which reduced the pressure on the defense and gave the team space despite the relentless West Ham attacks.

There is no definitive answer because perspectives always differ, as do the qualities of the players. When one of your players gets sent off you make a choice and hope that it works out. There is no such thing as a wrong decision, because you always have the perfect excuse that with ten against eleven you have more chance of losing than of winning.

That you still have a chance when playing ten against eleven is because a kind of primitive force takes hold of the ten remaining players, making them capable of achieving the impossible, while the eleven tend to put the brakes on.

The star of the team

When Eden Hazard was on top form, his markers would never let him out of their sight for a moment, so Hazard didn't need to keep up with them. Normally you would expect him to take up his defensive position when the other team had possession, since it's often only a matter of dropping back ten meters. If his opponent moved up past him then he would use the space and tell the player behind: "Look out, he's coming. Take over."

But later in the season Hazard lost his form and defenders would easily pass him: since he failed to move in formation and no longer made the difference in possession, Mourinho eventually replaced him. That can be a tricky situation for a coach; if Hazard didn't know why he was being substituted or left on the bench, the coach ran the risk of losing him.

Lionel Messi and Neymar are both fantastic players. That is beyond dispute. I'm interested to see how teams playing against FC Barcelona try to shut them out of the game without touching a hair on their heads or confronting them physically.

It's practically impossible. When these two don't have the ball they move into position. If you want to cut them out of the game you need to put pressure on the players feeding them. That brings you to Iniesta and Busquets as the principal passers. You need to tie them down. And then you still have to hope and pray that it works. Because if one of your players lets you down, then it's up to you as coach to intervene immediately.

In Italy I once saw a team play Barcelona in the way Chelsea successfully played them: with a block of four or five players at the back and a second defensive block in midfield and only a single striker and a false striker in front of the two defensive bulwarks. "Go on, do your best!" they challenged their opponents. They even let crosses from the flanks fly in. The widest defenders didn't pursue the forwards coming down the flanks at all.

For this kind of strategy, with two defensive blocks and no outside defenders, you need a big keeper and tall central defenders with a keen eye for crosses and who are powerful in the air. If the block is in position then there is hardly any way anyone can get through. That Italian manager didn't care how many crosses sailed in.

Me, with my Dutch background, I would have been worried having to defend against so many crosses. I would have been constantly thinking: get that ball out. For me, as a manager, the risk of exposing the team to danger like that would be too great.

Cutting out the star player

The best way to nullify a specific opponent is to cut off their supply of passes. If that doesn't work, the next option is physical confrontation. If all your players win their one-on-ones then you'll win the game. Only I don't know of any manager who plays one-on-one across the pitch. Sometimes you see pairs of players, but most teams defend by zone these days.

That is what made a player like Frank Lampard so dangerous. He roamed around long enough to lull the other side into a false sense of security and then suddenly he was there in front of the keeper. He never went in a straight line. And you never saw Lampard sprint. Despite the threat, you couldn't easily put a marker on him. What made it difficult was that he was really a striker playing from midfield.

How do you deal with him as a manager? Analyze his game, shake your players awake and keep them sharp.

At FC Barcelona the pattern is as follows: Messi drops back to midfield. The right and left wingers and the midfielders sprint after him and the defenders pass and wait for Messi's through ball. Extremely difficult to defend against. Any defender following Messi as he drops back leaves a huge space, which is dangerous as players move forward. As an opponent you're constantly faced with dilemmas.

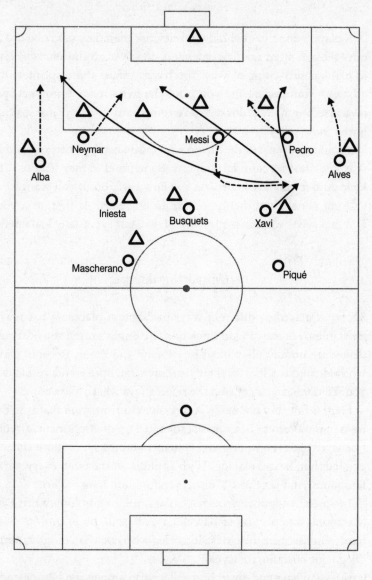

Messi's role at Barcelona before Suárez arrived: Messi drops back from the striker position to make space for other players and to receive the ball, and giving him various options to pass deep.

If players don't get behind your defense then they won't be dangerous. Yet you often see that defenders don't use all the available tricks
to block approaching players. You have to meet those sprinters literally with your body. Plant your shoulder in his torso, bring that sprint
to a grinding halt. It doesn't have to be hard or nasty. Just a simple:
boom, "Oh, sorry."

A smart player will hit the ground immediately when stopped like
that and start screaming in agony. Sometimes it may lead to a free
kick. And it may even cost you a yellow card, but if you want to win
and not get shafted then you have to be smart. At first, as a young
Dutch player I was amazed at what I saw, but eventually I adapted.

(Un)sporting defense

Soccer is played in different ways in different places. What may be
furbo in Italy is cheating in England. The English often consider smart
defending unfair. They liked Roy Keane and Bryan Robson, players
who ride into battle with their visor up, straightforward, visible, what
you see is what you get, and the referee says what's allowed.

Hard is fine, but not nasty. Aggressive confrontation that is so common in the Premier League isn't tolerated on the Continent, although
I believe that even in England Graeme Souness spent more time suspended than he did playing. With Souness on the pitch everyone was
fair game. And yet I would always choose him in my team.

In Spain, Andoni Goikoetxea had a similar reputation when Diego
Maradona was playing at Barcelona. A Basque by origin, he was as
hard as nails—he broke Maradona's leg with not a ball in sight, putting
Diego out of action for a year.

Gary Pallister and Steve Bruce were also among the best defenders,
yet with a completely different style: more open, with greater aptitude
for zonal marking. In the one-on-one tussles at corners and free kicks
they're hard but fair, typical products of the English school of soccer.

Claudio Gentile, the Italian who marked Maradona at the 1982 World Cup in Spain, was also hard and had plenty of tricks, although he was not overly dirty. He was a top defender, shrewdly holding on to his opponent, an arm around your body, nudging you out of balance, knuckles in your back, a tickle to your legs, an elbow slightly too high and all kinds of little things—whatever he needed to do to get the job done: cutting out the opponent. He was unique in achieving that without accumulating a stack of cards. A player you would love to have in your team, Gentile never lost control.

Pietro Vierchowod was of a similar ilk. As far as sticking to their mark goes, Gentile and Vierchowod were on a par. I never considered that Italians play nasty. I have a great respect for Italian defenders because I know the culture and the reasons why Italians defend like that. Winning is sacred, and if you don't concede a goal you can't lose. It comes from a profound instinct for survival, although in some ways it's almost comical. Think back to the way Zinedine Zidane fell into Marco Materazzi's trap in the 2006 World Cup final in Berlin between France and Italy. Zidane was furious, head-butted Materazzi, received a red card and left the pitch.

No one knows exactly what Materazzi said. Whatever it was, he got the result he needed. Although Zidane always seemed cool and never said much on the pitch, Materazzi knew that he had a temper from the time the French star had played at Juventus, where he had exploded with rage at various times. That's how Italians experience a soccer game.

Argentinians have an even greater instinct for survival. Add to that their technique and tactical insight and you have what is probably the most complete player. Argentinians pull out all the stops and are not afraid of being hard and nasty. They'll go beyond the acceptable without scruple.

For example, take Daniel Passarella. He wore the captain's armband when Argentina became world champions in 1978 and later played in Italy, first for Fiorentina (1982–6) and then for Internazionale

(1986–8). He floored me with a vicious and intentional elbow after his teammate Giuseppe Bergomi had failed to stop me heading in from a corner, twice.

Javier Mascherano of FC Barcelona, another Argentinian, is made of similar stuff. He often goes too far, but appears quite innocent. In the replay you can see him stamping his studs onto another player's leg. Which hurts. Tiny, unpleasant pinpricks. Even a soccer team like Barcelona needs a little of that occasionally. At least someone who bites back. I get a kick out of it. You need a shrewd player like that on your side. He frightens intimidating opponents. Sometimes it's quite funny the way they carry themselves: the holy innocent.

After the match

Depending on the result and the importance of the game, players may feel happy after the final whistle or not, quite apart from how they fared in the match. After a regular competition game you raise your hand in the air, thank the spectators and go for a shower. You did your job and the next game awaits.

After you win your first Champions League final you're in a state of euphoria and you only see afterward on television how you reacted. The level of ecstasy reflects the way the goals were scored. Last season, Liverpool players went wild after their 4–3 victory against Borussia Dortmund. The team seemed on the way out: they were 3–1 down in a Europa League quarterfinal at Anfield Road. If you manage to get the winning goal in injury time, against a better side, and a place in the semifinals, then naturally the players are ecstatic: a healthy reaction.

Psychology

Emotions such as anxiety and confidence may lie miles apart, yet on the pitch they are surprisingly close. Psychology coaches are increasingly common at soccer clubs. Although now they are generally accepted, this kind of thing used to be taboo and consultations were kept secret.

Psychology coach

I have always been open about my own connection with Ted Troost, who pioneered a style of physical therapy called haptonomy. I felt good as a result of his treatment and I've never made a fuss about it. At AC Milan we were also way ahead of our time in this. They had a team of psychologists at Milanello mixing with the players' group. No one thought it strange.

Besides individual sessions on request, we also did team sessions. We would all lie down on the floor and then the psychologist would say: "Close your eyes, breathe with your stomach and imagine a black-contoured frame. Put all your negative thoughts about what you can't do into that black frame. Now do the same but with a gold frame, and think of all the things you want to do and that are going well." Then he played the theme from *Chariots of Fire*.

There's no proof that it helped. But I know we won everything in sight with AC Milan, and we never ridiculed it. Medical supervision was uniquely important at AC Milan and the psychological health of the players was a part of that.

Another psychologist kept an eye on the relations between players in and around training sessions. He got involved in everything. If two players had a disagreement, he would intervene between them immediately and try to get to the deeper causes of the problem and to deal with it. Because he kept a close eye on everything he prevented things from getting out of control—disagreements hardly had an opportunity to develop in the dressing room.

I have rarely experienced such a large homogeneous group. We never had a chance to form cliques. The psychologist intervened straight away. It was all interconnected and felt really natural. Marco van Basten and Frank Rijkaard were in the same dressing room as me, but we didn't form a Dutch clique within AC Milan. The Italians treated us like their own and involved us in everything—outside Milanello too. If you couldn't adapt, you didn't belong at AC Milan. To avoid the risk of buying a player who didn't fit in, they screened you extensively beforehand. When they contacted me to suggest a transfer, the club knew more about me than I did.

When it came to Frank Rijkaard, at first the club had doubts—not about the player, but about his personality. He had signed contracts with Ajax and PSV, had fled to Sporting Lisbon and later he had moved to Real Zaragoza. They interrogated me and Marco endlessly about Frank. Happily we persuaded everyone that Rijkaard would be an asset for AC Milan. He was the missing link, with his strength, insight, stamina and ability to score.

You had to fit the club profile. How did you behave as a professional in the dressing room? And out of the dressing room? Were you gregarious? Everyone is different, but you have to work together. Respect for each other was an important principle. It is a key aspect of performing together.

Captain

To captain a team is something special. You represent the players and at the same time you're the person they come to, as do the managers, board, directors, media, sponsors and fans. Internally and externally, you're the figurehead. To be a good captain you need a sense of responsibility.

You need to have the right personality. A captain knows how to bring all the elements together. Not everyone is able to carry the responsibility for the team and its performance. You have to stand up for your players and the club. It's an important function, often even more so off the pitch than on it.

It doesn't really matter which position you play in—on the pitch you toss for the kickoff and have access to the referee if there's something you want to say or you want explained. That role on the pitch is more or less defunct these days, now that referees have stopped listening to players. Of particular importance is your negotiation with the directors or the board regarding bonuses.

Captaining the national side is an even greater privilege. You are representing your country. That captain's armband stands for something, although I feel that it should always be given to the person who emerges as the natural leader of the selected team. There should be no controversy within the group about the choice and the captain should be a first choice for the team; otherwise he soon loses credibility. Naturally, the more experienced members of the team are the first in line. In Spain, it is standard for the person who has been at the club longest to be the captain.

I know that selecting a captain can cause dissent in the team. So it's good to have some guidance from above to help the process along. In 1973, Ajax had won three European Cups, predecessor of today's Champions League. Instead of going for the compelling present holder of the position, Johan Cruijff, the Ajax players elected the calm, senior and introverted Piet Keizer as their new captain. Within weeks, Cruijff was on his way to Barcelona.

Reserves

For a player, the hardest thing to accept is being a reserve. It means being satisfied with second place, while you know that you really belong in the first team. A manager can never afford to neglect the reserves, because that leads to discord in the group.

In 2015/16, some of the Chelsea players began to complain. At first it was only the reserves, but then the first team began to express frustration too. Although Chelsea kept losing, José Mourinho continued to keep his first team unchanged. He wanted to show his confidence in them, but then the reserves began to complain that they never had a chance to play—a huge dilemma for a coach. Winning is one answer, but Chelsea weren't winning.

Members of the squad who aren't playing need more attention than the first-team players. Reserves are crucial, because with today's intensely busy schedules it's impossible to complete a full season with only eleven players. You need to keep your reserves sharp so they'll perform when you play them. The work this involves is done during the week. Let the reserves know they matter as part of the squad. At AC Milan the psychologists kept a particular eye on the reserves.

You also need your reserves to prepare the first team for the next game. At AC Milan we often played tactical games with the first team against the reserves. At other clubs the reserves would do their level best to show what they could do, but at Milan that wasn't the point at all, it was a tactical training session for the first eleven. Most important of all was for the second eleven to play their role as a practice team, to allow the first eleven to work out tactics.

No one dared go full out against the first team during tactical training. If anyone tried it, they were told off and given short shrift. Since we often changed the first team it was not uncommon for me to play with the reserves too. The object was to improve the first team. If the first team won that weekend, then we had won too.

Whenever I played against the first team, I never gave it the full 100 percent. Those games aren't intended for you to give your best performance. Sometimes you'll get players who go hell for leather in a training game, and then don't do anything when they get selected. It's fine to show what you can do during training, but never in a tactical practice session.

Premier League managers don't have an easy time of it, with their enormous squads of as many as thirty players. Players from every corner of the globe, each with his own culture. Try keeping all of them happy, especially when you have to tell someone why he hasn't been selected. After the third time, he says: "That's all very well, but I just want to play." In the end, players start to get annoyed. The advantage of such a busy program is that most players can expect to get their chance at some point. Then they have to show what they can do, which may not be that easy since the pressure is all the greater when you so rarely get a chance.

In the same way, reserves also get their chance to play in international games. Opportunities come when the best players are rested. Easy to say perhaps, but try going out there and taking over from Arjen Robben, Wesley Sneijder or Robin van Persie. Or stepping in when players like that don't want to play in an international, or play with the brakes on because their employer insists they come back without an injury, or that they can only play for one half.

Personal circumstances

You would imagine that a stable home life would be the ideal situation for a player. But everyone experiences that differently. What's important is to feel good. Some clubs advise young players to settle down quickly: family life provides a tranquil base and a place to build a regular routine. But what if you're always arguing with your partner? Or if there's a young child in the house who keeps you awake half the night? It's hard to lay down a definitive rule on this one.

At AC Milan they used to look at your qualities as a player and your behavior in the dressing room, but also at your life outside the club. What is your social life like? Do you go out on the town? Do you have a family? Any hobbies? How do you perform on television? These factors mattered when AC Milan were considering whether to accept me as a player.

Naturally, clubs have moved on over the decades. Life has changed since twenty, thirty years ago, if only through social media. These days, appearance is crucial. You don't need to have much talent to become famous and earn buckets of cash. Look at the Kardashians: a sign of the times. Young people grow up with these heroes and as club and manager you have to keep in mind what the fans want, without losing sight of the need to perform on the pitch.

Performance has to be paramount. If you have other things you want to be doing that's fine. It's important to enjoy the good things in life: expensive headphones, the latest phone, flash clothes with smart hats and intricate tattoos, fast cars, beautiful people; all the superficial things that people like to be seen with and that reflect your identity. There's really no point in objecting to that mentality. This is the young generation of today. Life goes on.

If you want your club to be a part of the march of time then you'll have to embrace change, not try to stop it, as long as performance on the pitch remains the priority and winning is paramount, preferably as a team. Because it's only natural that certain members of a club will get together and form cliques. And even if they're together, each of them will have his own agenda, because there's a lot of money to be had, with transfers, and with all kinds of commercial deals. For a top player, these can be even more lucrative than soccer. Those players have to be made to understand that it's because of soccer that companies are interested in them. If they lose sight of that, they'll lose their place at the top of the soccer pyramid.

Coping with fame

It's not easy to deal with instant fame and popularity. Everyone wants you. They never bring anything, they're always taking.

I regularly meet young players who have shot to the top and are having trouble keeping their feet on the ground or dealing with the concept of being famous. I always give them some of my time and offer a more critical opinion of them, since that's what's usually missing. I've got plenty of experience and I don't have a hidden agenda.

The most important lesson to learn is: dare to say no, even to people close to you, like your parents, brothers and sisters. They'll call you arrogant, big-headed, or say you're betraying your roots, but you have to protect yourself. It's not one person asking for something. No, there's a whole line out there. If you give them what they want, you'll be busy all day long, only you won't be playing soccer, which is where you're supposed to be focusing your energy and your attention. If you do something for one, you won't be able to send the others away. Dare to say no. You'll be criticized for it, but that's something you must learn to live with. Don't get involved, even though they won't love you for it.

Today it's hard for young stars not to be affected by how their lives have changed: they earn such extraordinary amounts of money. When you're young you want fast cars, a fine house, smart clothes, beautiful friends, I understand all that. But ask yourself this: is this good for my career?

The good people around you are the ones who dare to disagree. I understand the urge to follow the advice of your immediate family. Unfortunately, their critical faculties might leave a lot to be desired. The young soccer player is always the prince in the family, can never do anything wrong, not least because he earns lots of money and raises the whole family's lifestyle to new heights. Members of the family will probably see an independent business advisor as a freeloader. Just leave it to the older brother . . .

Diego Maradona is the best example of how horribly wrong that can go. When he came from Argentina to Barcelona, he brought a whole tribe with him: family, friends, acquaintances, an entire clan. It was doomed. His entourage lived in the city and Maradona was constantly distracted by them. Suddenly these followers were his principal concern and he hardly had time for his real business—playing soccer. He played well enough, but his focus was on what was happening in his household, off the pitch.

At Napoli they had a different policy and he was forced to reduce their number. Finally Maradona learned to say no. In Naples, Maradona played brilliantly because he no longer had to worry about his publicity-hungry entourage.

Mysterious forces in sport

FC Barcelona have the unusual quality of being able to play better with ten players than with the full contingent of eleven. While they sweep everyone off the field with eleven, when there are only ten on the pitch, Barcelona's players seem to become infused with an unbelievable power as they realize that they have to do even better to win.

When preparing for a match, one question is critical: what is your plan for when you find yourself facing eleven players and you have only ten on your side?

Do you want to make your defense as compact as possible? Because it's harder for the other side to play against ten players who are forming a massive defensive block, than against eleven who are playing to gain three points. But no, when they're down to ten players, Barcelona go the opposite route, piling on the pressure even more and playing one-on-one in defense. Astonishing, because you need to maintain tight discipline, far more so than with eleven in the side.

You realize that straight away when it happens to your team. It gives you an automatic mental kick. It's weird, as if you have another, undiscovered gear. Suddenly you'll see players marking half a meter away instead of three meters, you'll see players slide to try and keep the ball in play, you'll see more fouls, more reactions to the referee's decisions, players will encourage each other just that little bit extra and instead of turning sideways when a shot comes in, they'll face the ball full on even though they know it's going to hurt.

Are there really mysterious forces at work? Or is it just a question of mentality? And what happens when a team suddenly turns a huge deficit around in the last fifteen minutes to snatch victory? Does it smell blood?

Smelling blood

The perfect example of a team smelling blood is Liverpool in 2005: the final of the Champions League in Istanbul against AC Milan. No problem for the Italians, so it seemed at halftime with the score at 3–0 and an array of top players such as Maldini, Cafu, Nesta, Stam, Gattuso, Pirlo, Kaká, Crespo, Shevchenko and Seedorf. But then, as the second half started, Liverpool launched into an all-or-nothing offensive that brought them three goals in the first fifteen minutes. Eventually the English won, because AC Milan's players were so distraught that they missed no fewer than three penalties in the shootout.

It was when Liverpool got a goal back to make it 3–1 shortly after halftime that I suddenly felt that something was about to happen. A strange unidentifiable feeling. You sensed the fear begin to take hold among the Italians in the stadium, like an animal detects fear. AC Milan's players felt it too. Instinctively. Why? A kind of collective primitive power is released when you score, and you suddenly start believing in yourself. It's the same feeling you get when you enter a place and the atmosphere is good or bad. Without anyone saying anything, you feel it. Standing on the other side, you get such a boost of energy and confidence when you sense the fear in your opponents that it's almost an out-of-body experience. Instinct takes over.

I experienced something similar at the European Championship in 1988. We lost to the USSR in a group game and the Russians were stronger in the final too. Until we made it 1–0, and then 2–0. And especially the way Van Basten scored the second; you simply knew it couldn't go wrong after that. Not even when they got a penalty. Even then there was no salvation for them; Van Breukelen was supremely confident: he knew exactly which corner Igor Belanov would target.

You see that kind of thing at kindergarten. Put a group of toddlers in a room, place a toy car in the middle and leave them to it. The result is pandemonium and the survival of the fittest. This kind of behavior is a matter of primitive instinct. Do you radiate anxiety or confidence? The people around you pick up on it. If you walk around school all day with your eyes cast down, you'll be the victim, one hundred percent.

Is there such a thing as a bogey team? Well, even the best clubs in the world have a team they fear the most. In my day at AC Milan it was Verona. Manchester United don't often lose to Liverpool. It's hard to put your finger on the reason, because there is no reason. It's really a question of feeling. In some way or other, these clubs cannot abide each other and each time you wonder before the game: this time they'll do it. But in the end they never do. Until one day they actually manage it, like Liverpool did last season, when they knocked Manchester United out of the Europa League to qualify for the quarterfinals.

Another unusual phenomenon is that some teams manage to outperform themselves in one week and then a week later they slip up on a visit to a relegation candidate and seem to play at half power. At AC Milan we were constantly being confronted by opponents who gave it 110 percent and played on, or often just a little over, the edge of the permissible. For clubs like that, Milan was the most difficult fixture of the year. Of course, it made us even stronger and harder to beat. Oddly, when I moved to Sampdoria and we played those same clubs there was little left of that fighting spirit that they used to bring when they visited AC Milan.

While we had struggled at AC Milan, at Sampdoria we sailed through the match, sweeping our opponents aside. Naturally I wondered: how can that be possible? That palpable difference is incredible and it was an extremely odd sensation. I played against you the year before with Milan and then you had played much more fiercely.

It's a question of mentality. You know that you have to raise your game when you're playing a better team if you want a chance at gaining points. By contrast, when you play a lesser side you tend to think that it'll be an easy match. The first is always conscious; the second is unconscious. At AC Milan, my record tally for a season was nine goals; at Sampdoria I scored sixteen. Not because I was suddenly playing better. No, at Samp I was given a lot more space by defenders. At Milan, your opponent always kept uncomfortably close.

Sensing victory

People often ask players after a game: "When did you know you were going to win?" That's both simple and complex. When you're 3–0 ahead, you feel sure you're not going to lose. That goes for 3–1 too. Naturally, in April 2016 when Borussia Dortmund were leading 3–1 against Liverpool they thought they were on their way to the semifinal of the Europa League. So too Liverpool probably thought that the chances of survival were minimal. Yet it was the Germans who went home disappointed and Liverpool who progressed to the next round of the Europa League with a 4–3 scoreline.

When it happens, you get the feeling; when it doesn't happen, you know that it could have. Even though your instinct tells you it's in the bag, you still have to wait for the moment the ball goes in to confirm it. Sometimes the goal doesn't come and you feel strangely let down. But feelings won't win you games.

Superstition

Before a game, during halftime and even after a game, everyone has his rituals. Superstition is practically universal; I had my own superstitions too, though I often forgot them! I thought it was a good thing, because these little rituals help you get into the right mind-set for a successful game. You do whatever it is because it was what you did when you won a particular game. That's what you remember. It makes you feel confident of victory and lends you a certain calm.

To me, it's the same as for tennis players and golfers. They always have a pre-routine. Tennis players bounce the ball a couple of times and a golfer will do a couple of swings before actually hitting the ball or a few imaginary putts before actually putting. Just to get into the right mind-set. If you do that, it'll be fine.

I've seen a lot of superstitions in the dressing room. First the left boot and then the right. Wait as long as possible before going to the toilet. A slight touch of something or someone. At Anfield, all the Liverpool team touch the board above the players' tunnel on their way out. It says: "THIS IS ANFIELD." Some cross themselves a couple of times or touch the grass. These are all things with which to get yourself into a positive mind-set. I don't see a problem with it. On the contrary.

Us against them

Psychological warfare is a weapon with which to win games, and tournaments. During the European Championship in 1988, the Dutch coach, Rinus Michels, was having a tremendous fight with the board of the Dutch football association, KNVB. He turned those directors into our collective enemy and the effect was electric.

Managers also often use the media in the same way. Take Italy at the World Cup in 1982. The media were extraordinarily negative and Italy was still reeling from a huge bribery scandal a couple of years before. It almost prevented a player like the striker Paolo Rossi from going to the World Cup. The Italians began dramatically with three draws against Cameroon, Poland and Peru, squeezing through the group phase on goal difference. Everyone had something to say about the *Squadra Azzurra*.

That gave the veteran manager, Enzo Bearzot, his common enemy: he imposed media silence. Italy became world champions, beating Diego Maradona's Argentina and an amazing Brazil team. If you get a chance to create a sense of us against the rest, then as a coach and as a team you have to do it every time.

Tense and nervous

The tension you feel before a game is not the same as nervousness. Tension keeps you sharp, nervousness blocks you and may lead players to doubt themselves.

As a player, I was never nervous, but I needed that tension if I wanted to perform as well as I could. Then your antennae are in focus, and your body is finely tuned. For key matches for a national title, the Champions League or an international game for the Netherlands the tension is even greater. It often comes from having to succeed in an all-or-nothing situation. The importance of the match is raised an extra notch by the increasing media attention. And you face it in social settings too. Everywhere you go people ask about the game, and so it gains an extra dimension whether you want it or not.

As an analyst I was once asked to present FIFA's Ballon d'Or— Golden Ball—at the gala in Zurich. I had to do it live. It was quite different from analyzing games in a studio, but I didn't change my approach. We had rehearsed and they gave me a small room to pre- pare in on the day of the broadcast. The walls were soon closing in on me and five minutes later I found the room where all the other people working on the show were sitting. The producer came by just before we were due to go on and found me playing games on my phone and checking out news sites. She asked: "Aren't you nervous? Are you feeling tense?" Of course, but that's my way of channeling the tension: focus on something else. We spoke after the show and I said: "You thought I wouldn't make it and that it would all go wrong, didn't you?"

That's just my way of focusing. Everyone has to do whatever makes him feel good. It's something you learn in the dressing room surrounded by ten players with whom you're going to win a game. If you force someone to do something that goes against his character, it'll more than likely have a negative effect.

Spectators

Spectators can play a significant role in motivating a team. And they can be the death of a team with their jeers and whistles, white handkerchiefs, negative chants and cynical comments.

Fans can influence the game by their attitude toward the other side and the referee by whistling, shouting and chanting their disapproval. Whether consciously or not, it all has an effect on players and referees. Some players avoid the ball, find a place to hide and pray for the clock to reach the ninety-minute mark. If every decision the referee makes is followed by a chorus of disapproval then it's only natural for the official to react, even if unconsciously.

The home side's goalkeeper may waste time and never get a yellow card, but when the visiting keeper wastes time and 50,000 people start whistling and shouting, then he may very well get a yellow card without even having taken very much longer than normal. The spectators in the stadium can have a significant impact on a game.

In the Netherlands, the fans at Feyenoord's De Kuip stadium are especially intimidating. Kuip-phobia is a real phenomenon in Dutch soccer. It's ridiculous for players to be afraid in their own stadium, but it happens: it's reality. The expectations are always high—too high—and so they can never be realized. As a result a negative vibe develops that bears down on the players. So a team can be drawn into a negative spiral, the kind of situation Feyenoord have found themselves in for the last fifteen years.

Big games

Club games in the national league have a certain rhythm. You follow a weekly program and if you have international matches in between they often don't disturb that rhythm.

With the national team it's different. That's another rhythm entirely and the tension is distinct, too, if only because of the days you spend at the separate training camp. When you play an international game you're playing for your country: you're an ambassador for the entire nation. At decisive qualifying rounds for a World Cup or European Championship and other major tournaments I always felt that I was carrying a responsibility. That can get quite intense and the pressure can be huge. I didn't have too much trouble with it, though.

The momentum of a winning side is a great feeling. Or a victory for a team like Haarlem, which no one expected. Often those clubs allow you to play the way you feel. At Chelsea that was also true at first, although it changed the longer I stayed and the fans and directors decided that Chelsea might be good enough to have a serious shot at the title. When you get to the top you can't play like that any more, even at Barcelona, where the way they play makes it all look free and easy.

At the top, you have to get results. Every week, every game. That changes things. When "may" becomes "must," everything is different. The hardest part is to remain focused. That starts in training. The way you train is the way you play.

Just how serious that can get is something I experienced at AC Milan. When we drew, all hell broke loose. Silvio Berlusconi would come to see us personally to give us a talking to. On the Saturday before the next game he would fly in to the Milanello training complex in his helicopter. Then you knew what to expect. Three points from the next game were a must. The pressure was intense. You had to be able to deal with that if you wanted to play for AC Milan.

Often you need only to remain in focus and not get distracted. Players who let the huge expectations wear them down would never last there. Was a draw that bad? Yes, if two points made the difference between winning the league and coming second. Naturally people got upset.

As a club you have to grab every opportunity, just like a player. Failure isn't an option. At AC Milan they used to say: "No next time for you." So you have to be professional. Put everything on hold. Because if you make a mistake they'll dump you and you'll have ruined your future. Soccer at the highest level is not always fun. Especially for those who are balancing on the edge and their contract is up for renewal.

The tension in the Champions League is highest of all, and it gets even more intense the further you progress and the nearer you get to the final. The national cup competitions are always exciting, whether in England at Wembley or in the Netherlands at De Kuip. This is the shortest route to European soccer. Especially interesting for clubs not quite at the highest level, since they don't qualify regularly for the Europa League.

In England, managers don't take the League Cup very seriously. It begins in the autumn, a period that is packed with league games, European commitments and international matches. Later in the season clubs only rarely field second-eleven teams for FA Cup games. That's because the FA Cup is a major trophy in England, and it can make up for a poor season. Yet a long run in the Cup also has its dangers. If you take the competition seriously and always play your first team, you risk exhaustion, injuries and suspensions. Certainly for clubs already playing in Europe, it makes their program even harder.

On the other hand, if you make changes then you disrupt the rhythm of the team, although these days you have to rotate players. You'll never succeed in these competitions with just the one team. You'll come up against a brick wall at some point. A squad of twenty-two equally good players is no luxury, even though a professional should be able to play three matches in eight days.

It's a fine line. Managers have to keep a balance.

Look at the World Cup and the European Championship. Countries regularly qualify before the group stage is finished. That gives coaches two options: either to continue with the same eleven players, or to leave half of them in the team and replace the other half—for example, players on a yellow card, those who appear exhausted or have slight injuries—with alternatives. Often the substitute keeper gets to play a game in those situations, as a reward for waiting.

It's a risky choice. Marco van Basten coached the Dutch side at the 2008 European Championship in Austria and Switzerland and steered his country to the second round after two superb victories against the world champions, Italy (3–0), and the runners-up, France (4–1). In the third group game, against Romania, he replaced Edwin van der Sar with Maarten Stekelenburg and kept Orlando Engelaar. He made a further nine changes from the first two matches. The orange shirts won 2–0, so Romania received no unfair advantage.

But this wholesale substitution destroyed the team's rhythm for the quarterfinal against Russia. Van Basten reverted to the eleven players who had given Italy and France such a pasting. Yet the momentum had disappeared after eight days of rest and a little training and lazing about in the hotel. The Dutch struggled on into extra time, whereupon they were destroyed, 3–1.

Intimidation

As a player and manager I never intentionally set out to intimidate anyone. Later I heard that there were stories about how I intimidated opponents in the players' tunnel because of my height, but I never gave it a second thought. I never did anything I shouldn't have. As club soccer has internationalized, top players often meet before the game in the tunnel. Two Brazilians or Argentinians who know each other from their national squad who find themselves on opposing sides in an FC Barcelona–Arsenal match will naturally be happy to see each other. Top soccer players learn to separate how they play from the rest of their life, so they can still throw everything into winning the game.

At the European Championship in West Germany in 1988 we heard Tony Adams encouraging his team in the English dressing room as we stood in the players' tunnel: "Let's kill the bastards!" he was saying. We all burst out laughing. "What's he saying now?" It seemed rather forced and not in the least intimidating. On the contrary, we were amused and relaxed despite the pressure of knowing that the losers would be going home. We won with three Marco van Basten goals, 3–1.

Intimidation may work for a while on young players who have only just started their careers, but I think you should be professional and focus on winning. Players will always try to intimidate opponents on the pitch. I don't like that: you should impress, not oppress.

Respect

As a player you have to accept team tactics and team discipline—that's your primary task as a professional. And yet within those team tactics you also have your own individual ones. For the player it's about taking the right decision at the right moment. The more right decisions you take, the more time you have to carry out those decisions. It's all about speed of deliberation and execution.

It's about things like: when do you get involved in play? When do you stay in the background? When do you go deep? When do you shadow the man you're marking? When do you give him a few meters, entice the player to have a go and do exactly what you want?

There are hundreds of situations like that. If you know what you want and you make the right decisions and execute your plan at the right speed then it'll happen the way you want.

After I retired from professional soccer, I played for AFC, an amateur soccer club in Amsterdam. Just for fun. A group of friends in the first eleven on Saturdays. I never got kicked so much: those amateurs really took me to task. They take the ball, pass it well, and again, look around and finally they pass it to your feet. Meanwhile there's an opponent breathing down your neck who gives you an almighty kick as the ball reaches you.

To which you'd normally say: "Why don't you play the ball?" Only the foul wasn't intentional and he meant no harm. He is just too slow and puts others at risk quite unwittingly.

Later, this team developed into a mix of amateurs and former professionals and internationals including Stanley Menzo, Aron Winter, Marco van Basten, John van 't Schip, Rob Witschge and Wim Kieft. A team of forty-somethings playing fit young men in their twenties, who still couldn't keep up, although we were practically standing still while they played. It's a matter of being able to think fast, which gave us a huge advantage and created lots of extra time for us. The youngsters didn't stand a chance, even if they were in peak condition.

To avoid a game like that getting out of hand, you need to anticipate the situation. Don't be haughty or arrogant, but go and meet the youngsters, go to their dressing room and say: "Hey guys, enjoy the game. Have fun." After chatting a little and shaking hands you'll find the game will be pleasant enough and you can still win because you operate at a much faster speed.

One touch, second touch. Soccer is about letting the ball run and exploiting the moments when you can make the difference. And then suddenly the ball is in the net.

That's what makes soccer fun: playing in a way that doesn't get you into difficulties.

Don't put us down!

In the same way, different playing standards can be found at the top of the soccer world too. And Barcelona approach teams that are obviously less talented as we did at AFC. It's absolutely crucial not to disparage your opponents or to ridicule them. When players look for revenge they're a danger to life and limb. In fact you often see big teams tone it down once they can't be overhauled.

In their heyday, Manchester United had an unsurpassed ability to read a game. Their victory in the final minutes in the 1999 Champions League final against Bayern Munich at the Nou Camp in Barcelona didn't surprise me at all—despite their 1–0 deficit after ninety minutes! Even in such a dire situation, that team could still raise its game above that of its opponents and take the initiative. It's a mental question, too.

Bayern Munich's big mistake was to think that they had already won. That made United mad, especially when the Germans brought off Lothar Matthäus and he paraded to the bench in triumph, enjoying his substitution, made for the benefit of the crowd, to the fullest. It was like a red rag to a bull: just what Manchester United needed.

What United did then in two minutes of injury time was amazing, with two goals by Sheringham and Solskjaer. The Germans complain that it was pure luck, but it certainly wasn't. This was a favorite United trick: making a difference in the final minutes, domestically and internationally.

AC Milan had a similar experience. Three days before the

Champions League final on May 18, 1994, Johan Cruijff's FC Barcelona were crowned Spanish champions. Everyone in Spain felt that there wasn't really any need to play the final, the winner was a foregone conclusion. AC Milan were still struggling in Serie A and Barcelona had their head in the clouds. Even Cruijff said it was a mere formality to pick up the trophy four days later.

In Italy and especially at Milanello, everyone was livid at the superior tone of the Catalonians. They saw red and a quite different AC Milan were unleashed against Barcelona. By halftime the score was 2–0, with two goals by Massaro. In the second half Savićević and Desailly made sure of victory—the final score: 4–0.

The lesson was simple: always show respect to your opponents. Even if you're playing against amateurs: shake everyone's hand, pat their shoulder, exchange a few friendly words, stay humble. That takes the pressure off and releases the tension that makes an opponent kick like a wild animal, doing everything he can to stay in the game, but without success. If you chide and challenge an opponent, you're asking for trouble. And there's simply no need.

It could cost you the Champions League, as we saw in 1994 and 1999.

National teams

Luis Suárez handled the ball on the goal line in the final moments of the quarterfinal against Ghana in the 2010 World Cup and was sent off. Nevertheless, Uruguay progressed to the semifinal against the Netherlands in Cape Town. It wasn't fair, but in Uruguay Suárez was the hero. In Ghana they'll have cursed him, but in Uruguay no one told him: "Luis, you shouldn't have done that."

Playing for your country

The same thing happened to Thierry Henry in 2009 when he scored against Ireland after having brought the ball down with his hand. It enabled France to proceed to the World Cup in South Africa. Unfair perhaps, but the French claim that Henry was acting in the country's interests. Difficult to accept for a purist, but we don't live in an ideal world, not even in sport. A Ghanaian or an Irish player would probably have done the same in a similar situation. If you asked Suárez or Henry, they would probably tell you that they wouldn't do it again if they had the choice, but theory and practice are different when it comes to playing for your country.

It was touch and go, but Henry didn't get sent off, and didn't even get suspended. Looking back, it is a minor blemish in his career. For a few days it was the big story and then it was old news and now no one even remembers.

When you play for your country you go that extra yard and the pressure on the game is so much greater. In England, too. There Manchester United's Ashley Young is often booed for diving, but if he pulled the same stunt for England and England got into the final as a result, then everyone would suddenly be cheering. There's so much more you can do for your country and suddenly everyone judges you by a different standard.

In international soccer it's well known that referees unconsciously adjust to the way these players behave. So, for example, English players can't tackle the way they're used to in England, but a referee knows that the English are attached to their way of tackling and will take a slightly more tolerant view of their infringements.

That nuance doesn't extend to the World Cup and European Championship. Before the start of either of those tournaments, referees are pumped full of instructions. They are drilled to perfection. And they carry out their instructions because they want to stay in contention for major games and advance their careers. Referees who want to make it to the end of the tournament shouldn't even think of straying from the designated path.

When I played for Dutch youth teams we always played honest, positive soccer without any tricks. We played for the joy of playing and did our best to win, but we never sailed too close to the edge. It was as a young international that I first encountered the Latin soccer culture. Young players on those teams did everything they could to win. They sat on you, kicked, pulled your shirt, whinged, dropped to the ground and never stopped nagging—to the limit and then some more. Because we had no idea how that worked, we always came out the losers. It was an entirely new soccer experience.

Naturally, after years of experience abroad, we later learned that in the service of our country, when wearing an orange shirt, it was permissible to bite back. Paul Gascoigne once got an elbow in his face from Jan Wouters in an England–Netherlands game at Wembley. He broke his nose, was brought off and turned out later to have broken his cheekbone too. Nothing nice about that, but it was how we played the game twenty-five years ago.

Gascoigne was playing at Wembley and was entertaining the

spectators, but was up against Jan Wouters. Not a player like Roy Keane. After a couple of reckless two-footed tackles he suddenly got an elbow in his face. No one saw it. That's how it was in those days.

We once played a qualifying game away in Cyprus and found ourselves facing an extremely competent and troublesome striker. Ronald Spelbos, a defender for AZ and Ajax, hit the fellow squarely. After that we heard nothing more from him.

National anthem

Every player experiences the national anthem at international matches in his own way. Sometimes it depends on the tune. When I explain the words of our anthem to foreigners, their jaws drop. German blood? The king of Spain? Their jaws drop even farther.

We Dutch have an anthem in which we honor our former occupiers, Spain. "That's not something to be proud of?" they ask. Then it's me who's lost for words. I used to mime the verses when the national anthem was played, although I was more than proud to represent the Netherlands.

The English, Americans, Italians and French take this bit seriously and draw inspiration from their anthem. It won't win you the game, but it creates a sense of camaraderie. A packed Wembley singing "God Save the Queen" makes a lasting impression on English players and on visitors. And it gives England's opponents just as big a boost. Who wouldn't want to play in such an amazing atmosphere? It might leave a young player paralyzed by nerves for a moment, but if you're capped and playing at Wembley, then you've probably built up a bit of experience.

Dutch infighting

One thing the Dutch are known for above all is their infighting during major tournaments. Whenever I'm invited as an analyst for a World Cup or European Championship, they always ask: "When are the Dutch going to wreck their own chances with another row?"

That's the reputation we have abroad. I actually experienced it at the 1990 World Cup in Italy. The Netherlands were European champions and big favorites for the world title. Marco van Basten, Frank Rijkaard, Ronald Koeman and me: we all had another two years' experience, we were between twenty-five and thirty, at the peak of our (soccer playing) lives, and yet it all went sour.

It started with the decision by Rinus Michels, director of technical affairs, to appoint Leo Beenhakker as coach rather than Johan Cruijff. Entirely against the wishes of the players, who had specifically asked for Cruijff. That Michels made a point of mixing with the players every day made everyone angrier still. Then there was a certain friction between guys like Van Basten, Koeman and the captain—myself—and some of the others. The image that many of the players had of themselves was all wrong: having won the European title, they thought they were better than they were. Moreover, we Dutch have difficulty lodging in such large numbers in such confined quarters for a month without complaining. We always end up saying something.

Other national teams bond when the results are positive. Only the French suffer from the Dutch syndrome. Players are supposed to camouflage the disunity so no news of it reaches the outside world. Naturally it affects the team's performance, although not always.

In 2014, the Netherlands came third in the World Cup, but Robin van Persie couldn't hide the fact that he'd had quite enough of Arjen Robben's conduct. Before the Argentina game, the semifinal of the competition, he walked onto the pitch for the warm-up ahead of his teammates because he refused to wait any longer for Robben. It seems a minor incident, but at such a big tournament with such huge media attention, it was bound to explode.

The Netherlands lost, and then for days the debate in the country was all about the Van Persie–Robben tiff, instead of the unexpected chance of a bronze medal. Happily, a unified Dutch team beat Brazil four days later to gain third place.

The Dutch like to tell each other blunt truths. And not just on the soccer field either. I've often been told we act like we're the professors of soccer. Italians are particularly keen on pointing this out, even though they seem to talk about nothing else themselves. But we analyze ourselves silly. We debate tactics openly in the press, as if we were talking to a fellow manager rather than a journalist.

The Dutch like to solve everything with tactics.

Dutch school

Dutch tactics are based principally on the 4-3-3 system, with the central midfielder connecting to the striker—triangle tip forward—or dropping deep toward the two central defenders—triangle tip facing back. The two other midfielders move in the opposite direction. Since this is the tactical system that most Dutch teams employ, opponents have learned how to deal with it.

Simply put: disrupt the buildup by the two central defenders, lock the midfield down and then in the main you've got the Dutch where you want them. There is usually no real response, although these days teams playing a strong opponent tend to switch to a 5-3-2 formation. The Dutch team came far with this formation at the 2014 World Cup. It is reactive soccer, and that's a dirty term in the Netherlands. Yet the tactic is gradually winning ground: for example, when PSV almost eliminated Atlético Madrid from the Champions League.

The 5-3-2 system assumes that the other side has possession, while Dutch soccer culture is all about keeping the ball yourself. Broadly speaking, you play soccer because you like playing with the ball, not because you like chasing your opponent. We want to see creativity with the ball, not think about formations when we don't have possession. Which is usually what happens for about half the game.

Yet 5-3-2 is not necessarily defensive, because when you switch to 3-5-2, it becomes a highly aggressive tactic. See how Juventus tackled Bayern Munich in the Champions League.

Dutch teams often get into trouble when they play against two strikers. This often results in one-on-one marking at the back. Every long ball into the space behind the defense can be extremely dangerous. That is how Atlético Madrid threatened PSV last season in the first knockout stage of the Champions League. The keeper, Jeroen Zoet, saved PSV three times in one-on-one situations. Dutch players aren't used to them.

How do you solve this? With a 5-3-2 formation, but in principle the two central defenders have to learn to play against two strikers.

Dutch soccer managers should spend far more time on other systems than just 4-3-3: both on how to play them and how to deal with them, ensuring that Dutch teams aren't constantly being surprised and are able to anticipate the tactics of their opponents. I only ever played 4-3-3 in all the Dutch youth teams I played in as well as at Haarlem and Feyenoord. At PSV we played 4-4-2, but often so aggressively that it became a sort of 3-3-4. In Italy, I was taught the pure 4-4-2 and at Chelsea it was 5-3-2. In effect, I learned to play all these formations. Young players should get to know all of them too.

Last season I invited Arrigo Sacchi, my former manager at AC Milan, to give a guest lecture at the Dutch football association, KNVB. It wasn't just a whim. I wanted to hold up a mirror to Dutch educators. He was ruthless and began by saying that he loved playing against Dutch teams. Always 4-3-3, lots of shuffling about in the buildup, slow positional play, no fast switching and constantly trying to reach the players on the flank for a cross to the striker. In other words: incredibly predictable. Always the same and never a surprise.

It was music to my ears, because this is what I had been saying for years. It's 4-3-3 all the time, possession soccer and slow buildups from the back with no deep passes. It's only logical that Dutch soccer no longer makes a difference forty years on—especially since there are no stars left to make a difference individually. We like to talk about tactics, but we forget to look for solutions and innovations for ourselves.

The Dutch consider themselves progressive, but they have effectively come to a standstill. Concerned about this situation, the football association convened a symposium to find a way to drag Dutch soccer out of the mire. Meanwhile, there is a master plan to improve the way youngsters are taught. As long as we recognize that 4-3-3 is a great system, but not the only one.

International innovation

Some teams have played a crucial role in the development of soccer. In retrospect they were twenty years ahead of their time. Take, for example, the total soccer concept developed by Ajax in the early 1970s and the Dutch national side of the same period, dubbed *"Laranja Mecanica"*—the "Clockwork Orange." Or what about Liverpool in the late 1970s and early '80s, or AC Milan in the late 1980s and early '90s, or Ajax under Louis van Gaal in the mid-'90s, and FC Barcelona today? All of them innovative teams that introduced a different way of playing that caught on internationally.

Before Frank Rijkaard arrived as manager, Barcelona had won few international trophies. Since then the team has adopted the style of play developed by Ajax and Johan Cruijff almost fifty years ago, although now with a contemporary ensemble of players: short, lithe, intelligent, with power and pace. The package differs from its predecessor because soccer has evolved. Yesterday's defender played differently from today's defender. In those days you only had to feint to one side and you were through and ready to cross. Today, wing backs are all forwards who stopped on their way to the top. They defend in different ways. Wide defenders would love to move up and join the attack.

Two national teams have missed out on these European developments, whether consciously or not. They play the same way they played forty years ago: Argentina and Brazil. That they still compete with the best testifies to the timelessness of their kind of soccer. In fact their success depends on the presence of individual talent.

Argentinians play purely physical soccer, with an incredible mentality and a heritage of powerful individuals such as Mario Kempes, Diego Maradona and Lionel Messi.

Brazilians love technique, and when they have a striker like Pelé, Romário, Bebeto or Ronaldo, they can make a difference at the highest level. It is due to these players that Brazil have been world champions so often.

Brazil lacked a top striker at the World Cup in 2014 in Brazil, and the Brazilians were shocked at the result. The way the Germans demolished them with their team spirit and their technical baggage has left a deep scar. In Brazil, the soccer world has been reexamining its situation. The side were never a tight machine. Although Neymar performed exceptionally well, the rest lagged far behind. He needs a better team to back him in future.

New developments

As the number of cameras around the field have increased and the soccer talk shows have multiplied, along with other social media, soccer has changed. Tear into an opponent the way players used to thirty years ago and the whole world comes down on you like a ton of bricks. In the old days such fouls were hardly ever noticed.

The atmosphere at the training ground is also transformed. As an eighteen-year-old, if you weren't listening you got a sharp kick and you flew three meters into the air. It was all part of a hard learning curve. These days it's difficult to imagine, but back then the older players made sure you listened: you were playing with their money and their bonus. Young against old at training sessions: those were battles and blood flowed. All that has changed. I wouldn't say improved or worsened, just changed. When I came to Chelsea, the second eleven trained in shorts. The whole season, rain or shine, winter too. Those poor guys were cold, that's for sure. Their bare legs froze out there on the pitch. Not especially healthy, but in those days it was all part of the game.

Commerce

In my day, soccer was just beginning to become commercialized, both clubs and individuals. I didn't have a sponsor for non-soccer-related products, such as pants, watches or perfume. I did do a commercial for a car, but that was all. That company provided a fleet of cars for the club.

I had a soccer-related contract with Adidas for boots and kit. I was an Adidas man, and even had my own Adidas line of clothes. After I was transferred to AC Milan, I switched to Lotto. I had to, although I wanted to stay with Adidas. However, my contract was with Adidas Benelux and since I was going to Italy, Adidas International would have had to take me. But they had no idea who Ruud Gullit was. I was too obscure for them to offer me a contract, so I switched to wearing Lotto boots. Their own design, by the way. A year later I won the Ballon d'Or as world soccer player of the year. Now I'm back with Adidas.

Nutrition

Food is important. Although little attention used to be paid to nutrition, today much has improved. At AC Milan they were years ahead of their time. I took the initiative and took a tolerance test at Milanello, because it's good to know if you have an intolerance for anything in particular—which is different to an allergy, by the way. I discovered I should avoid yeast, cocoa, caffeine and milk. It really helped, because I genuinely felt a lot better, which naturally affects your performance.

When I was appointed player-manager at Chelsea, I introduced that same tolerance test, because it had helped me so much. You should have heard the players, especially the beer drinkers: "F*** hell, f*** intolerance for yeast, no f*** beer. Are you f*** crazy? I am not gonna f*** do this shit." I said: "You don't need to do it. It's just so you know. You can do what you like with the result, I'm just giving you the information. If you try and avoid those products you'll feel better and sharper."

At Chelsea I decided to switch to nutritionally balanced meals. Again, the same chorus of complaints. "No f*** gravy. Where's the gravy and where are the potatoes?" I said: "If you want to eat something else go out tonight with your wife to a restaurant and order whatever you like. Have a tandoori and a piri-piri. Here in the club you'll eat what you need to be able to perform."

Technical aids

As long as technical aids don't affect the pace of the game I'm happy to see them used, only not without limits. Goal-line technology is a logical development, but technical aids to help determine if a player is offside are more questionable. It's a gray area and even with such help the same discussions will still arise. So what's the point?

Whether or not to appoint a second referee, a so-called video referee, parked in the television editing van to help decide about issues such as fouls and yellow cards? I doubt that's a good idea. It would still be a subjective decision, because one referee may say a foul is worth a yellow card while the other may say red. It's hardly an improvement.

That subjective element is best illustrated by the various television programs in which games are analyzed. Whether it's in England with Gary Lineker, Peter Schmeichel and Robbie Savage or in the Netherlands with Jan Joost van Gangelen, Ronald de Boer and Pierre van Hooijdonk, we always end up talking about penalty decisions. If we as soccer experts can't agree and each have a different opinion, what do you expect from a video referee?

Many referees thought that Jamie Vardy of Leicester City deserved a penalty against Arsenal last season. I and other former players saw that Vardy deliberately looked for the Arsenal defender Nacho Monreal's leg and was going for a penalty. Should Monreal have been penalized by the referee, Martin Atkinson, simply because he couldn't pull his leg away in time? No, of course not. To be able to make an informed decision, you need to have played at that level. The referee would argue: "But he touched his leg." Sure, but Monreal could hardly have sawn it off.

A video referee would also have doubts—decisions would be the opinion of an individual, just like Atkinson's decision. You can agree or disagree. The debate continues. No problem, because discussion is one of soccer's charms. Just that you don't need a video referee to have a discussion.

My experiment would be to introduce an additional referee. Not in the middle of the pitch, but on the touchline or behind the goal, like in handball and field hockey. It works fine in those sports. The same authority of course and with respect for each other's decisions. It would be unworkable if the two refs disagreed about whether to give a penalty or not.

With two referees you could have one outside the penalty area when a corner is taken, and the second closer, without getting in the way of course. Refs could determine for themselves at what angle to watch what happens in the penalty area. As long as they don't both watch the ball, because then there's no point in having two officials.

Of course, having two referees makes the pitch smaller: it's harder to make a decision after sprinting a hundred meters to see what's happening than after sprinting fifty meters. I'd love to see an experiment along these lines at top level, although it's obviously a difficult matter.

Media

Then, of course, there are the journalists. You can shout out the strangest things when the adrenaline is pumping through your veins. If you just had an enormous release of emotion or disappointment, then you should count to ten before telling the media what you think. I tend to remain relatively calm, and I try to keep a sense of control.

Those interviews after the game are usually the same in every country for players and managers alike. Why did you win, or lose? How does it feel to have scored? Why did you substitute so-and-so? Did you see the foul and what do you think? Did the referee influence the result? Did you notice how angry that player was to be substituted? Sometimes it's fun to give an opinion, although often it's routine and boring.

In the Netherlands, reporters like to sit in the manager's chair and discuss tactics. Or they say you were wrong to do this or that, and tell you how to do better in future. Then you just sit there and listen, and wonder: man, what are you talking about?

Epilogue

Soccer is a game in which people make mistakes: that makes analysis interesting and relevant.

Pundits who analyze games use statistics more and more. That will only increase, judging by the way they do things in America, although it's hard to encapsulate a game in figures: except for the result, of course. I usually ignore statistics when I analyze a game, or I use them as an interesting detail. That Manchester City never win a European game in which they have more than 50 percent of possession tells you nothing about what went wrong or right in a game, or where the mistakes were made and how to avoid them.

Insight into the game is essential for my kind of analysis. How do forwards, midfielders or defenders try to correct mistakes and how do they try to prevent mistakes? Soccer is more than action and reaction: good players anticipate situations.

That is one of the reasons why you can count the number of great World Cup finals on the fingers of one hand. Two sides aiming for perfection in a soccer game is by definition boring. Teams playing at the level of a World Cup final hardly make any mistakes. When no team makes mistakes, the game soon becomes dull and predictable. The perfect execution of a task, of their tactical assignments: this is what players at the highest level do, especially in a final. Those players are good at it, otherwise they would never be where they are after a six-week tournament. The length of such a major international tournament often takes its toll on technical players who make a difference at the top. Guys like Messi, Ronaldo and Robben have already had to give so much on the way to the finals of the tournament that they are exhausted in the knockout phase. Which is why Mario

Götze—another crucial player—made all the difference in the 2014 World Cup final in Brazil between Germany and Argentina. Messi had already spent a huge amount of time on the pitch, while Götze had largely been used as a substitute. Whereas Messi was obviously weary in extra time, the substitute Götze had the strength to score the winning goal for Germany in the 113th minute. He had been on the pitch for twenty-five minutes.

In fact it was also a matter of anticipation, of adaptation to an impending situation: in this case by the manager, Joachim Löw, who used Götze for ninety minutes only in the opening game against Portugal, and then brought him off the pitch or used him as a substitute, or left him on the bench, as in the semifinal against Brazil, which Germany won 7–1.

Adapt and anticipate is a theme that runs through my whole career as a player, and something I have always tried to do. One of my teachers, Rinus Michels, said: "Never underestimate your opponent. Never base your strategy only on yourself, because your opponent is preparing for you. Your opponent will disrupt your game plan, so how are you going to adapt to counteract your opponent's move?"

That tactical contest often remains invisible, especially for a neutral television watcher. During halftime, the television analyst does exactly the same as a manager. In the Netherlands and England they have their own soccer culture and identity and they sometimes hold on to their traditions for too long and against their better judgment. It's something that I look out for when I watch a game. I don't like it when teams head almost willingly to the slaughter simply because the other side appears better on paper. Try a trick or two. Have a go.

Never imagine that as a manager or a team you're too big to change. I like to quote a story in this context about the late Muhammad Ali, one of my heroes. George Foreman was defending his world heavyweight title against Ali. The fight was between the greatest boxer of all time—Ali—and the world champion—Foreman—who was bigger and stronger. The fight, the "Rumble in the Jungle," took place in 1974 in

Kinshasa, capital of Zaire. Ali had already been written off by most pundits, but he figured out a way. Instead of dancing around the ring, he clung to the ropes and let Foreman hit him, one round after another. Gradually Foreman grew tired and then Ali started to box and knocked him to the floor. If the best boxer of all time wasn't ashamed to adapt, which club, which team and which player can afford not to take account of and adapt to what their opponent is doing? No one, not even FC Barcelona with Messi, Suárez and Neymar, the so-called MSN attack.

We all know pride comes before a fall. Atlético Madrid eliminated Barcelona for the second time in three years in the Champions League, because Barça refused to change their tactics; they had no plan B. And everyone knows that at some point every team gets exposed. To prepare and to delay being exposed as long as possible, that's what managers and coaches are for.

How Atlético Madrid managed to stop Barcelona doing all the things they had planned is something I particularly enjoyed. Not every purist or true aficionado of good soccer—which is what I am— may have appreciated it, but they had to do it to win. In top soccer it's all about winning. If you don't win the battle, you won't win the war. Strategy is essential and you find it in tactics and the approach of individual players on a technical, a tactical and also a psychological level.

Soccer is also undeniably a mind game. If you can gain an advantage on that level then you shouldn't neglect that either as a manager or as a player.

Managers and players of all kinds of teams are continually involved in developing soccer as a game. That evolution is the reason why teams never manage to win the Champions League twice in succession. Even a timely change to the selection still fails to break the pattern. That evolution may start with a detail of a particular tactic: for example, a striker moving five meters closer to the opponents' goal or five meters farther away. As an analyst I keep looking for that sort of clue in every game I watch. Or I gauge whether players are able to read a game, or when they decide to accept that the game is a draw or when they sense it's time to play winning soccer. A team with a wide winning margin can afford to offer spectators something to enjoy; if the advantage is small, then winning has to be the priority.

That's how I watch soccer.

Ruud Gullit profile

Player

		Games (goals)
1979–82	FC Haarlem	91 (32)
1982–85	Feyenoord	85 (30)
1985–87	PSV	68 (46)
1987–93	AC Milan	117 (35)
1993–94	Sampdoria	31 (15)
1994	AC Milan	8 (3)
1994–95	Sampdoria	22 (9)
1995–98	Chelsea	49 (4)
		471 (174)

Caps

1981–94	Netherlands	66 (17)

Manager

1996–98	Chelsea (as player-manager)
1998–99	Newcastle United
2003–04	Netherlands under-21s
2004–05	Feyenoord
2007–08	LA Galaxy
2011	Terek Grozny

Trophies as player

FC Haarlem	Erste Divisie Champions 1981
Feyenoord	Eredivisie Champions 1984
	KNVB Cup 1984
PSV	Eredivisie Champions 1986, 1987
AC Milan	Intercontinental Cup 1989, 1990
	European Cup 1989, 1990
	UEFA Super Cup 1989, 1990
	Serie A Champions 1988, 1992, 1993
	Supercoppa 1988, 1992, 1994
Sampdoria	Coppa Italia 1994
Chelsea	FA Cup 1997
Netherlands	European Champions 1988

Individual

Erste Divisie Footballer of the Year 1981
Dutch Footballer of the Year 1984
Dutch Footballer of the Year 1986
Golden Boot 1986
European Footballer of the Year 1987
Knight in the Order of Orange Nassau

Trophies as manager

Chelsea	FA Cup 1997